MONEY FOR NOTHING...

AND YOUR PROPERTY

FOR FREE!

How In My First 12 Months I Bought 74

Properties Worth Over £12,000,000- with

None Of My Own Money!'

The Passive Investments Strategy

BY

Andy Shaw

This book is designed to provide competent and reliable information regarding the subject matter covered. However, it is sold with the understanding that the author and publisher are not engaged in rendering legal, financial, or other professional advice. Laws vary from country to country and if legal or other expert assistance is required, the services of a professional should be sought. The author and publisher specifically disclaim any liability that is incurred from the use or application of the contents of this book.

Published by Andy Shaw

Third Edition

ISBN: 978-0-9554041-1-5

Copyright © 2007 Andy Shaw

Visit my website www.AndyShaw.com

In Andy's new book 'Money For Nothing And Your Property For Free', there seems to be the perfect blend of "Mindset and Strategies". This combination will elevate anyone to their financial goal by just following this recipe.

-   *John Childers*

TABLE OF CONTENTS

5

Author's Note

What if I told you that in a few hours you could learn how to create more money than you will ever need – for your children and their children's children? What if I told you that you could get that money for nothing; perhaps even for free? What if I told you the expertise you need will be easy to grasp and will stay with you **forever**?

Would you believe me?

Or would you think I was just pumping out some tired scheme or sentiment?

Well… this is a moment you will look back on and smile. You are about to reach the fork in the road. In the next few minutes you will find yourself at a significant turning point. You just do not know it yet!

When the time comes, the choice will be yours. Will you succumb to your doubts and walk away? Or will you see your scepticism for what it really is… fear of what lies ahead?

If you will suspend your doubt and face your fear as you read the words that follow, my promise to you is this:

<u>I will deliver on the statement I have made above!</u>

Andy Shaw

Note: - Specific dates are mentioned in the book to enhance your enjoyment and understanding, the book was originally written in March 2006.

Introduction

One of the greatest opportunities a published book offers is a public forum in which to thank the people whose encouragement over the years has made you the person you are today.

Just as your own lives are measured by the efforts invested in them, I too have reaped the rewards of the efforts invested in me. The faith, trust and inspiration that have guided me are the greatest riches of all. They mean more to me than mere words can ever say.

This is my first book. It represents a lot that I have learned as I have gone through life. And so, to everyone I have ever met, spoken to, worked with or read from, I say thank you. Learning from your successes and failures has made me who I am today.

I would also like to take a moment to say a few words about the thinking that inspired this book. There are many great property investing books out there. Unlike most that you might read, this book offers two unique features. The first is a practical guide to creating wealth using one simple property strategy as the vehicle. This is only the first step. Much, much more important than merely creating wealth, this book also reveals the strategies that enable you to keep your wealth and make it grow.

The fact is, almost anyone can create wealth. It takes real skill and knowledge to keep hold of it forever. Many authors of this type of book have not actually reached that second phase yet. Their success was driven by their unique personality and the special circumstances they found themselves in. They are less certain about making long-term wealth strategies work for anyone, least of all you. Their books often skate over the 'how-to' parts, leaving you thinking, *'I want to do it, but you haven't shown me how.'*

Unlike those publications, this book gives you all the information, tips and website tools you need to make it happen for you! I must make it clear at this point however, that they are not free. You will need to subscribe to membership of the site but this is fully satisfaction guaranteed so there is nothing to stop you subscribing, downloading what you want and asking for your money back. However, it is my intention to retain your membership by offering a risk-free guarantee, and delivering ongoing real monetary value to you. My site's primary goal is to show you how to significantly build on your net worth year after year. www.AndyShaw.com

When a revolutionary new idea is presented to the world, it takes a bit of getting used to. My team of editors and advisors agreed that the mind-bending concepts I offer are guaranteed to raise eyebrows and generate plenty of questions. Questions are good, I replied. It means that my readers are engaged in the creative process. Before long, the theories I put forth will be accepted as fact by those who are ready to take on the exciting challenge that unlimited wealth can bring. Whether everyone reading this book takes up the challenge is up to them to decide.

If you are used to reading property investment books, but you have not seen anything new for a while, you may be in for a few shocks. The concepts I outline have been touched on but never explored in a way that shows how to maximise their effects.

For those who have never read a property investment book before, you should find it both revealing and rewarding to see how easy it really can be to build lasting wealth if you approach it correctly.

For those who are used to taking cautious steps in life, I urge you to brace yourself! You may find my coaching style a little hard hitting for your taste. To those people, I say that there is plenty of time for subtlety when the money's in the bank.

Finally, a few quick words to the team that makes the dreams come true: A special thanks to my best friend, Phil Doolan. Without him, this material would still be a file stored on my computer, a project waiting to happen. Phil and I have been friends for years, building businesses up from nothing. Our partnership, like our friendship, just keeps getting stronger…Thanks Phil.

Next, to Alison, who is so much more than just my wife: To my life partner and best friend, thank you for your unfailing patience, loyalty, love and understanding. We thankfully share a wonderful life together; she is the person I love most in life and I want to thank her for letting me go off in whichever direction I choose and always supporting me whatever happens. Her support and tolerance are unbelievable, and my business partner, Greg, believes she deserves a medal, for still being married to me nine years on. I love her more with every passing day.

To my business partner, Greg Ballard, what can I say? It has been 15 years and it just keeps getting better every day – ha ha! But seriously, our bond goes further than friendship and we have a strength together that words

9

cannot describe. Anyone who has ever been in business knows that true business partners – especially good ones – are very hard to find. We have both learned and grown through our business lives and relish the opportunity of learning more each day. Well, I am very fortunate to have a great business partner in Greg.

To Adrian Daniels: your unique mindset is changing the way I think, keeping it fresh, making it grow. Adrian is always there and will help by going above and beyond what could ever be expected.

To my good friend, Peter Halm, for his inspiration to spread the word. I was just too busy doing it myself. It was his idea to actually start going out there and talking to people about it. If he had not badgered me into it, I would not have started down this road when I did and I may have never let my techniques out.

To Nicola Cairncross, who inspired me to see my skills in ways I never knew.

I would also like to thank my wonderful Personal Assistant Lindsay. None of the things that I do would look anywhere near as good as they do if I did not have somebody as clever as Lindsay looking after me, and making sure that I do everything I have committed my time to.

To my business mentor and friend, Mike Grimes. Mike came along at a time when I had reached my own fork in the road. His blueprint for business became my bible. In his own words, he was the old man in business teaching the young man in business how to do it. Both Greg and I are, and will be forever grateful, Mike.

I would like to pay a special tribute to my Uncle Dave and my Aunt Sylvia. My Uncle Dave was the person who first inspired me to go out and become a multi-millionaire. He assured me from the age of 13 that I had what was necessary to do it, and the bits that I had missing, he told me, I would find along the way. He said: "The people you need will come to you. You just need to be able to recognise them when they do." Boy, was he right! Those words have served me so well, and they can serve you too, if you believe them.

After his death in the '90s, my Aunt Sylvia - who was a fair bit younger than Uncle Dave - carried on her support for me. Unfortunately, she passed away last year. She told me how very proud she was of what I had managed to achieve and she told me that Uncle Dave would have been proud as well.

Thank you to my mum and dad. They have always been there for me and supported me through all my business ventures. When they were both retired they let Greg and I use their home as security to enable us to expand our business. My mum and dad are wonderful people; they can both be a little strange and Dad's a bit of a space alien at times, as anyone who knows him would agree! I would just like to say that I love you both very much and thank you for everything you've done for me. I hope I will always continue to make you proud.

And finally, thank you to Bill Evans, to whom I will be forever grateful because he was the first person to inspire me into a lifetime of reading. Bill gave me my first self improvement book, 'In Search of Excellence' by Tom Peters.

Thanks to all.

And thanks to you for allowing me to take the time to honour the people who have made it possible for us to begin an exciting journey together.

Are you ready? Then it's time to get you started on your own road to wealth!

1

The Backbone Of Real Wealth Creation

As a lot of my readers will know, I am very big on the whole wealth creation thing and I consider Long Term Property Investing to be the **backbone** of *real* wealth creation. I am also doing quite well in other fields, such as the Internet and business, as this book will show later. This year I have also set aside time to get back into stock market trading. I did that for a short time just before property and I was not at all bad at it. But property turned out to be the absolute **backbone** of everything I have created so far and is where I really excel.

The point of this book is to show you how easy it really can be to build a solid investment portfolio and how over-analysing everything is what stops the vast majority of people from ever reaching their goals. This book will show you how any damn fool can create wealth through property investing. It will also show you that you do not need to go to an expert like me. You will become the expert in a very short time if you follow the system I am going to present to you here and on my website.

So take heart. Once you understand what to do and why, all it takes is a belief in yourself that the decisions you make are right for you.

In a nutshell, the single most important step to creating long term wealth through property investing is to buy a property – <u>any property, that is</u> – and hold onto it. As long as they did not make the <u>silly mistake of selling it</u>, anyone would do well over time.

That is it! That is what hundreds of property investment authors take hundreds of pages to tell you.

I am going to focus on just one way in this book to make serious long-term wealth. I am not going to generalise over too many different strategies, as a lot of property investment books seem to need to do.

To give you an idea of how much you can learn in property, I could write 100 books on different styles of property investment. I could write an entire book on each chapter title in this book, and I could probably write a book on each paragraph. That is how much you can really go into detail on property investing, how many angles there are. Everywhere you look, there are new angles with new ways of creating money.

This is going to be very, very specific about one particular area, one strategy that most people will know about if they have ever owned a property before. And if they have not owned a property, it is probably an area they will know about because they have rented.

The subject of this simple strategy is enormous. So, I am going to be skipping over a hell of a lot. But that will not hold you back, or it should not hold you back anyway.

Anyone can do this, anyone out there, anyone in this country, probably anyone in the Western world. Anyone can put this strategy to work in their local property market. They do not have to be anything special. They do not have to have huge credit ratings or anything like that. They do not have to have lots and lots of money. They just have to be inspired to do it, and they must have a desire to start with. They have to believe they can. If you can manage to find a passion for it within yourself, then boy, does this get easy!

In your own markets the maths may and probably will be different than the examples I give in the book. New mortgage products and new ways of calculating mortgages are becoming available every day. Interest rates will change and therefore the exact style will shift slightly but in the end you'll still be able to make it work as long as you remember the rules about cashflow that I explain later.

2

The Learning Curve

When I first got into wealth creation, I had not read any of the gurus whose insights can save you money, heartache and time. It was not because I thought I knew better than they did. It was because I did not know anything at all! I did not know that the world of wealth creation mentors and self improvement books even existed and had no idea there were places you could go and be taught how to create wealth!

In my ignorance, I assumed that creating real wealth – like anything else – was something I had to sit down and figure out for myself. Unaware of all the books on the market, I just got on with it. I found ways to do things and reached conclusions that many of the experts do not seem to share in the material I have since discovered and read.

This does not mean that I urge you not to read their work. Having valuable information at your fingertips and refusing to use it would be worse than crazy! You will find all kinds of fantastic insights on property by reading Dolf de Roos. Michael Gerber gives unbelievable insights into business in his book, *The E-Myth*. There is a link on my website to it that I strongly urge you to use. Robert Kiyosaki's *Rich Dad Poor Dad* is only one of several excellent books in a series. *Retire Young, Retire Rich* is my personal favourite – what a read - but make sure you read the full series in order. It is excellent. All of these and many more can be linked to from my website:-
www.AndyShaw.com

The purpose of my book is to show you how to create wealth for yourself without too much expertise; in fact, with very little expertise; and if you want to, with no expertise at all. It does not get any easier than that.

You should, by the end of this book, have all the bits you need to know to get on with it yourself, to go and do it. That is what this book is all about.

And so, because of the length, I am trying to keep it short so that I do not overload you with too much stuff. I want to give you just what is needed for you to make an informed decision about whether you want to do property investing or not. And I want to give you an exact plan of achieving it.

By the end of this book, if you still won't do it for yourself, if you look at it and think, no, there is not enough money in it for me to give up a couple of weeks of my time; no, it is too much time; or no, it is not for me, I still really have a fear, **I will show you another way**. I will show you a way that you can have all of the benefits of property without any of the effort. I will show you how to get other people to do it all for you!

I am emailed weekly by property investors who say to me things like I've been in the business for five, ten, twenty years and I already own ten, twenty, thirty properties, but until reading your book I didn't understand it in the way I do now.

Those people go on to make extraordinary gains after reading this book, one person bought another thirty properties (to my knowledge) after reading it. This book shows people how wealthy they are and removes all of the bu****it that is in the media, which frees them up to create substantially more.

To all of you that have never gotten into Property Investing before, you will see that all the seemingly hyped up marketing that goes with my book isn't hype at all. Just us trying to get the message over that this is a must-read.

It was suggested by a book reader that when I re-edit this book I include a few of the testimonials I've received to show people how the 'average' person can really achieve this. This would let people know that the read is well worth the effort and it might then help more people to achieve wealth.

So here are a few of the many testimonials I have received from people who were probably just like you before reading my book.

"Your Book is a TOTAL DISGRACE !!!! Yes you heard that right !!!! A TOTAL DISGRACE ....that it isn't in the Hands of EVERY SINGLE child, mother and father on the planet !!!! WHAT AN AMAZING BOOK :- It's AMAZING and I just wanted to thank you sooooo much and anyone who was involved in its making. I've been a fulltime Property Investor for one year. I've read all the books, been on all the seminars and I believed I had all the answers... For the first time in my investing career I feel as if I could be actually purchasing 3/4/5 Props at any one time and it's all thanks to you :-) Thank you for taking the time to write this book. I now see how people can buy 100 props in a year !?!" - Mark Chapman

"The book made me think in an entirely different light. It is quite simple to understand and completely opposite to what property gurus have written in the past." - Brian Hamilton

"I just wanted to say WOW, WOW and WOW! I am reading your book and I'm about half way through. Already it has changed my life by changing a lot of my thinking and beliefs regarding money and abundance. WOW! That's saying something as I'm a person who is very logical and not easily persuaded at all. I am so excited. I feel like your book has woken me up after being asleep at my job for 15 years. I now have the passion and the drive and feel alive again. I have been touched by your honesty and down to earth no nonsense approach when you talk about your first hand experience. Thank you so much for sharing this most amazing experience and journey." - Karen Strutt

"I think it is the best thing I have ever read and I have already had offers accepted on two one-bed flats in my chosen area. Thank you for writing this book and sharing your knowledge. I have already started telling people that the day I read it was the day I knew my life would change and believe me, from where I come from, for people to think a book can change your life is a leap of faith." - Paul Heaton

"Congratulations on the launching of your book. I have just read it for the first time ...it's an excellent, insightful and thought-provoking read. I believe it should be a reference book for the uninitiated and for people who need a bit of motivation!!. What I find particularly interesting is your ability to instil a sense of urgency and clarity on paper ...not a gift too many authors have." - Michael Tracey

"The Book is the BEST read ever and I was cross-eyed after reading 15 chapters non stop! It is better than Rich Dad Poor Dad as it is more practical, down to earth, and it is British! You are also DRIVING people to 'do it'." Ken Ward

"I have just finished reading your amazing book tonight. I have been reading some self improvement books over the last couple of months (Rich Dad Poor Dad, Think and Grow Rich etc.) and I have learned a lot but to be honest with you, this was the only book which made me set my goals while I was reading it and I wrote them down as I was delaying it all the time. I do not know how to express my feelings but I am so excited and determined and cannot wait to buy my first property. I enjoyed the book a lot. It is just fantastic!! By buying your book I have made the best investment in my entire life. Thank you for sharing your knowledge and experiences in property investment with us. I have not put the knowledge into practice yet but I am sure I will and be successful." - Yasemin Turan

(Do you know how long it took me to find six favourable testimonials? ☺)

Seriously now, this book is for you if you have been searching for the way to easily become wealthy and have been let down in the past, when the get rich quick scheme you thought would sort you out didn't even get you slightly wealthy slowly.

This isn't a get rich quick scheme; this is a get rich CERTAINLY scheme. I used it to get rich quickly but I am not recommending that, because now that I know it is a certain way to wealth then I know how easy it is to do and it's not going to be ripped away from you if you don't make it happen now.

This is something you can do now, or come back to in 20 years time and it will still certainly work. The maths may change and I'll be updating the book like I am now every couple of years but the techniques can be used when you are ready. This is not a 'jump in now or you've missed it' message. But if you do jump in now then it will work for you because it makes you wealthy whether you want to continue with it or not! This makes you money despite you!

Now-that message when you start to believe it shortly, may cause you to get somewhat excited. That's why one of the most common questions I am asked comes up. People say to me, 'Andy, I get it. It is unbelievable. The trouble is that my wife/husband is a sceptic and they think this is just another hair-brained get rich quick scheme that won't work. So how can I convince them of how simple it is?' Well, towards the end of the book I will be giving some ideas to help get your partner to open their eyes a little.

3

Feedback – The Cornerstone Of Success

I truly believe that I have achieved success thanks to feedback. Whether I get feedback from close friends, business associates, bank managers or clients; whether the words are full of praise or anger, they never fall on deaf ears. Why? Because those words help me grow.

I have bought property for dozens and dozens of clients. I have bought property for family and friends and obviously a seemingly endless amount for myself. And feedback is one of the most useful tools in my bag of tricks because it keeps me from losing sight of my goal. Just because I may think I am making the right choice does not always make it so. The only way I can judge is by getting feedback, whether it is good or bad.

This book covers a lot of bases for me but I wrote it to cover one main thing for you, and that was to inspire you into action. In their feedback, a lot of people have told me that I motivated them, and that worries me a little because a motivated person will go cold when not spoken to regularly, whereas an inspired person will go and make it happen for themselves.

My policy towards feedback has not changed. Please tell me if I have inspired you as hopefully some of your messages will help to inspire others to change their lives too. And if the feedback is bad then I invite that too.

Without negative feedback, how can I hope to improve what I show people? Please send your feedback to feedback@andyshaw.com

4

Why You Should Listen To Me

Success is predictable. As my friend Gill Fielding says, all you have to do is check the right boxes. Do your due diligence, make sure that you're happy with the way things are going and you will be able to predict your own success.

Success is not a mythical thing that only the cleverest people on earth can achieve. How does Richard Branson do that, or how does Donald Trump do this? Their success is predictable to them -and you can make yours predictable to you! Of course there is an element of risk in all ventures. Some of the greatest successes you see these guys have could have been speculation. If you go out to bat enough times, you are going to hit a home run or two.

But at the core of what they do is predictability. You have to do something that's predictable. And what I am going to show you in this book - this one technique that everyone can use, will help you to achieve predictable success. Both success and wealth **are** predictable and above all, they **are** easy.

I was chatting to a friend of mine, Terry, the other day. (A lot of you will know him for his simple, but effective method of Nerve Release Therapy – "Tiukaan").

-- A quick sidetrack here: I have endorsed his unbelievably simple cure since he changed my life a few years ago and believe me I do not endorse things lightly! I had a bad sciatic problem and I was fortunate enough to have him relieve 99.9% of it by his very clever treatment and I avoided surgery altogether! If you have tried everything else and you just can't shift that pain, or worse, you are facing surgery as I was and you want a more 'sane' option, then email me for his contact details. If you would like to read the full story of this experience, and how the treatment has helped so many others that I have recommended to him, then visit my site. --

Anyway, I was chatting to him over the weekend and I said, 'Yeah, I am writing a book.' And he said 'Oh, yeah? What is the title of the book?' And I said 'The title is *Money for Nothing and Your Property for Free.'* He paused and I said, 'What do you think?' He said 'Sounds too good to be true.' And I said, 'Yeah, it does sound too good to be true, doesn't it? Funny thing is, it isn't.'

I am nothing special. People view us (Greg and me) as special because we had a big business, or they perceived it that way. We employed well over 100 employees plus we had a lot of sub-contractors. We had 25 -30 vehicles. We had three factories with five different production facilities. We had over 100 pieces of machinery. It was considered a successful business. I considered it a bit of a pain in the backside and a huge millstone around my neck.

Don't get me wrong. When we first started it, I had a lot of fun making it work and I really, really enjoyed myself. I was production-trained as an apprentice. I loved that and I loved the installation side. Some of the people I worked with were just fantastic and I made some really good friends. Though it was a struggle at times, I think it is fair to say that I enjoyed every day – it just wasn't fulfilling my life plan if you like, but I had a lot of fun, as I do with everything I do.

One day I realised that the life I wanted was not going to happen if I carried on doing what I was doing. I realised that owning this business was the same thing as having a job but without the benefits. I said, I want more. I wanted more than I had got there. This was not enough for me.

When I was 13 years old, my millionaire Uncle Dave sat me down with my brother and asked us a series of questions. When each of us had answered him as best we could, my uncle gave my brother a fiver and said, 'Well done. You can go and buy a lolly in a little while.' My brother ran off happily to play.

Then my uncle turned to me and said, 'I have got something to tell you.' He was a smart man, my uncle. He knew that I had been hoping for a fiver as well. He said, 'I am going to give you something far more valuable than five pounds. I am going to tell you your future.'

He said, 'You are going to become a multi-millionaire. You are going to go out into the world and you are going to create a lot of money. You are going to have a fantastic life and you are going to help a lot of other people to do the same. Most importantly, you are going to have great fun doing it.'

'But,' he said, 'You are missing some key elements that you will need in order to be able to create this money. But do not worry. There are people out there who will have the skills and talents you will need. Some of them

26

will become your business partners. You have got to wait and they will come to you. Just be ready when they do.'

Wow! Still blows me away when I say it now.

I could have taken that several ways. I mean, to be told that sort of thing at the age of 13.. But I took it the right way and, sure enough they did come to me. It was years later and only a few years ago I read about manifestation and I realised that I'd been practising it for years. But that is for another book and time!

I was very fortunate when I met my first business partner, Greg. We were both quite young, about 18 or 19 years old. I recognised him the instant he walked into the room, and I had my back to him as well! I do not know why. He just seemed to have a sign on his head that said 'He is the one to go into business with'.

Since that day I have found that a sign is present on a lot of people I meet, but what is written on it is often very different. But that is for another book and time as well!

Okay, back to the point and skipping forward several years, Greg and I were at lunch with our business mentor, Mike, in October 2001. We had done quite well since he had first come to help us when we'd had a bit of trouble in the '90s. Back then, he had been sent by another friend to help us.

Mike was about 55 when we first met. He says we were like frightened rabbits at the time. After looking things over, Mike said, 'I am going to help you and I am going to show you how to stop these sorts of problems ever occurring again. But I am not going to just sort it out. I am going to teach you how to sort it out. I am going to fill in the blanks for you' and over the next few weeks he gave us the real foundations for good business.

At one point I said, 'Look, you know, why are you helping us? Why help us at all?" And he said, 'Well, it is like this. I am the old man in business teaching the young man in business how it works. This knowledge comes with a price and the price is you have to go on and you will have to do it for other people as well.' And sure enough, we have been fortunate enough to have been able to help quite a few people out since Mike passed on the skills. It's when I save someone's business using the skills he taught us, that I get my greatest pleasure in business.

Anyway, I was at lunch with Mike and Greg in an excellent Chinese restaurant in Worthing. We used to go there at lunchtime, as it was Mike's favourite; it was always packed in the evening. It is a very large restaurant. But in the daytime, it is nice and quiet so we had the restaurant to ourselves.

We were sitting there, enjoying lunch and the conversation. I was coming out with yet another idea for something and I was trying to sell both Mike and Greg on this fantastic idea I'd had for some new business venture or whatever it was. I can't even remember what it was to this day.

Suddenly, Mike cut into my presentation. 'Look, Andy,' he said. 'All of your ideas are excellent but they all lack one thing: money. If you have not got the money, then they are useless. Besides, you have already got enough business, you do not need to start any more.'

Like a giant switch inside me, something flipped and my life changed. So I turned to Mike and I said, 'All right. I will go make us some money then.'

Now, up until that point, I had virtually forgotten what my Uncle Dave had said to me. It had come back to me in my late teens , because I lost my way in my teenage years as most teenagers do. It showed up occasionally over the years and then it came back to me later that evening.

I suddenly realised that I had not achieved the goal that my uncle had set me, which was to become a multi-millionaire. I had forgotten to do it!

So, I had to go away and learn about money and learn how to make money. I did not know what *creating* it was at that stage.

You know, I used to think it was automatic. You go into business, you build the business up, you get good turnover coming in, and you get reasonable profits coming in. Then the bank looks after you and you go out there and make lots more money. And you know, up until lunch that day, for no reason at all I still believed that; I really thought that was what was going to happen – *naivety beyond belief!!!*

Sure enough, that was complete rubbish. Or as Blackadder would say, there was only one problem with that plan: it was bollocks!

I had been working for 18 years when I decided to dedicate my efforts to achieving real wealth. It took me less than one year to make my first million. I was a multi-millionaire a couple of weeks after that.

5

Beginner's Luck

The reason I believed so completely in my Uncle Dave's prediction of my future was because he knew what it took to be wealthy. He had told me that I would be wealthier than he was because I had qualities he didn't have - persistence and desire. But most of all, he'd said, I had passion. All I had to do, he had added, was focus it toward my goal.

So there I was, a millionaire in waiting and no sense of direction, so I went out and bought a copy of the Sunday Times Rich List. I figured that rich people knew where the money was, so I'd just copy them. I read it from cover to cover.

As I read up on all these people I started to notice where they kept their money. Again and again, I saw that this one or that one had made his money or kept it in property. By the time I was done, the number was staggering: Something like 60 to 70 per cent either made their money in property, or now kept the money they had made elsewhere, in property. And I thought, that's a hell of a lot. There has to be a reason for it.

I then researched property prices, inflation and deflation. I kept thinking, maybe I should look at what I have done in property. I have always been a big history fan. I believe you can predict the future by looking at the past.

I had bought my house, the one I was sitting in, about a year before. I'd paid less than it was worth, but I'd spent money on it so I didn't feel I'd made money on it. I'd just turned it into a nice home. I also owned another house that I had bought in 1988. It's near a shop, near a parade of shops, and near a school.

When I bought it, it was considered to be a rundown part of town. Originally, it was owned between me, my brother and another friend. The friend pretty soon left because he couldn't pay the mortgage. And unfortunately, because of negative equity, when Alison and I decided to get married in 1997, my brother had to give us money to remove his name from the mortgage. After that, what with the business, I didn't think anything more of property and wasn't interested in buying. I was more interested in saving because we were not making a lot of money at the time. Business got better and the better it got, the busier it got and I still didn't think about property for its own sake.

So my second house was an exercise in keeping up with the neighbours, or in this case, my business partner. Greg had decided it was time to buy his first house. His decision made me take a second look at our finances and the market in general. I did a bit of digging and discovered that with the deposit I had sitting in the bank, plus the money I could get out of the house, we easily had enough to buy a bigger house than Greg was looking at. In the end, we bought a property nearly twice as expensive and I managed to keep my first house as well.

When I began looking at property as a path to wealth, I had one house worth £450k and another worth £130k. Though I didn't know it at the time, I already owned an investment property. Before I had even started my journey, I was halfway to my goal!

I had also bought another house in partnership with Greg earlier that year. We had been looking at buying a house that could be extended. That way we would have a 'hospital' job for our building teams in the lean times. It was one of those ideas you have each year, but you know you probably won't get around to.

Then one day one of our employees came and asked for help as she was going to be evicted from her home. As she worked for us I knew we could be sure the rent was paid. (She and her husband are still renting the property five years later and are always up to date with the rent and are excellent tenants).

I said to Greg, 'Look, why don't we buy a house and rent it out to her? If we do that, we get to keep the house and control the hospital job on it. She can let us in to do all the refurbs when we want, and she gets to live somewhere. We get a house that the mortgage is paid on and we get a job for our builders.'

Greg thought this was a great idea. I did too, especially because I didn't have to put any of my own money into it. So we said, 'Yes, let's buy a house.' Greg picked up the phone to a local estate agent that we had done some work for and we said we would like to buy a house. He said, 'What do you want to buy?' We said, 'We want to buy something where we can put an extension on the side of it.' He said, 'I have got just the house, right around the corner from you.'

So we agreed to meet him. Five minutes later we drove the 500 yards down the road to this house. Got out, looked at it, spent five minutes looking around inside it. Went outside, told the agent we wanted it. We used our trained negotiating skills, to haggle the owner down to the full asking price and we bought our first property. There. That was it. Done, no regrets as we had *actually* taken action.

Our research was non-existent. Our looking at the market was non-existent. We did not know if we were paying the right price or not. We paid the full asking price because we did not know any better. This was in March 2001.

The property purchase took three or four months to complete. Nowadays, I look at three or four months as being nothing at all but at the time, it seemed to take forever. The sale was completed on the 31st of July, 2001 and Greg and I had our first property together. We both felt pretty good about it and thought we might buy another one the next year. Our employee couldn't believe her luck when we managed to complete the purchase a few days before she was to be evicted.

When the deal had finally closed, I was looking at the prices of property because someone had said to me in a pub that he couldn't believe how much a certain property was selling for. When I looked at the property he was talking about, I saw that it was in the same area as Greg's and mine. The asking price was the same as we had paid for ours, and yet ours was much bigger and in a better road. So I thought ours might be worth more. I called the agent the next day and sure enough, our house was now worth

£135k to £140k. I got out my calculator. It had gone up in value £25,000 in 4 months!

I did another calculation and worked out that £25,000 wasn't far short of 25% of our whole group of companies' net profit. As I stared at the numbers, I realised that we did not need to employ 100+ people; we did not need several factories, all under lease; we did not need over 100 pieces of machinery; we did not need 25+ vehicles; we did not need to give personal guarantees; and we did not need suppliers. And we would never again need credit control! All we needed to do to make that kind of money was buy property.

We had just made more money by mistake than we ever had when we were trying to make it. I took my calculations to Greg and said all we needed to do was buy a few more properties over the next few years and we would be doing okay.

So, I am sitting there in September with a comfortable sum in the bank, some of which was about to be spent on a second property that Greg and I had agreed to buy. We called this property the Yellow Peril. It was painted bright yellow. I mean, this house was visible from outer space. It was a Victorian end of terrace, nothing special at all and we could not extend it. A teacher was selling it. We bought from the same estate agent again. He wanted to sell it for £105,000, but he had not counted on our new amazing negotiation skills. We managed to buy it for £102,000.

We were negotiators! We had learned how to haggle with the pros by the time we were on to our second property – okay, I admit it: we were still rank amateurs, but £3,000 was a lot of money at the time.

After we had agreed to buy it, Greg kept delaying for some reason. He did not really like the property so he did not want to buy it. I kept saying, buy the house, buy the bl***y house. In the end, we had an argument about it. No, to be truthful, we had a blazing row. Very unprofessional, but we did – it was our style at the time.

I said, look, we just buy the house. He said, 'Is it that good a deal?' I said, 'Yes.' I said, 'The house, I think, is worth more money than we are paying for it. I think over time it will go up in value." I do not know why I said that. I just did. Because I had not evaluated it. I was just coming out with some rhetoric I had learned somewhere along the line.

We weren't getting anywhere, so finally I said, 'Look, if you aren't going to buy it with me, I am going to buy it on my own.' That got him because he did not want to miss out. Greg got it done quickly after that and we completed that deal on 1st October 2001.

At this time one of our other employees came to me and said he was going to have his house repossessed unless he sold it. I thought, why not? So we agreed to buy his property as well. This sale was completed 14th Feb 2002.

Even though I was doing all of this with property, I had not stopped to think that I could make this into my business. I just looked at what we were doing as something you did with your money after you had earned it in a real job.

When I was looking at my own property buying history, I found myself wondering if the Yellow Peril had gone up in value. I called the agent and he said, 'Yes, it is now worth £125k - £130k.' So we'd done it twice: earning nearly 50% of our companies' net income by taking some money from one place and putting it in another.

I thought, I am a property investor now. I own two properties with my business partner, with another one on the way; I own a property with my wife and I own my own home. So, what has this taught me?

The first thing that popped into my head was, 'Hang on a minute, what if we could do this more often?' The second thing I realised was that the profit we had made on the property would not be taxed unless we sold, and if we re-financed we would not pay tax on any of the equity that came out, unless we sold in the future. I thought, 'Well, that's pretty good.' (Don't worry I'll cover this truly amazing little gem in more detail later and tell you how you can use it to fund your life forever ☺)

So I thought, 'Okay, property seems to be quite good for us, and I really like the no-tax thing.' So I looked deeper and I started to research the market. I tracked my property back and then I tracked my dad's property back. My dad had bought his house in 1971 on the 4th of January and he had paid £5,400. Thirty years later, his house was worth, in my opinion, £160,000. It was really hard to take in. I thought, 'It's gone up in value so much over that time, surely it can't be repeated.'

I am a bit of a formula nut on Microsoft Excel and I just started writing this spreadsheet. I back-tracked house prices that I knew about. Then I went out and started asking friends and employees, everybody I knew in fact, to tell me how much they had paid for their house , and their previous houses. I asked what the price was when they actually completed the sale as compared to when they were viewing the property. I tracked a lot of house prices in a lot of different areas for a lot of different types of houses.

Then I went and did all the research I could in the library, because I had not learned to use the Internet properly at the time. The earliest properties I found were from 1901 so it was over 100 years' worth. Some of the research I did, though, as it happens, was not necessary.

I finally decided to focus on the late 1960s to early 1970s, as the property market trend line in Britain changed significantly about 1966 (I've since then discovered why but it's not relevant for the book). Since that time, prices have more or less doubled every seven years. Actually every 6.74 years, to be precise.

I am a big believer in the thing they put on the History Channel: if you want to know the future, then look at the past. Yes, I know I have said it before, but it bears repeating as repetition is a master skill!

So I thought, 'I wonder if that means the prices today will go up in future?' And I thought, 'well, let's run a spreadsheet to do it.' And I ran the spreadsheet.

Almost immediately, I had a setback. The house I had bought in 1988 should have been worth more than it was. According to my calculations, it should have been worth £300k if this formula was right. And it was not worth that at all. So the formula was wrong.

Then I thought, 'Hang on a minute, was that the only answer?' What else could it possibly mean? So I decided to use my parents' home as a calculation base because their ownership covered a thirty-year period from 1971 to 2001. Actually, this was into January now, so it was in 2002 when I first got to this point.

I am being specific with the dates for those of you who will be going and doing the research to verify what I'm telling you, and checking what the market was doing about then. You should find my predictions quite inspiring – even though I say so myself!

Anyway, I used my parents' home and my first house as a basis for my predictions. My parents' home was worth about £135k and mine was worth about the same. I thought, 'They're both worth that same money today, so let us see what that tracks back to.' When I tracked it back, it revealed to me that when I bought my house in 1988 for £65k, according to my spreadsheet it was really worth £33k - £35k.

I thought I couldn't have paid twice as much money as the house was worth because if I had, then there should have been a big market correction straightaway to restore the prices to the way they should be.

And then I thought, 'No, that is too simple. I cannot have found a baseline for property that easily.' So, over a period of time I went and did more research in different areas. I managed to establish a baseline for where the property market was as a whole and more importantly, where it was in my area. I wrote two spreadsheets. '*What will it be worth*?' and 'What did you buy it for?'. The results were pretty impressive. I was able to tell people what they had paid for their property and if they had bought well or poorly, working on an ever-increasing baseline for property.

I'd go to friends and ask, 'When did you buy?' They would say, 'I bought in August.' I'd say, 'So you actually negotiated in March?' 'Yes,' they would reply. 'Well,' I'd say, 'You paid this amount for your property.' They always said, 'Yes I did. How did you know?'

I would go to other people and I would know what their properties were worth now, based on what they had paid for them. I had concluded, somewhat simply, that the property market was something that went up in value over time. 'Right,' I thought. 'That's fixed. If I buy property and wait, it will go up in value over time.'

When I ran the program forward I noticed something else. I noticed the first property Greg and I had bought was not worth £135,000, but actually 20% to 30% more. Again I thought, 'Well, that cannot be right - or can it?'

I could feel I was getting somewhere, even though it was taking all of my free time to research and test the spreadsheets. I sat there with Alison sitting next to me on the sofa. She was heavily pregnant with our little girl, Sarah, at the time. I was sitting in front of my laptop for 18-19 hours at a stretch, just crunching these numbers, coming up with graphs and different reasons for this and different ways to do that.

As you may have guessed, I am a bit of an amateur analyst. According to Greg, I write spreadsheets the size of Asia to actually work my figures out on. I was analysing them forwards, backwards, up, down, every different way I could think of. I was trying to understand all of the different factors that made the property market move differently at different times; why some areas would go down one year and an area twenty miles away would rise 30%-40% over the same period.

I was trying to analyse what had gone on. I looked at many different aspects of property investing and many ways to make money from property. I looked into why banks loaned money and how they made their money. I looked into money multiples and investigated ways of using the same money at the same time for different investments.

Eventually, I was able to predict what was happening. Well, at least I felt I was.

I reached the conclusion that the property market as a whole was undervalued. At the same time, even though all my calculations without fail showed it to be as undervalued as I thought, my rational side was saying that the numbers couldn't be right; that I had to be wrong. If it was undervalued, everyone would know and they would all be buying.

And that is when I came over all shaky. I have had several real revelations in my life. Every time I've had one that I am absolutely certain of, even though I cannot always say why, my hands start shaking. It has proved quite a useful guide to tell me when I am onto something.

I spent the next few weeks checking my information. I could not believe that I was right, especially when you bear in mind that it was all over the news about an imminent property market crash because it had risen sharply in the previous few years.

But I knew differently. What had actually happened was that the property market was busy correcting itself from the years when it *should* have been going up in true value but hadn't actually shifted. I figured out that what had happened in the '90s was that the market had overcorrected. And the property market had stayed so flat because the whole economy at the time was flat as well.

After that, it took too long to come back up. As a result, the curve looked like it was too sharp. The press simply refused to believe that the trend could continue. They wrote what they thought and everyone agreed. The last thing on nearly everyone's mind was that the market was 30-35% undervalued. They did not know or had forgotten the underlying rule: that property doubles in value every seven years.

It is there, whether you can see it or not: Whether the property market is flat or not, it is still going up in value. That was the underlying truth I had figured out from my endless hours of research. I'll go into more depth on that as well, later on.

So I thought, 'Hang on a minute. If I know the property market is undervalued, surely if I were to buy property now, I'd make 20-30%.?I can raise £50-£60k from different sources and go out there and buy maybe four properties.'

So I looked at ways to raise money. I had to come up with new ways to raise the sort of money I needed because I had not got the reserves to really capitalise on my research. I had what I felt was a dead cert with no money. I had an amount of money that I never touched and I was tempted to use that, but in the end I didn't.

Obviously, I was looking at acquiring the maximum amount of property possible, based on the limited reserves I had. I could buy five properties and have a total value of, say, £600k. When the market lifted – based on my calculations – I would stand to make as much as £180k. That number proved to be a pretty big carrot! This was like, WOW! FANTASTIC! I have got to get into that.

We had the Annual General Meeting for our business lined up in early February. Greg knew I had been doing a lot of research, but he did not know what I was up to. I told Alison I was going to announce my property investment scheme at the AGM and explain that I thought we should all go into property because the market was undervalued.

When the day of the meeting came, Alison wished me luck (I still believed in luck at that time. Of course now I know otherwise – but that's for another time).

At the meeting were our external auditors, our company accountant, our in-house accountant, our bookkeeper, Mike, Greg & me. When the numbers had been accounted for and all the reports were read, we were very pleased with the company's results. We had made significant progress in all of our businesses – not significant profits – but they were all profitable and all pointing in the same direction.

When we had discussed everything and had finished patting ourselves on the back, I stood up and started drawing up my plan on a big whiteboard in our old boardroom.

I said that I had been doing the research and had worked out that the property market was 25-30% undervalued in the UK. 'Not only that,' I added, 'It is going to go up in value over the next six months by that same amount.'

Instantly, everyone jumped into their cars and went to the local estate agents and bought some property. Really? Of course not. They all started sniggering and laughing.

I said to them, 'No, no, seriously, I am right. I think we should sink as much money as possible into property. We will all make a lot of money this year.' They just looked at me and carried on sniggering. They went, 'Yeah, right. You're pretty good at analysing stuff, Andy, but no, not this time. If the property market was that much undervalued, everybody would be doing it. There are people out there who are a lot cleverer than you and they do not think the market is undervalued. In fact, the experts say that the market is very over-priced at the moment and if anything, there's a fall in prices coming.'

I was pretty cool about it. I said, 'All right. Okay.' If they did not believe me, I thought, it had to be because they did not understand that my uncle had told me I was going to be a multi-millionaire or that this was the vehicle.

At this point I hadn't figured out that my suggestion that we go into the property market and bank on a market rise was not investing. This was pure gambling, nothing more. I will cover that essential difference properly later.

43

I went home feeling pretty down. I had shown my peer group and they had laughed at me. I was now beginning to doubt my own findings. Maybe I was wrong, maybe I had mis-calculated somewhere.

I went in and started watching the telly. Alison said, 'How did it go today, then?' And I told her, 'Not very well. They all laughed at me.' I asked what she thought. She paused and then said, 'I think you should take every penny we've got and do it. You're right, they're wrong. Just Do it!'

I told you Alison has always supported me, but this was and still is the time she supported me most. I was so confused and let down that I very nearly took the wrong turn. If she had not said what she did and inspired me with her support, I probably would have.

It almost doesn't bear thinking about, because if I had taken that wrong turn, all the lives I have changed and all the wealth I have created, and all the help I have been able to give people just wouldn't be there. I would probably have been one of the guys in the pub saying that I had predicted when the housing market was about to rise and did nothing about it.

I went in the next day and said to Greg, 'All right, this is the situation. Just to let you know, I am doing this whether you want to or not. Whether anybody else does it, I am going out there and buying property. I am right and you are all wrong. I am going to raise the money I need and I'm going to buy as much property as I can.' He said, 'Fair enough, but I think you're mad!'

Later that morning I went out and viewed five properties and bought three. I did not do too much negotiating; I more or less paid the asking price on two of them and on the other I knocked the price down a bit. I came back to Greg and I crunched the figures and said, 'Look, if I'm right, I've made £120k today.' Greg took a look at my calculations and went, 'You are right, they are wrong. I am in!' From then on we bought properties together, but those first few were the seeds to my own portfolio.

From that point on we just went hell for leather and it got a little crazy. The following week we went to Portugal and Spain, on a previously planned trip because we had been talking about buying villas. We looked at plenty of villas in both Portugal and Spain. We had not really decided what we were going to do until we came back and said, 'No, let's go for this undervalued market scheme and buy all we can in the UK.'

So I went out and started buying and buying and buying. I realised pretty quickly that I had committed far more money than we actually had. I decided to pay the full asking price to keep the vendors happy now, as I knew we were going to be messing them around later when the sales neared completion.

Greg said, 'How are we going to fund all this?' And I said, 'We will have to figure that out when the time comes.' At that point, I was just going out and getting my name on deeds before the properties went up in value. I wanted as many as I could get my hands on so that when the time came, I would make a small fortune.

I thought, right, okay. I will buy 20-30 properties and will try and hold on to as many as possible, which is what we did.

In the meantime, we had to find some money. We raised money on the three properties we had and we both re-mortgaged our homes. We raised money on credit cards. We raised money on loans. We raised money from family. We even went to bridging loan companies known as hard money lenders. We raised money from friends as well; anywhere we could get it, we did not hesitate to borrow it. We raised money to buy all these properties because we had a 50-1 shot that we were certain was going to pay off.

One thing we had going for us was our reputation. We were known for our honesty and integrity so people trusted us. We looked for ways to compensate them properly and our guiding principles of never missing a payment and always paying money back when it was due led to more funds becoming available. So we kept buying.

One day, we had lunch with Mike. I think it was around June. Greg and I chatted about how we were going to break to Mike what we had done. Since it was my idea, I had the pleasure of doing it.

He was eating his soup when I told him we had bought 23 properties and he nearly swallowed his spoon! He said, 'Just how the bl***y hell have you done that?' I said, 'Well, we don't really know actually, but we've done it.'

Anyway, we completed the first one in May. After that it was just steady completions, one a week, two a week sometimes. Almost as soon as the ink was dry, I was setting the new properties up for re-mortgage so we could keep the money coming in. We had to keep going because at that point, I was able to buy properties for the prices pre-what I thought the rise would be. I had thought by now (it being summer) that everyone would have figured out that a market rise was upon us.

Unfortunately, the rest of the market didn't know there was a rise out there. So, when I was instructing the valuations for re-mortgage, they were coming back with a lift in value but not enough of one. In other words they were not coming back right by my calculations.

I thought, 'Why are they not valuing the property correctly? I paid £110k for it and it is worth £140k today. Why don't they know that? Okay, so I've only owned it five days, but it is worth the money. Why aren't they seeing this?'

Suddenly I realised what the problem was: I had been so caught up in getting the deals done, I had not told the Worthing property market it had gone up in value. I know this is amazingly arrogant, but that is exactly what I thought at the time.

So I thought, 'How am I going to do this?' I decided to put back on the market, and this was in July, ten of our properties that were in key locations, even though I had no intention of selling them.

One of my little strategies had been to buy properties that were on roads that I went down. As I was driving through Worthing, I wanted to see my properties because it gave me a little buzz, you know, a little bit of an ego trip to remind myself, that property is one of mine!

I have found that continually re-affirming your decisions in life and patting yourself on the back when you remember an achievement you have made is very important to your inner self. I have never been someone who beats himself up over every mistake. I look at mistakes as yet another positive way of moving forward and it has always served to protect me from losing heart when I make them. As Henry Ford said, mistakes are just an opportunity to begin again more intelligently , so they are to be relished and learned from, not feared.

So, most of my properties were in key locations and people could see them as they drove past. I said, 'We're going to put them back on the market at the price they're now worth.' I had to get Greg to talk the estate agents into putting them back on the market at a price they did not think was reasonable. One particular estate agent said, 'Oh, I can't do that. You paid £120k for it. You can't put it on the market for £170k. It's not worth £170k!' We said, 'Look. Do us a favour. Would you please put it on the market for that?'

We finally managed to put all the properties on the market, thanks to Greg's wonderful persuasion skills. Then we sat back and waited. In just two weeks we watched the property market in Worthing lift to the price that I had said it was worth all along. Now the estate agents were valuing everyone else's properties at the prices they had put my key properties on for. I had trouble getting my head through doors for a while after that!

At that time, as my strategy was a market rise, I wanted to be in tune with the feelings that were running through the town. I was speaking to most of the agents on an almost daily basis. As they were the people running the property market, all I had to do was get them all facing in the same direction to achieve my goal. So that is what I did.

The agent that said he could not put the property on the market for £170k rang me two weeks into my test and said, 'Andy, just to let you know, I've just put another customer's house on the market for this same price. I don't know what to say to you, and I don't know how you knew the market was so much under valued.'

Okay, the market had lifted and Greg and I, with all of our properties, made our first real wealth overnight. We never had a problem with a single valuation for those properties.

We had bought 30-40 properties at that time with another 25-30 in the pipeline, each of which had made £30k-£60k. I had bought quite a few on my own as well and I had also bought several for my parents.

It wasn't all roses. We also got it wrong a bit as well. We ended up losing a few and it cost us a lot of our reputation. To this day, some agents still don't think they can trust us. This is very unfortunate. Everyone makes mistakes when they first start out and we had proven ourselves as responsible businessmen long before we had got into property investing. But some of the agents whose deals went sour just haven't figured out that we are in the business that they make profit from and they can make very good profits from selling to people like us. I think that it is very much an English attitude, and I find myself guilty of it in other areas quite often.

In the end, it worked out for us because we managed to hold on to a lot of property and made our first fortune, even though it was just a house of cards at this stage. It is one of our guiding policies now, to never and I mean **never,** back out of a deal. When we do a deal now, the people we deal with know that the deal is done and the sale will complete.

I had set myself a goal in October 2001 of creating wealth. At Christmas 2001, I said I wanted to be a millionaire within two years. It took me seven months to become a paper millionaire. It took me another two weeks to become a multi-millionaire. I had been in my working life for nearly 18 years. It took me 18 years to make my first million. It took me two weeks to make my second.

The trouble was that this had just been a speculation that I had got right. This was not a replicable system so therefore it would be of little use to me and no use to you going forward.

6

Success Is No Gamble

That was it, goal achieved, financial freedom and independent wealth were just a few short months away. We were done, right?

Wrong! As I sat there, thinking back over the steps I had taken, I realised that all I had done was gamble. This was not investing. This was at best speculating, which was not sustainable, and was wholly reliant on the property market going up!

If I was going to become a 'property investor' and carry on buying property, I had to take the gambling aspect out of it. How the hell was I going to do that?

By this time we had, as I said, quite a few properties with another 25-30 due to come in at some point in the next six to eight months. I went back to the drawing board after the realisation hit me that I wasn't clever at all; I had simply guessed on a market rise and, based on some intensive research, guessed correctly. Having to revise my thinking was a bit unsettling because I had really thought: "That's it. I have discovered my way to wealth. I have done it. You know, I am there." Some people might say I was, but I was in search of a strategy to build constant, sustainable ever-increasing wealth, and what I had done did not qualify, not by a long shot.

I started to look at what I had actually accomplished. I had reached my goal of acquiring a lot of

51

property that would go up in value year-on-year. I had become a millionaire and this was a realisation that gave me great pride.,, I had achieved the goal my uncle had set for me, which was to become a multi-millionaire. What I had to do now was figure out a way to achieve predictable success.

We had about 35 props on the go so we probably had, between the portfolio with Greg and my own portfolio, between seven and ten million pounds worth of property we had bought or were buying. It was an enormous amount of money at the time. Quite unbelievable really. Don't get me wrong, it is still a huge amount of money today. It is just that, compared to the wealth I have gone on to create, and much more importantly, am creating all the time, it is a small amount of money in relative terms.

I suddenly realised that I had actually achieved probably all I would ever need to achieve in property. But I did not feel wealthy. I did not feel rich. I had achieved it because I had recognised that this five million pounds worth of property was going to go up in value at 10 per cent a year as an average over time. So, if I wanted £750,000 a year, I had already done it.

There was something really important about it. It was more than £750,000 a year created for myself, Alison, Greg and Helen.

And do not think I did this all myself, by the way. Greg played no small part in this, I can tell you. He might not have chosen the properties, but he held a hell of a lot of this together. Without him, this would not have happened.

I realised that we had created a £750,000 yearly income that had one other great advantage. If I did not sell any of the properties there would be no tax to pay on that money! (I'll come back to this in more detail later.)

I thought, 'Well, hang on a minute. All I have to do, if I want a £1million a year income, is to own £10 million worth of property.' It seemed pretty logical to me then and it still does today. The truth is that it's not always easy to get at this money even though it should be. So rather than rely on 10% equity release a year, I rely on 2% and the rest is a bonus. So if you want £20k per year tax free then you need a £1million pound portfolio. Simple eh?

Greg and I were already there. The property was going to produce easily three or four times what we were earning, made even easier because of the tax advantages. So I thought, 'That's a good thing.'

I don't remember who said it, but someone once said, when you see a big success, someone took a big risk. Boy was that true of us, but how blissful we were in our ignorance. I can tell you now that I am so risk averse that to think about the odds that were stacked against us is enough to give me plenty of sleepless nights.

We had made our money by gambling on a market rise. This was a really bad way to build our future, as it would simply be a matter of time before we tied up too much money in property, or worse still, we ran out of cash by taking a deal too far.

If we were just buying property, we would have to do what most other long term property investors did: We would have to buy and wait until the property had gone up in value enough to pull our money back out. Now, I know I have said it goes up in value 10% every year, but that is an average taken over time. This means that some years, you have to wait. That is where great cashflow planning is essential.

The problem with that style of purchasing, the 'buy property and wait' method, is that it is just not fast enough for me. It is really what I call 'old-style' property investing. It is still a sure-fire winner; a very, very safe way to invest. I mean, you are at risk for longer because your money is exposed longer. But you are virtually guaranteed that your rental incomes are not so tight, that if the market changes shape slightly, you are not in a cashflow deficit situation.

So, while it is a lot easier to do it that way, it is a lot slower as well and I had no interest in doing it slow. I have tried making money slowly and I have tried creating money fast, and fast seems to work better for me. I had already created 85% of my net worth in under six months, which was less than 3% of my working life. This meant that 97% of my working life had created just 15% of my net worth. Under the circumstances, you can see why I wanted to take this to another level!

Do those figures demonstrate the power of leveraging what works, or what! We'll get back to that in more detail as well.

Quick side note: the book has been written as my story so that it inspires you to get into property investing. And by being written as a story it is not as dry as a lot of property investment manuals. But that doesn't mean that there isn't clear instruction in here on how you can do it too. There is also going to be a lot of profound knowledge that will give you some reality shifts- -so you'll definitely want a highlighter pen and you'll probably want a note book and pen.

Back to the story. I wanted to buy property that was under market value, instantly refurb it where needed and revalue it for more than we paid. To achieve this on my terms, I wanted to buy property with a 107-110% mortgage. Unfortunately, there are not many lenders out there who will do this and the ones that will, won't do it on 50 props a year.

So first off, I needed to be able to source property that was below market value (BMV). Then, and this was most important, I needed to be assured of getting the property valued for what it was really worth at the re-mortgage stage. So, for example, if I am seeing it on January 1st, I know that I will complete the purchase between the beginning of April and the end of May. I know that it will take four weeks to refurbish the property. It will take a week to instruct the re-mortgage and get the valuer into the property. Then the re-mortgage will take, say, eight weeks. This means that I was looking at a cycle of probably six months.

If I say that it's an average property cycle of about six to seven months, then I want to design my system so that it can meet that criteria. So I have got to know on January 1st, when I agree to buy the property, what that property is going to be valued at in July or at the end of June. So, that is what I did. I came up with a system that allowed me to do exactly that. How I was going to negotiate the properties down to the price I needed to pay and how I was going to find all the properties I would need.

I had never heard the term 'motivated seller' in those days and when I did hear it,, I did not know where to find them. I just knew that I had to flush them out if I was going to find property at the price I wanted to pay.

I knew how to get the properties to value correctly; how to get the tenants to pay premium rents; how to find the right mortgages. The lot. So I came up with a system that would do everything else. I had already worked out that my cash was only exposed for an average of three months in a property, which meant that if done properly, I could use the same cash to buy four properties a year.

One of my strongest features as a property investor is that I am completely unemotional about property. To me, haggling on a property deal and not chasing deals comes naturally. One of my weaknesses at the time was the harm we had done ourselves at the beginning, buying a few too many properties and having to let some of them fall by the wayside. As a result of that experience, some of the estate agents thought we were a flash in the pan and, at that time, they were right. They looked at us as people who had come along, didn't know what they were playing at and would be gone tomorrow. It meant that I had to fight a lot of the estate agents who wouldn't sell me property because they were afraid I would not complete on it. They were quite right to be afraid at the time because I was pushing the envelope, to say the least.

I went to Greg and said, 'I have redesigned the system. It is based around math now. We don't need to worry if the market is going up, down or is static. I have taken the gambling aspect out of it and what we have got now is property investing pure and simple. I can now predict success in what we do. I can get our exposed money out in less time and re-use it faster. I think we should go again.' He said, 'What do you mean, go again?'

I said, 'I think we should go and raise some more money and go and buy another load of property.' He freaked. He went, 'You are absolutely bl***y mental. What the bl***y hell do you want to do that for? There is absolutely no need to do that, we've made an absolute fortune this year so far. Why do you want to put all that at risk?'

In his own words, he said to me, 'Thanks to you, you've put us in a position where we are going to be financially secure for the rest of our lives. What the hell do you want to go and put us both under more pressure for?'

I said, 'Because I have a new, improved system and I want to give it a proper test.' And he said, 'Well, I don't think we should. I think we should talk about this another time. Let's complete the ones we're buying now and then decide.'

I said okay but I went away and thought about it and I decided to do it anyway. At the time, I had a need to try this new system out; it was like an uncontrollable urge to just do it. From my point of view there was not even the slightest chance of failure.

I said to Alison, 'I am going ahead, even though Greg does not want to. I need to do this and I want to do it now.' She said, 'What do you need from me?'

'I want to get together with you and my mum and dad one afternoon. We are going to get on the phone and raise the money I need to do this.'

And sure enough, we did it. I left work early one afternoon and between the four of us we raised £150,000 worth of credit, which I put in my bank account. I used about £80,000 and kept the remainder available as cashflow.

As soon as it was in the bank, I just went for it. I started buying property. Within a month I had agreed to buy 20 properties, plus another 25 that would not complete that side of Christmas. They would complete in January, February and March. I had picked some vendors who would allow me to complete transactions early and some late. This allowed me to use the same money to buy multiple properties at the same time.

As I kept buying, I kept getting better deals. I got better and better at finding the deals and negotiating the purchase. I did not fail to complete on a single property. I was in control and knew exactly where I could go with it.

I did not tell Greg what I was doing for about eight weeks. By the time I did, I was close to exchange on the first four or five. Again he said he thought I was mad, but I knew I was right.

I had got my cycle times down. It was not even taking six months to do it most of the time and my money was exposed for no more than about 6 weeks. Several of the props were actually re-mortgaged before the first mortgage payment came due. I was buying the property and then I was controlling the time, dragging it out to make sure the cashflow landed from a re-mortgage in time to complete the next deal. I had the properties refurbished, if they needed anything at all in a week or 10 days at the most.

Most of the time I arranged an eight-week completion and was in at the exchange, refurbished it and started the re-mortgage four-six weeks prior to completion. The quickest I ever got one of these to work was two days and that was because I did not need the money for two days, so I took it easy on the solicitors and bank.

I had the valuers going round, sometimes before the carpets were going down. Most times, they were giving me the valuations I wanted because I had negotiated the property so well and I had got the right valuation.

Don't get me wrong, I wasn't 100% on every deal. About 85% came in valued on target and about 15% were coming in with only okay valuations. I factored these into my calculations and carried on. I would take it the way it was and the ones that did not work first time, I went for re-mortgages a second and even a third time within a one-year period.

I was refinancing at such speed that when my money was exposed, it was only exposed for a very short period of time. Of course when I say my money, it was not really my money: it was money I had borrowed and that money was now only exposed for an average of six weeks at a time. So, I was turning the same borrowed money seven times a year. One pot of money allowed me to buy seven properties.

Somewhere along the line, I got even better at buying and cutting costs. I not only got my money back, I was also getting surplus cash out of every property I bought. I worked out that each property produced, at first re-mortgage, an extra £6,999 cash. Wow! So not only was I

59

buying them and getting my money back, I was getting just under £7,000 in cash from each one. This obviously meant that I could buy more.

The money was just coming in, and I was getting more and more and more of it. So every six weeks, as an average, I had an extra £40,000+ coming in, over and above what I needed, tax free! Which meant that I could buy more. I projected this success forward and bought more.

In 2003, my purchasing went through the roof. My improved system was making the previous year's gains look just reasonable; the portfolio I held with Greg was growing at warp speed too. The old style property investing I had started with was already a distant memory and the new technique just kept getting more efficient. In 2003, I think I bought 40 or 45 properties for myself, and something like 30- 35 for Greg and me. It was something ridiculous like that.

7

Making A Good Thing Even Better

Anyway, it worked. By the end of 2003, going into 2004, I had started buying a few different types of properties out my standard buying pattern, outside my core strategy. At the time my standard buying pattern was anything from studio flats to three-bedroomed houses. I had bought a few out of that style because I wanted different types of property investments.

At the end of 2003 I bought a big house opposite the one I live in, as I did not want any neighbours. I was intending to holiday let it. However, we now work from that lovely house and I have a lifestyle that's simply fantastic!

I bought a big property down in the New Forest, a six-bedroomed place near where my Aunt Sylvia lived. It was originally for her, but she decided it was not what she wanted and that we should either sell it or rent it out. This was just a lovely home, a holiday home in the most wonderful tranquil setting, with a really nice stream running through the garden. I tried to sell it in 2005 but could not get the price I needed to cover the expenses. As this property had never been bought to make a huge profit, this was not a traditional property investment.

After six months or so, I made the decision to spend a further £30k and fully transform it into a beautiful holiday home. I had always wanted to try that strategy out and this seemed to be the obvious choice and because I intended using it myself, I added a few little luxuries that I wanted.

I tried to look at it from the point of view that, when I was staying in this sort of home, what would I like? It is the attention to detail that is lacking in most holiday homes I have rented. You can tell that these places are just moneymaking tools for the owners. I wanted to treat the people who stayed in my home like honoured guests, the way I like being treated myself. So I put full Sky TV in two of the reception rooms downstairs and in two of the main beds upstairs; I put DVD players everywhere. I added a pool table, games tables, two playstations, big TVs. These and countless other little touches were added to make the people staying there really enjoy their visit and love the home. I thought, if they like it, maybe they will come back.

I researched the holiday-let companies and decided to go with one and set up a website to promote it myself. I thought I would give it two years and tweak and tune the concept before deciding what to do next.

Well, what has happened from the moment I started it as a holiday let in Dec 2005, is that it has been taking bookings. I had thought, well as long as it covers its costs, when it is not rented we can use it as our holiday home. So far, it's been very difficult to get in it! Part of the reason, I think, is because it is in such a wonderful location: it is right in the centre of Fordingbridge, but it feels like it is buried in the New Forest and it is totally unique. All I have managed to get are a few days with the family and close relatives down there. I am determined to get a weekend in October, but so far it is not looking good.

I did manage to get in towards the end of 2006. I made several changes to what the property had to offer, and I rewrote the property description for their catalogue. Then, in 2007, this property became one of their top three most rented properties. Not too shabby for a beginner to the market!

Sorry! I drifted off there for a minute. The trouble is when I am testing and experimenting with a new system, which is what this is to me, I just find it fascinating to watch it develop. When I have this holiday-let thing right, I will be telling people how to do that as well. Anyway, if you would like to hear the updates on my first holiday home, *Parsonage Cottage*, as I post them, go to my website and as things happen I will let you know.

Anyway, back to the point. I made the classic mistake of somebody who gets a system to work and then gets bored. I got bored with the business of going in and buying a house, or buying a flat and making £20k or £30k. It was boring, it had become routine. When it became boring, I went off the rails a bit and I started buying other property investments, all of which worked, with one exception: but they did not return money in the same way.

Don't get me wrong, I made plenty of money at them, but I did not make the sort of returns that I had made spending £10k or £11k on small deals which went on to make £15-£30k in just six weeks. I did not make anywhere near those sort of returns. So I quickly went back to my small deal style and carried on making excellent returns. I realised that the reason it had become boring was that I had gotten really good at it. When I realised that, it inspired me to do it some more.

cherry-pick them. This meant we had plenty of spare deals as well. In fact, we had too many spare deals.

When I first started, it was like picking up fruit that had fallen from the tree. Now, I had to pick the ripe ones off the tree, unfortunately. So, it was a little more work but there was always plenty of fruit and I rarely needed a stepladder. While it was always available to me, property is seasonal and there are particular times of year when the market bears a lot of fruit and you have to be ready to bring in the harvest.

In 2003 I had bought like a crazy man and I needed to wean myself off the crazy buying in 2004. The problem was, I had actually become addicted to buying property. I could not get my fix unless I bought a property. I would come home at the weekend and Alison would say, 'How have you done this week? Did you manage **not** to buy any?' And I would say, 'Well not really. I bought two or three' or 'I have had a really bad week. I bought four.' Occasionally I would say I had done well, I had only bought one. I was buying for friends and family as well, of course. I liked making other people money too; it was fun when I was buying for them.

For me, however, it had got to the stage where it was almost painful. While it was boring buying all these properties, I needed to buy them because I kept being offered deals that were too good to pass up. When you're making £30k out of a £15k outlay in just six weeks you simply have to pick the money up. You can't leave it on the table.

Anyway, I gradually started to wean myself off them. By this time I had come up against other problems. I could not own this many properties because finding enough lenders was proving difficult. We had not been around long enough to establish the kind of reputation the hard-core portfolio lenders demanded. Most of them would not touch us because we did not have three, four or five years of accounts. This put a ceiling on the number of mortgage lenders we could go to. I ended up buying 16 properties in my mum's name, because I had nowhere else to put them.

I was reading in the paper the other day that they are relaxing the rules on this now and many more lenders are coming onto the market with £5,000,000 and £10,000,000 portfolio lending, which I could have really used a few years ago. In the end, I had to start buying in my friends' names as well because I had literally run out of space with all the mortgage lenders.

While it frustrated me no end, it also forced me to slow down. In the end, it actually weaned me off my addiction. I look back at it now and I think what I did was absolutely crazy. It was just mental. Yes, we have had a fantastic result but, as I said earlier, when you see a big success it means that somebody took a big risk. Well, we took a big risk and it was so stressful. It was like being back in the manufacturing business again.

The risk we took is just not necessary to create wealth. Yes we did it quickly, but if I had to do it again, I would not treat wealth like it was something elusive and I should grab all I could while it is there. Now I know that wealth, like success, is predictable, sustainable and relatively easy. It is when you don't have it and you are trying to find the way, that it appears to be so elusive.

At that time, one of the real powers of property had not really hit me yet. And that is that you can have all the money without the stress. You do not need it. That is just one thing that I should have learned earlier.

So there I was, forced to ease back and prevented from chasing every deal. Over a period of six or seven months I learned to buy only when we needed it. And the funny thing is, as we did that, our buying became better still.

We then focused on honing our buying skills instead of going out and viewing all the property, putting loads and loads of silly offers in and waiting for some of them to come back. I mean, it had been nothing to offer on 25 properties in a week; nothing at all! On a week where eight to nine of them came in, it was great.

But now, we do what was once unthinkable. Get this: we actually wait until the money is available before we go and buy the property. Yes, I know it is a bit crazy (see I did listen in the end Brian!), but I am getting on a bit. After all, I am going to be 40 next year.

Julian and I worked on getting our buying skills better and forging stronger relationships with the estate agents. In other words, instead of going out and viewing 25 properties and putting 25 offers in, we'd go and view four properties, put two offers in and buy one. This meant that 25% of all the doors we walked through we ended up owning.

We got better and better. By the end of 2004, we had our average down to one purchase for every 2.1 doors we went through. In 2005 we were buying one property in every 1.5 doors we went to. In 2006 the market has been a little hard. We are averaging 50% so far, meaning that we are buying one out of two that we walk through.

As we got better, we found that we were able to leverage our time as well. Instead of taking four hours to locate two deals and buy one, we found that we were able to spend three hours and buy two. If we wanted to buy two properties, Julian would spend 40 minutes to an hour looking for four deals; he would speak to the agents on them; we would go out and have a look and we would buy two. This was phenomenal!

Because of the math and because of the system and the finance path, as I call it, we now knew virtually to the penny where we were going to be at the end of each deal. We factored in rental voids. We factored in every possible fee you could imagine. We factored in all of the refurbishment void and the time it took for the rental agents to get the tenant in.

In this period of what I call the quiet time, we started to work on improving how quickly we got tenants into properties, improving the efficiency and the managing agents; making sure the managing agents were better. We really plugged up most of the holes in the bucket. In the early years we did not care as much, but now we had the time because we had become more efficient.

In the early years, we had quite a few tenant issues with late payments and no payments, and we dealt with these poorly. This is madness to me now. Now it is a case of, I want to charge premium rent for every single one of my properties, and we do. We charge on average between £25 and £50 a month more for our properties than most other landlords charge and we get it because we strive to provide excellent quality properties for our tenants.

We very seldom have people paying late and we simply do not have people who do not pay us. Rarely do we have tenants that we have to evict. In the first few years, I think we evicted about six or eight tenants. Now, I would say if we have to evict one tenant we will have had a bad year on tenant issues, and when you think about the size of the portfolio, this is an impressive statement.

What we discovered, when we were going through all of these purchases and we were buying too many, was that we weren't tidying up our systems behind us. But now, because we can buy to order, we are in control of every aspect of the investment. Our main focus now is on improving these already working systems. We work on one at a time, and as something comes up, a new fault for example, it provides us with the opportunity to make the system better.

Our property buying experiment that began in 2002 showed us that traditional business was hard, but property was easy. What we do is just make the easy way easier and there are no limits to what you can do in property. It just gets easier and the deals just have more zeros behind them.

The point is, with property, you can make an easy thing easier every time you look at it, if you just put a little effort in. You can improve it and then continually improve. This applies to all aspects of life as well. You can improve your quality of life easily by looking at yourself more, and by examining how you are interpreting situations that present themselves to you. I go into this in a lot more detail on my website.

With property, the return on your efforts is multiplied. If you've become 10% more efficient and you've got 20 properties, the effect is very large indeed. (Yet another reason for not selling by the way.) With business, you always have another little bomb going off somewhere. Somebody did not turn up for work for this reason or that one. The local chapter of the Hell's Angels has issued a death threat against this bloke. That really happened by the way, and believe me, that was only a seven out of 10 on the weird events scale. Employing over 100 people and another 30 sub-contractors was absolute madness!

Lots of businesses like our previous group of companies employ hundreds and thousands of people. We had not set our systems up to allow us to expand to that degree and by the time we were in a position to improve the systems and knew what we had to do, we had worked out that we did not want to be in that industry any more.

We had the choice of sorting the problems out, which would have taken several years, or we could get out and apply what we had learned to the business of property investing. At that stage we were so fed up with the staff problems, the choice was easy.

While you can get a few crazy bits and pieces occasionally in property, it is nothing compared to the things we dealt with in our previous business. The nature of the work seemed to attract a number of people who were of the lowest common denominator, if you know what I mean. Of course, the vast majority were decent people who worked hard but some were just not good employees. To emphasise that point, one year we sacked more than 50.

The stories we got from people were beyond belief and at times, hilarious. When I tell some of them, people can't believe I am not exaggerating – but believe me when I say we've heard it all.

8

It's All About Choices

I have told you all this to try and get a simple message out. The message is that everyone can create wealth through property if they choose. It is a choice. You can choose to do this. I showed you in my little property story, all you need to do is buy £100k of property to make, on average £10k/year, forever. That is it. If you want to make £100k/year forever, then you buy a £1,000k worth of property.

And yes, I know you're thinking it can't be that easy, right? Wrong. It is that easy, and the <u>choice</u> is yours, whether you choose to believe me or not. It is up to you. Remember property will continue to make this money whether you are in it or not. It will make this money despite you.

Also remember, you can do what I go on to suggest in this book and have the property and still not risk your money. You can do that and still not believe me and that is fine. All I want you to do is take action and buy property and have no money at risk. Then just wait and see what happens!

Choice is something that is really important to me. It has given me freedom. Choice is freedom. When I was in business, the manufacturing business that is, I had several millstones around my neck because I had leases to pay and other things like that. I also had leases for machinery that was depreciating in value.

Now I have mortgages and while most people consider them millstones, I consider them to be my best friends. Those mortgages last at least 25 years. The property goes up in value, it does not depreciate. What is more, I am not paying the mortgages. My wonderful tenants are paying my mortgages for me. The least I can do is make sure that they live in nice homes and keep paying for them. Because they are providing me with one hell of an income and I am very, very grateful.

So, *property gives me choices* And it can give you choices about what you can do with your life. You don't have to do what everybody says you have to do. You don't have to have a job and you don't have to go to work for a living. You can choose to do what you want.

I have chosen to give up some of my time at the moment to someone who has helped me with my weight loss. I am not getting paid for my help because the sort of money I would charge is a lot more than this business could afford. But because I want to help, property has allowed me to choose to help.

How it happened was, I had a go at them in one of the sessions I was in. They were saying that they thought their marketing was really quite good. I told them that their marketing sucked. I said, 'You should have a six-mile-long queue outside your office with a six-month waiting list to get into this room. The population of this country is 25% obese and they should be desperate to come and see you.' I was right; their marketing sucked. When the woman who owns the place asked me for my help, I agreed to help her.

She asked me the other day, 'Why do you continue to help without charging for it?' I said, 'I have not been charging you because I made a choice. I made the choice because **I wanted to**. I believe in an abundant way of thinking that, if you give, more will come back to you in other ways. I don't expect it to come back. It just does.'

She told me that she believed in abundance too, but she thought I was helping too much and that there must be another reason. I told her, 'No, it's just because I chose to. I can do whatever I want because I own property, lots of it, and it has given me the choice in life to enjoy myself and to do whatever I want.'

Most people look at what I have done as a great financial achievement. The bank managers for example. When I was in the manufacturing industry, I used to say all they would do would be to spit in our general direction. You know, when we walked into banks it was like you could feel the cold atmosphere coming from them.

They had this attitude of, 'What did you want to come and see me for? And don't think that I'm going to give you any money!' Do you know what I mean? We had bank managers that we thought literally hated us, do you know what I mean there? Not in a nasty way, but because the industry we were in was not the industry they liked.

The bank managers only helped very occasionally. At one point we had cash flow problems from hell. We desperately needed a £20,000 overdraft. The bank was not interested in helping us until we agreed to put our house up as security. To get a mere £20,000 overdraft! It was dire to say the least.

Now that I am in the business that banks love, bank managers no longer spit in our general direction. They roll out the red carpet whenever I am courteous enough to go and see them. Most of the time however, they come to see me, and I am very fortunate that I have ended up doing business with people I like in the banks.

I am very fortunate that I have very good relationships with two bank managers I use quite often, and I have got another two that I use occasionally. The two I use most often are both really nice people and really easy to get on with. They also make commercial decisions, which is very important to me. I understand the restrictions they have to work within, so we work together.

For my initial purchases now, I tend to use commercial lenders, as I buy properties of higher values and types that do not fit standard buy-to-let mortgages. Most of my investments when using commercial lenders for a while were done through limited companies where I am just one of the shareholders.

The vast majority of my properties are in single names, but for a while I made the mistake of listening to the so called property experts and accountants who preached to me all the great tax advantages of limited companies. Basically I was suckered in because I wrongly believed that because these people sounded like they knew what they were talking about, they actually did. I was wrong and so were they. Limited companies are for use with a different style of property investing, one that tries to mitigate as much tax liability as possible for the eventual time when you sell. But, since I am teaching you never to sell, they are absolutely useless. The reason I got into property was for the money. If I make money in property and I make that money in a limited company, that money isn't mine – it belong to the limited company. I didn't get into this to make a company wealthy. I got into this for the cash I can pull tax free every year for the rest of my life. This is something you can't do in a limited company and therefore they are of little use to me.

As I said, most people look at what I have done as a great financial achievement. Now, here comes another very important point: what I did was not one great financial achievement. It was an accumulation of hundreds, if not thousands, of small efforts and sacrifices that no one ever sees, appreciates or understands. Put together, they amount to a massive achievement.

We put in so much work to make this happen. I mean, just imagine that you can't complete on a property until a re-mortgage has happened from a previous one. And just imagine the person that you're buying the property from is jumping up and down and basically about to pull that property away from you.

So, you have got to tickle through the re-mortgage and you can't give them a completion date until you have the re-mortgage drawdown date. You have got the pressure of the estate agent on the phone, threatening not to offer you any more property. And you haven't got this going on for only one deal. You have got this going on in a dozen deals all at the same time because, as soon as one of them goes, another one starts. This went on for the best part of two years. Pressure, pressure, pressure. We made lots and lots of little financial transactions exactly like this that produced a monstrous result.

Now, our portfolios are worth tens of millions. Several of the properties I own value at over £750,000 and the cheapest property we've got is worth about £85,000. And the cheapest we paid was about £55,000. We have also got a spectrum of property. We have only got eight to 10 in the £400,000 to £750,000 level. The vast majority of our property, the other 200 odd, are in the £165k average. Our other property is now held in limited companies. Those portfolios are growing nicely and at a more reasonable pace of around 20-25 more props every year.

I am desperately trying to get some messages across, through writing this book. As you can see, I am trying to tell people that they do not have to worry about money again if they just get into property. I am trying to tell people that everyone can be wealthy -and you do not need to be clever to be rich.

The problem is that what I have just told you in the last few chapters is probably making you think that you do need to be clever to be rich. And, yes, if you want to become a multi-millionaire in two to three years, you really need to **get** clever. What I am telling you is you do not need to do that. You can become a millionaire or a multi-millionaire just by ticking a few boxes and waiting for time to help you.

If you want to do what I have done, then you have got to go where I have been.. You have got to learn what I had to learn. But, if you just want to become wealthy easily, without too much effort, and get on with your life and have a bl***y good time, then I am here to tell you that everyone can be wealthy. And I am here to show you how you can be wealthy through property investment without any of the stress.

And the reason I can show you the shortcut is I have done every area of this particular style of property investing. There are obviously angles that I have not covered yet, and I will do so over the next few years. I have explored so many avenues that I can show you an easy path and remember *you really do not need to <u>be</u> clever to <u>get</u> rich*.

I have also got to correct a mistaken impression. If you believe that people with money are evil, I am here to tell you you're wrong. Since I started this journey, I have met some very influential people and I've been invited to amazing places. I have found that, mostly, rich people are nice people as well.

I started wasting some money a few years ago when I started buying a collection of super cars. I bought a few Lamborghinis, a few Ferraris. I bought a Koenigsegg, a few Mercedes. And basically, I have been invited to everywhere. You name it, I have been invited. Some of the nicest people I have ever met are the people who also collect cars.

I met a guy who does not live too far away from me who is considered to be second-generation wealth, but he has taken his father's business and made it a lot better. He is so friendly and so nice and his wealth makes me look poor. What is more, when you first meet him, you would never know the level of wealth this man has, and what a decent, honest, nice person he is.

I have got to say, it is very rare that I bump into a wealthy person who is not a really nice person. Usually they are generous and giving because the advantage of being rich is that you have so much more you can be generous and giving with.

I was helping a lady the other day because she had asked me for my advice on property. She came to see me and she has a massive income, over seven figures a year. One of her desires is to set up a charity because she wants to help children from an area in Africa where she grew up. She lives very frugally on £35-£50k a year. I had to virtually pry it out of her that she does actually have one excess, when she goes away on holiday she buys first-class plane tickets, but that is about it. She drives a normal car, lives in a normal house; well, maybe it is not that normal. And thanks to her wealth, she has so many options open to her. What she wants to do with her money is to set up a charity and she needed my help and guidance.

Frankly, this lady has enough money to live the rest of her life on a beach if she wants to. But she doesn't want to do that. And she is not unique in this. I am telling you that in my experience, this is what rich people are like. You create money and you give some of it away. That is what it's all about.

There is another thing you should always remember: You deserve to be rich. You do not deserve to be poor. In the western world, we should go out and create as much money as we can because there are people out there who are not as fortunate, who are not living in this area of the world. If we have an opportunity to go and create wealth, we must act on it as our duty.

Some parts of the world do not even know what creating wealth is. So you have to do it. You have to make that choice. You have to go and create as much money as you can. You have to have the best life you can because they would want that opportunity, that opportunity that you and I have. I am thankful that I will never end my life thinking I wish I had taken that chance or I wish I had tried a little harder. But most people do not take risks and in fact do nothing at all. The funny thing is that by taking no risks at all they are taking a far bigger risk than I would ever take, the risk of a failed life. That's what I started to see when Mike reminded me that I wasn't rich, so I decided to change it and you can change your destination too. You deserve to be rich and all you need to do is check the right boxes. You owe it to yourself and to all the people who do not have the abundance of opportunities that surround you.

What is more, your family deserves to be rich, too. You have the ability in your hands right now. You are looking at it. You are reading from it. This is the instruction manual for your personal wealth creation. I can show you how to do it, yes really! It is not hard, believe me. I can show you other ways to become wealthy too and achieve financial freedom, I can show you several easy ways on the Internet or in business and some of these are just SO clever! But the simplest is shown in this book.

It is up to you to take the next steps. The choice is yours.

9

The More You Know, The More You Grow

Currently, I am sitting in The Marriot Hotel, in Grosvenor Square in London. Its 6.41pm on Sunday 23rd April and I am about to stop writing/editing this book and attend day two of a stock trading seminar. And I will be sharing these experiences as well on my website, <u>when</u> I have fully understood them myself!

Quick questions:

1. Why is it that we as adults do not go to more seminars? There are no wealth creation skills taught at school, after all!

2 .Why is it we stop learning when we finish school? Is it because we think that the learning phase of our life is over?

We think, as adults, that we learn through experience, every single day! While that is true in part, the fact is that our experiences only teach us if we're willing to learn. It took me becoming wealthy before I realised that I needed to go and learn and carry on my learning throughout my life.

I now attend four to eight different seminars/year minimum, and my wealth creation skills are growing all the time because I have a plan for them. I planned to evaluate all of the five ways to create and hold onto wealth and learn them one at a time. I planned to do it over four years, while my life carried on. So why am I the odd one out? This is not a particularly clever plan: I just wrote it down and am actioning it.

Ever since attending my first seminar I realised that the vast majority of people, for sure the 99% who retire poor, are missing out on a really easy way to increase their wealth and so I'm now passionate about getting as many people as possible to see the benefits that these seminars can bring to their lives.

Ask yourself this question: If I attended more seminars, would the likelihood of me learning something increase my chance of becoming wealthy? I know what you are going to say: They all cost money. Yes, some of them do. The one I am on now, for example, is about £1,000/day and I can easily afford it. The money is irrelevant to me as I know there is always going to be more! I know that my portfolio grows in value by £40k a week, tax free; I know that my web businesses and my company bring in money too. Under these circumstances, spending £2k to come on a seminar is nothing.

But no matter the price, seminars to me are the best return on investment there is on this planet. It does not get any better than learning a skill to create money once, paying for it once and then being able to repeat it and use it as much or as little as you want for the rest of your life!

There are countless offers out there that give free taster seminars or even free three day seminars. Yes, they are there to up-sell you to full courses. But that doesn't mean you have to buy and it doesn't mean you cannot learn anything. It is very rare that I will buy a course at a seminar but I learn immense amounts from attending. You can go to them and get a taste of what they feel like first, see if their course fits your plan and then decide whether you can afford it. You can't decide that from the chair at home; you do not know what's on offer.

If you want real sustainable wealth however, with no other fuss then all you have to do is what I have written down in this book. But if you go to some of these seminars, you are going to learn things that will change your life. You will meet future business partners and new, like-minded friends. To me these seminars have become like school outings with all the best bits from school and none of the bad. Also, it is fun to learn new things and flex the old brain matter occasionally.

Sorry. I drifted off again for a second, but you can see that I am quite passionate about this subject.

Of course I can show you how to be a success in business and all of that can make you wealthy, without a doubt! All of it requires skills that can be learned and mastered. But with property you have one big advantage over the other ways of making money. With property, I can show you how it will work despite you! That's right! Even if you get it wrong it will still work, no matter what. All you have to do is actually start and then it takes over for you and makes you rich. Can you handle that?

Property is a wealth vehicle that works despite what you do! It is immortal, like in the film Highlander. It will live forever and work for you for free forever and pay you to work for you forever. Unless you cut off its head, of course.

This is why **Property is the Backbone of Wealth Creation** and if you're at the beginning, it's the best place to start.

However, if this is not the vehicle of your choice then maybe one of the others I talk about on my website would better suit you. After all what do I know, I have only made millions in a few short years.

There are obviously people out there who have done better than I have. Maybe you can find one of them to listen to. If you can, please tell me so I can listen too.

Now I am going to answer a question that I get asked on my blog. For some reason it is one that keeps coming up: Why am I wasting my time writing this when I can be out there making more money? Those who doubt a good thing when they see it assume that my wealth creation strategies do not work. If they did work, I would be out there doing only that.

As I explained to the woman with the weight loss business: The answer is, because I choose to. Just like everything in life is a choice, this is a choice I have made for me. My life is not just about making money. In fact I view money more as a method of keeping score.

It's a bit more than that though. I believe in the Universal laws and one of them is about giving, and I believe that you can't out give the universe. The way I figure it is that I can have everything I want if I just help enough other people to get what they want. So this is me trying to give the Universe more than it can possibly ever give me back :)

We have improved our business with our time and money leveraging methods so I can afford to make this choice. We also buy to order, if you remember. We only have so much money with which we can buy and believe me, we work it pretty hard.

I rarely invest any more without my business partners, as it is far simpler for me to have them with me on all deals and take a smaller cut and have 'nothing' to do with property, other than strategic planning. So with a structure that limits the money we can invest and the time we can invest it, beyond the nods of approval I give to Julian's decisions, my actual time spent on buying property for myself, for clients, for family, for friends is probably, I don't know, half an hour a week. Currently we are agreeing two-three properties a week. Next year we should be agreeing a lot more than that so I may need to put in an extra half-hour a week.

We rarely invest with our own money, or should I say our own borrowed money. We never ever actually invest with what I call my real money and when we do invest, we have two other ways of doing it. One, I have negotiated such a good deal, with both the vendor and the banks, that there is no investment required; or Two, we go in with silent joint venture partners where they provide 100% of the required funding for 25% of the profits. We now have several 'JV' partners and this enables us to buy at a controlled rate without any need to rush, because you can easily make more money, more easily from deals if you slow them down and focus.

You also have to bear in mind that I like to vary what I do to keep me on my toes. If I just did this all the time it would be so very dull, and I want balance in my life.

For me, property investing is just part of it, not all of it. By writing about what I do, I get feedback and ideas from people I never would have met, if I had not written. Barely a day goes by now, where someone does not ring me or email me and tell me that I have changed their lives for the better. Can you understand the true pleasure I get from helping? Do you see now why I am *'wasting'* my time writing!

Hopefully that answers the question. But if I have failed to answer it to your satisfaction, perhaps I should write a book on the answer, if you know what I mean?

I am also very involved in the Internet and that is part of what I want to do, because the creative ways there are to make money online just blow my mind. I love the marketing of our business, Passive Investments. I really enjoy trying to improve our service to our clients, not because we can't afford to pay somebody else to market the business, or improve our systems, but because I really enjoy doing it and I really enjoy learning the master skill in business – marketing!

That is why I do this, because I enjoy it. If I did not enjoy it, if I did not enjoy writing this book, I wouldn't do it because I don't need to. For those who don't believe what I am saying, I can't help you. The only way I can possibly help you is for you to look at your life and think, would you want to help people if you could? Well, I can. I want to help as many people become wealthy as I can while I am here, and I want to leave as many directions for as many people as possible for when I have gone.

Why not, after all, if there is always more money out there? Why can't everyone become rich? Yes, it's a good sentiment. There is always more money out there. It is not as if by me helping somebody to become rich they are going to take money away from me in the future.

We just did a training course aimed at teaching the skills I am laying down in this book. At last year's Wealth Creation Conference we decided to do this course to help people get into property investing. It was a very high cost course at £10k, but it came with a pretty strong guarantee from us. If someone offered a guarantee of your money back if you didn't make at least £20k you would think the only problem with that guarantee, is could they afford to give me my money back. But when that guarantee comes from several multi-millionaires, it is pretty strong.

We only wanted to do it for a few people because the idea was to make them a lot of money by teaching them how to create wealth through property themselves. So we went out and pitched our product and four people bought it. They had partners and we ended up selling another one after the event as well.

Anyway, the core of the product was this: we will teach you how to do it in property, we will give you full mentoring support, we will do full email support, we will supply you with a forum. What we want from you is, you have got to have the money to go and buy at least one property. We will help you buy that property. We will evaluate the deal for you. We will make sure that you buy the right one. And we guarantee to make you £20k or we'll give you your money back. This course happened two months ago at the time of writing, and so far, I think there are three properties being bought with a profit of around £90k for just one of the people on the course.

The point is, we want those people we have just taught using our techniques to create wealth for themselves. Before you ask, we are not doing that course any more. The purpose was to prove it could be done and get their testimonials, such as: this is what they did; and this is how good they were at doing it; and this is what they helped me make; and this is what I am doing now; and these are the choices it has given me in life.

A home study course we are building off the back of that course is under construction now, but you don't need it. You will achieve the same success if you just use the techniques in this book and apply yourself.

Back to the point: There is always more money out there. Every year, every day, more money gets created. So, by showing people how to do this, by teaching people how to do it, it is allowing us to help other people to get wealthy. Those people will go on and help other people and they in turn will help other people to get wealthy. And hopefully over time, it will change the lives of a lot of people just like the ones we help.

10

Assets And Liabilities

What is your most valuable asset?

I consider that I have six assets of value to me. I am going to give them to you in reverse order, as follows:

My least valuable asset is my earning ability. My earning ability was based around the amount of work I had to do or could do; how much I would get paid for the services I provided and things like that.

Well, my earning ability is really not that important now because I have other things that produce my income for me. If I were to lose it all tomorrow for whatever reason, my earning ability would be important again. Since my asset protection plan is running very, very well, my earning ability is not as important as it once was.

Number five on my list of valuable assets is my business relationship with my partner Greg. I am very fortunate in business. I really am. As my Uncle Dave said to me, you will find the people that you need. Greg is an unbelievably clever man, despite the fact that he appears, to some, not to be. He is very, very good at what he does. He understands that because we are selling what people want, his job is simply to show people how our service will benefit them, and then they can make up their own minds. And at his core he is also a very giving person. I am very fortunate to be in partnership with him.

I guess you could say that Greg's the front man. I tend to get the glory because I am the one who finds the deals and comes up with the majority of our direction. But without Greg, these things would not happen. Together, we make a great team. And our relationship is a very valuable asset to me.

Higher than that, in position four, are my two children, David and Sarah. They are so fantastic that I cannot put into words what they mean to me. I am somebody who never wanted to have children. Now I consider myself to be so fortunate to have experienced what having children is all about. I can see it from the point of view of people who never want to have children and why I believed that not wanting to have them was the right thing.

Now I cannot begin to tell you how they have changed and continue to change my life. I am educating them on not having to go out and work for a living, on asset creation rather than wage earning. I view them as a great asset going forward and, hopefully, my relationship will grow with them over time because I view them as being the future of my life.

Third on my list of my most valuable assets is my wife and my relationship with her. She is not just my wife. She is my life partner, my best friend. I have been with her since 1988. And there's nothing I cannot talk about to her. Nothing I do seems to phase her, whether it is a hair brained scheme I'm going off on or a good idea, she will support me in whatever I want to do.

She gives me the freedom to go off, research foreign property, do my seminars, trainings, whatever. I get to go to wonderful places around the world, just wander around and have fun. And she gives me the freedom to do what I do best and supports me in every way. So, thank you.

Second on my list of valuable assets, I believe, is my health and wellbeing. Without your health, you can't do anything. I had a shock hit me in 2003 when I had an incredible sciatic nerve problem. My back had a slipped disc and I could not get it fixed. Chiropractors, Osteopaths, Reiki healers, Acupuncturists, you name it, I tried it. None of them could fix it. Finally I gave in and tried conventional medicine. I had private medical cover, so I was whisked through the system and within a few days was told I needed back surgery.

I was certain there was another way, but the pain was simply impossible to bear. I had decided to have the surgery when, just five days before I was due to go in, a chance meeting introduced me to the person who fixed my back. It is quite a story and it is available to read on my site. I truly believe my positive attitude sought that person out for me. Was it luck or was it determination to prevail? Well I don't believe in luck!

He is the only person in this country, probably the western world, doing this particular treatment. If you want to know more, please email me and I will let you have his details. Unfortunately for sufferers in far off countries, he is only one guy and he does his treatment in Worthing. As you can imagine he is usually booked up, but if no-one else can help, I think he could. He is now training two other people in his technique and it is just incredible what he does. I simply cannot put into words what he has done for me, and now what he has done for my family and friends.

You would be amazed at what he can cure with a non-invasive technique that is thousands of years old that no-one seems to have heard of. I have seen him relieve 99% of the arthritis in my hands; a condition which is apparently untreatable by western medicine other than by painkillers. I have seen him cure life-long migraine sufferers who had been told that their condition was only treatable with painkillers. I have seen him cure shoulders, necks, elbows, knees, ankles, you name it: if it is attached to the nerves in your back, he can probably help.

I was on thirty painkillers a day when I went to see him and he told me I had to stop taking them. I said they were what was keeping me alive but he said I had to stop. The next week when I went to see him, I was on just one pain killer a day and it was the last pain killer I have ever taken in relation to my back!

Other than that, the only other health problem I have had, if you could call it that, was that I was overweight until very recently. I had gradually put on weight when I stopped going out on site and went to sit behind a desk. I had put down the tools, but I carried on eating in the same way I had when I was burning off all the food. Last year when I was working on the Wealth Creation Conference, I came to the conclusion that I could not go out and teach people about wealth unless I treated my body correctly as this was the one area still left undone and it really messed up my life balance chart.

Please don't get me wrong, I did not lose the weight just for everyone else. I did it for me and for my family. But I also thought that, as my body was a reflection of my psychology, I simply could not have myself in poor physical condition any more. I had to turn that part of my life around and lose all the weight. And I did. I am still on the diet as I am editing this and I have got just thirteen days left before finishing stage one.

I've been on the diet for nearly seven months and have lost 9 stone 5 lbs. By the end, I will have lost nearly 10 stone. I will have changed the way I eat in that time and I will never be fat or overweight again, which is a nice position to be in. To achieve this goal, I had to change my beliefs about food and am currently changing my beliefs about exercise. I have learned that I chose to be fat and now I have chosen not to be. Before I started, I set myself a goal and designed a plan for my weight loss, my weight management, my exercise, my re-toning and then finally, the rest of my life.

My well-being now comes from having complete balance in my life, a balance in all different areas: emotionally, spiritually, in business, with my children, with my wife, in every area, my holidays, my personal development and my goals. I have really got a balance with everything, which I did not have a short while ago. The balance I have will not stay as it is now; I know that my standards will improve and my choices will change, and then I look forward to adjusting my balance.

I know what some of you are thinking, he has listened to Anthony Robbins, and you are right. I started listening to him on Friday 21st April 2006 **(two days ago).** I had never got round to it before, but my plan was to listen to his courses this year. Funny, how I chose to change my thinking before listening to his excellent course.

He makes it quite clear on his course that it is not him, it is you that makes the change and he is right: he is just there to show the way. Simply excellent, I can't wait to listen to day four of Get the Edge.

I have a very good friend, Brian Hughes, who first told me about life balancing a few years ago and since then I have used a simple Excel charting spreadsheet to see how I am doing. What it does is shows you, by using a graph, where the balance is missing in your life. I go in occasionally and I enter where I feel I am at the time. It is amazing how this all changes shape depending on where I am and what I am doing.

So, I do this thing regularly now, every three months, to try and remain balanced with everything. And obviously, my health was something that did concern me and I think I was definitely on the road to diabetes, but I recognised it in time. I have now lost the weight and, you know, I feel great. I washed my wife's car at the weekend and for the first time I can remember, didn't even break into a sweat.

And this brings us to the top. There is one more asset that is even more important than all the others and that is my time. My time is the most valuable asset to me. I am using time to get the most out of life in all different ways. I try to make sure that I don't waste any of it. I also try to make sure that I enjoy every moment and have fun with it.

Time is a very, very valuable asset. To get the most out of everything I do, I structure my time very carefully, making sure that I have fun and enjoy myself while I am doing whatever it is now that I want to do. In this world, whether you are a Bill Gates or a homeless person, we all have the same measure of time, and each morning that measure is topped up. It is up to the individual how well they utilise their individual measure of time and how much they appreciate the moment they are currently in.

I spend as much time as possible doing each of the things I want to. I moved my business to my home, or just opposite, so that I could be closer to my children. I now get to have lunch with my little girl, who is not at school yet. I get to have breakfast with my family. I don't go to work until later, not that what I do could really be called work. I come home when I want. I take them to school. I get to know them as I am always around. To me, the most important time I have is the moment I am in right now. The past is the past and I cannot change that, the future has not happened and I will deal with that when it does.

Please don't misunderstand me here. Time is not precious, but my time *now* is extremely precious.

11

Why 100 Per Cent Return On Investment Is For Amateurs.

Let me ask you a question. What is your favourite Return On Investment? You think about that and I will tell you in a little while, what my favourite return on investment is.

First I will tell you a little story about the Money Gym Property Investment Training Day we were asked to do for our friends, Nicola Cairncross and Judith Morgan. Greg and I went along there a few weeks ago. Greg, as usual, did a fantastic presentation about the power of property and what it can do and how it can really change people's lives.

While we were there, Nicola chucked a local paper at me and said, 'Go on, then. You think you're so clever.' In front of everybody this was. 'Go and show us you can pick a deal.' I had previously stated that I could pick a deal in no time at all, and it did not matter which town I was in or anything. I can find deals wherever I go. A bit like Robert Allen did with the no money down thing in the '90s, though our property market is not quite so much the promised land as the American market is. I first read about that from Peter Jones in his book 'An Insiders Guide To Successful Property Investing' which has some very good things to say on property investing, but there are still great deals everywhere.

Anyway, I went out of the room and looked through the paper. It took me about half an hour. In that time, I found six possible deals. I then got on the phone to Julian. 'Julian, here's six deals I found. Can you call up the agents and find out the details on them? Find out what sort of deal we can get and run them through our system to find out how the maths work out.'

I gave Julian an hour, maybe two hours to do those bits as I was away from my desk. Later, I went back to him and said, 'All right, how did you get on?' and he gave me the feedback.

I went back into the room. In a little while Greg called me up and said, 'Right, tell us how you got on.' So, I showed the first deal. I said, 'I looked at six deals. Now let us evaluate the first one.' I put it out and I showed that the first one would produce 191% Return on Investment (ROI – this is quite an important abbreviation) in six months.

Everyone was like, well, that's pretty good, you know. I'd have had a bit of money left tied up in it but, basically, through equity creation and the money which would have been returned through refinancing, it produced approximately 191% ROI. Everyone was quite impressed.

So I asked them, 'What do you think?' They said, 'Well, it's pretty bl***y good.' So I said, ' Yeah, it's not bad. But it doesn't excite me.' They were shocked and asked me what I meant. I said, 'Let's look at the next deal.'

The next deal produced about 400% ROI in the same sort of time frame. When I revealed this there were shocked shouts in the room like, 'Bl***y hell! 400% ROI. That's fantastic! Wow!' I said, 'Isn't that a good deal?' And they said, 'Yeah, that's a fantastic deal.' I said, 'Well, I don't think so! I don't think it's a very good deal at all and it does not impress me much! Let us look at another investment.'

The next investment produced a whopping 950% ROI. Everyone was again shocked. '950% ROI! What? In only three months? This is fantastic.' I said, 'Yes, it's really good, isn't it?' People were shocked to believe it is possible to make a 950% ROI in such a short time frame and from any paper. It made what I was showing them look absolutely brilliant. A little bit of cash was tied up in the property, but it produced a hell of a ROI.

I said, 'Well that more or less diminishes most other investments, but it doesn't excite me very much!' They asked, 'Why's that?' So I told them, 'It's not enough.'
'What? 950% ROI isn't enough?' I said, 'No, it's not enough for me! I don't want a 950% ROI. It's a pathetic ROI and if that's what I got for myself, my business partners and my clients, I would have complaints to deal with.'

I asked, 'Is there anybody here who would like this deal now, as it stands?' About five hands went up. I said, 'Yes, I can see why you like it, as it isn't bad after all, is it, 950% ROI. There aren't many investments in the world that give you that sort of return on investment, is there?' Then I said, 'Hang on a second. Let me show you another deal, and we will see how you feel about this one after that.'

99

I showed them the fourth one. And the fourth one produced a massive 3,635% ROI. The room went silent and then went, 'Wow!' Everyone was shocked. Without fail they all said, 'That's incredible.'

I said, 'Yeah, you see what the power of property is? What other investment gives you these sorts of returns on a regular basis? A few minutes ago you were looking at that 191% ROI and thinking that was good. Then you were looking at 400% ROI and couldn't believe that. Then you were looking at the 900%. And now you're looking at the 3,600% thinking you wouldn't even get out of bed for the 191% ROI. So, 191% ROI is for pure amateurs, isn't it?' And they all said, 'Yes, it is!'

I was at lunch a couple of years ago with a very good friend of mine. He had seen us grow into property and thought it was just a flash in the pan and that there would come a time we would return to our previous business so that he and I could work closely again, because we had both enjoyed it. He was right about me enjoying working with him and it is one of the very few things I miss from our old business. He has watched us in property and can't get it into his head that we are now experts in this field. It just does not make sense to him and he is fixated on a 20% market fall coming. I can't help him, because my words have no meaning to him.

It never ceases to amaze me that I can empower the lives of complete strangers so easily, but I can't help one of my closest friends at all.

Anyway, we were at lunch and we were arguing about property versus. shares. Not that I have anything against shares, of course. It is just a different market and after evaluating both I had decided to create wealth in property first. I was saying you cannot compare the two as the returns on property are just so much greater than the stock market. He turned to me and said: "Look, in the last nine months I have made nearly a 20% ROI. You would not turn your nose up at that would you?" I said: "I would not get out of bed for that return!" Obviously he didn't believe me. What can I say?

Anyway, I drifted off there for a bit. Let's get back to The Money Gym. I said: "3,635% ROI – do you think this is a good deal?" And they all went: "Yes, that's a fantastic deal!" I said: "Well, I don't think it is. I think it's mediocre and I wouldn't buy it. So anyone here can have this property if you want it, if all you want to make 3,600% ROI, because I am not interested in that and nor are any of the people I buy for!" Everyone was just stunned into silence and I paused to let that really sink in.

I said: "Let me show you another property." The property they saw returned all the money to me and it returned some cash to spare: £2,000-£3,000 approximately. It returned all my capital invested to me and it returned an extra cash surplus.

I said: "What do you think the ROI on that one is?" After a few seconds it was clear that nobody knew. And I said: "It's infinite. It's **an infinite return on investment** and infinite is my favourite ROI. When I buy property, I always look for an infinite return!"

Well, the room went silent again as everyone tried to get their heads around that little wonder. I have none of my money in it and I have some cash come out. I am looking for an infinite return on every investment I make. I achieve this in at least 99% of all of the deals we ever buy within 3 – 6 months of buying them.

I asked: "Hands up who'd like that deal now?" Every hand went up! I said: "Yeah, I thought you would all like that one. Well, there is one even better than that!"

I showed them the last deal. And the last deal looked the same as all the others, because they all looked more or less the same. They were nothing special. They were all one-bedroomed flats (thought I had better mention that at some point).

As for the last one, though, obviously it produced an infinite return on investment, as this is standard to us but it also produced £10,000 cash out as well. So, it gave me all my money back and £10,000. Well you can imagine the response in the room, even though they were all feeling pretty drained at the time.

Now, I had found that deal sitting in a local paper, without trying. It did not take very long. I offered that deal to the people in the room if anybody wanted it. I don't know if anybody took it up, but I would imagine no-one did because that would involve taking action and doing a small amount of work to produce an incredible return.

As human beings we are work averse. It is far easier for us to remain within our comfort zones and not venture out to the unknown. This means we would not do something easy, simply because we have not learned the process for doing it. At the same time, we would not hesitate to do a year's work to produce the same result. We – and I am including me here – often behave just like sheep. If you want wealth, you need to recognise when you are doing that.

I offered both of the infinite returns on investment properties. No, I offered them all. It was up to them. It did not bother me because we didn't need them, because we only buy to order. Just because we found a deal does not mean we have to jump in a car, rush over, find it and buy it. Bear in mind this was just out of the local property paper and over the phone. We had not actually seen any agents yet, where we would always find better deals.

That is not the point. The point is, the ROI always wants to be infinite. Now, how can you always find infinite ROI's? We will come back to that a bit later in the book.

Here's what I do: I buy a property for, let us say, £100,000 and get an 85% mortgage on it. So, I've put in £15,000. Let us say my legal costs are £1,000 and let us say my refurbishment costs are £4,000. So, I have spent £20,000 in total acquiring a property that's worth £100,000.

I then get that property re-valued for £130,000. I then get a new mortgage on that property for 85% of £130,000, which gives me a mortgage of £110,500. That pays off the original £85,000 mortgage, it gives me back my £20,000 and it leaves me with £5,500 surplus cash. That's it. That is how you do it. Right?

It's simple for me because I do it all the time. I suggest you re-read those paragraphs until you understand the theory, change the figures and get them to work for you.

So now I have a no-money-down deal. It has taken three to six months for me to get my money back, but there is none of my own money in it and I have got £5,500 cash in my hand and I have got a tenant in the property paying the mortgage. It is all done with conventional lenders, conventional valuers, nothing out of the ordinary. This is just a system!

So, if you know that skill and if you've got that skill, what would stop you buying as many properties as you want? Nothing! That is why it didn't stop us. That is why we were able to buy several hundred properties with no money, or at least with none of our own money.

In fact, I have never put any of my own money into property other than to cashflow my own mortgage and as we know, that's just a temporary arrangement. (See if you can figure that one out. I will explain fully what I mean later).

Greg had to put his own money down, unfortunately, because he did not have a house he could re-mortgage to pull the equity out of. But I have never put any of my own money into property. Even my first house, my dad gave me the 5% deposit. So I have never put a penny into property of my own. I have paid mortgages, that is all. Later, we will come to how I actually make it so that the mortgages are free as well. By the end of this book, I will have shown you how all your property investment has been and always will be free!

So, that is how you get your money back. You go to one lender and, get them to give you the mortgage on it. They give you the mortgage and you buy the property. , You then re-mortgage the property after you have bought it and you get the money back out of it. That is it. Ta-da!

Back to Return On Investment. What happens after a year or after two years, when that property has gone up in value again? What is the Return On Investment then? Because you have not got money in it, it is still an infinite Return On Investment, isn't it? So it is an infinite Return On Investment for the rest of your life. That isn't bad, is it? Yeah? I mean, each year we are getting an infinite return on our investment.

However, I don't think that's a completely realistic way of looking at it, so what I have ended up doing is looking at it another way. I have ended up having to go, all right, well, what is my equity in the property? Let us say my equity in the property is £20,000 and the property is worth £100,000 and the property goes up in value 10%. Then my return on my equity investment is 50% a year. Obviously even looking it that way, 50% ROI for virtually zero work every year for the rest of your life, is not bad. So did you get that? I will go through it again.

A property is worth £100,000. I have got £20,000 equity and an £80,000 mortgage. The property goes up in value about 10% percent. So my property is now worth £110,000. I have got £20,000 equity in it and I've made £10,000 pounds return. So therefore, I have made a 50% return on my equity, even though you could say, "No, that's rubbish because, basically, that isn't your money anyway, so it's an infinite return.' But I'm going to decide to count *after* I have had my initial money back all equity and say, well, I have got a return X on my equity investment.

So when you see the figures come out monthly or annually on the TV and they say, "The property market hasn't done very well this year: it has only grown by 8%

compared to the FTSE 100 which has grown by20%", I just smirk and think amateurs. I mean, it is like comparing a pillow to a solid rock and saying the pillow is much softer. Pathetic amateur investors hold good people back by advising them poorly. When I see 8%, I don't think: "Oh, the market's done bad." I think: "Well, not bad: That's about 50% increase on my equity!" *50% is not bad for money you can't touch!*

People who tell you to pay off your mortgage and that sort of thing don't know what they're talking about. Please stop saying that, people, because you simply do not understand how property works!!!!! People who think you make more money by selling property are just showing their ignorance, but we will come to that later.

Let us look at other Returns On Investment. You know, we don't even need to talk about ISAs and PEPs, do we? So, personal pension plans and things like that, SIPS. Yes, they can be good; they are very good, tax efficient vehicles. But, they do not give you the sort of Return On Investment that this will give you, and they definitely will not give them to you for the rest of your life.

So, let's look at an ROI based on your time. I am going to show you a technique in this book where, for let's say a total of three working days a year you will be able to create yourself more wealth than you will need for the rest of your life, comfortably. Let's say it was three working days a year and that is if you want to buy two properties a year as well, every year going forward. If you don't, then it is a lot less than that.

Now, all of this is well and good, but what about the tax? What effect does that have on your ROI? If you are

106

earning a decent income, then 40% of everything you make is taxed, while in property you only pay tax when you sell. So if you don't sell, guess what? You don't pay tax. Is that a good thing or a bad thing?

Also, you have got rental income. You will have to pay tax on your rental income, but there are ways to mitigate that as well. So you could end up not paying any tax at all, legally, above-board, playing by the tax man's rules. Why? Because you are in something that the government wants you to be in. They want you to provide properties for people to rent because they are an inefficient provider of housing, as I think Robert Kiyosaki says.

The government gives you tax incentives to get into it. We'll come on to more of the tax benefits of property later, because it really is like the cherry on the top of the cake.

Right. This is simple. Most semi-intelligent people can grasp what I have said. You buy a property below market value. You put in your 15% deposit. You then refurbish it. You go to another lender and re-finance it. The second lender gives you what the property is really worth now. Pretty simple system. Gives you an infinite Return On Investment. Right? As I said most semi-intelligent people can grasp this and do it and achieve it.

So when you hear people say they are making 20% per year, do you think you will ever be impressed again? Don't get me wrong, each investment has its place in a true wealth strategy but Property Investment is real wealth's backbone.

12

What Do You Want?

What do you want? And more importantly, why do you want it?

Not knowing what you want, or why you want it, is one of the biggest obstacles you have got to overcome to become rich and get started in this one particular style of property investing. As with any other achievement you want in your life, the biggest obstacle you have to overcome is actually yourself. Fortunately, there are ways you can get around the problem.

Without knowing what you want or why, you are doing yourself more damage than you know. The key to getting around it is simple and easily skipped over: goal setting. It is simple. Yeah, yeah, yeah. We have heard it all before. Right? No

Goal-setting is the master skill in life

According to an expert on this subject, Brian Tracy, (his book: *100 Absolutely Unbreakable Laws of Business Success* is one of the best books I have ever read, by the way) less than three percent of adults set goals. According to me, that is why less than one percent retire financially free. You should—no, if you want wealth, **you must** set goals! And set them in all areas of your life.

Lloyd Conant, founder of Nightingale-Conant, the biggest supplier of self-improvement courses, said: **"Success is goals and all else is commentary."**

Think about that for a second.

"Success is goals and all else is commentary."

So everything else that you do, *everything else* is just commentary. Talk, in other words, that gets you nowhere, unless you turn the lessons you learn into goals.

Success is about setting goals. Success starts with and comes from, well-set goals. That is what you have to do. You have to work out a strategy and set goals because if you do not set goals, you will not win. You will not get there. You will not achieve what you want. Success is goals. It is that simple.

If you do not set them, you will not achieve. You will not do it and you will fail! If you just keep them in your head, then they are just a dream and you will fail! Put them on paper and then they are a plan and you MAY succeed. Get passionate about that plan, and you WILL!

Now, let's look at the actual goals themselves. You have to set focused, measurable, achievable goals. It is no good saying: "I want to be the best looking person on the face of the planet." It is completely unachievable, even if you are absolutely gorgeous. How can it be judged that you are the best looking person on the face of the planet? It is immeasurable. So, it is not focused, it is not measurable and therefore, it is not achievable – it is a sh*t goal – doomed to failure. The only achievable thing you would glean from that goal, is that goal setting does not work! Real clever!

However, what you can say is "I want to excel at this particular subject in this particular time frame. I want to have this particular result and this is why I passionately want to achieve this goal." This way, you can set a focus for it, you can set a timescale and, the most important thing, it can be achievable. There is no point saying: "I have got £10 to my name. I want to be a billionaire a week on Tuesday; actually, can you make that Monday, as I fancy going to a club Monday night?" It is unachievable.

To give you an example of an achievable goal, I wanted to set myself a financial target. The financial target is a sizeable amount of money. I gave myself 20 years to achieve it. I am referring to my main, long-term financial goal. As it turns out, I will achieve this goal in just 12 years. I am just three years into it and I have already shortened the timescale from 20 to 12 years. So, already, just by setting that goal and working towards it, I have taken eight years off the end target. You can do this too.

To achieve goals, you have to have passion built into them!

First off, there is a difference between desire and passion. Desiring something is when you see a Ferrari or a Lamborghini or a Porsche or a Koenigsegg and you think: "Boy, I'd like to have one of those. Yeah!" You desire it. Or you think: "I would love to be thin!" That's desire. Passion is something completely different.

Passion is refusing to live without the thing you desire.

I don't know who said it first, but it is so true. I heard it again from Steven Pierce recently at an Internet seminar: **Passion is refusing to live without the thing you desire.**

I refused to live without being thin and in control. And I got passionate real quick. And as soon as I got passionate, I achieved it in well under 50% of the time I had given myself to achieve it in. From initial concept to setting the goal was two months; it was another two months to actually put the plan in place to achieve the goal; and then actioning and achieving it was another five months. Similarly, I had set myself a two-year time frame to achieve a certain level of wealth and I achieved it in just seven months. You know? That is the difference between desire and passion.

I had always desired wealth before I reached that point. Then all of a sudden, I got passionate about it. I used to desire being thin. I would desire that. Then all of a sudden I got passionate about it and learned how to do it, researched it, figured out what the hell was going on. Learned what I needed to learn and that was it. That is it. I will never be fat again. I lost over nine stone in under seven months. I am now a thin person for the rest of my life because I am passionate about being that way.

I know what it is like, thinking you cannot be thin, because I have been there. Now I know that you don't need to be fat; that it is something I used to choose to be, because being fat and lazy was easier than finding out how to be thin and stay that way. I found an easy way to do it. I then decided on all of the plan:
1) lose weight
2) re-educate myself on my eating habits
3) tone up

4) carry on with my life, using my new education.

Each of those four headings has a number of sub-headings, of course. I put the overall timescale to each element and the total. Then I wrote down when I wanted to achieve it by and a series of markers – mini goal setting, I call it – to make sure I am on the right track. Then I wrote down all the reasons why I wanted and needed to achieve this goal. Then I sifted through all of those until I found the one real one which I could get the passion behind and I put that at the top of my list of five reasons why this was going to happen. If you want to know the five reasons or you want to read the full story, or you want to know how to do it, it will be on my website if I ever get round to writing it down.

I now knew how to do it, when I was going to do it by and, most importantly, why I was going to do it. And I can tell you how to do it as well. I'm more than happy to tell people how to do it because I am passionate about the subject. I am currently just over seven months into my twelve-month goal. Does anybody think I will not fully achieve it?

I am still passionate about property too, and can never see a time when I will not be. Not just for the unbelievable wealth. I am passionate about trying to help people make money and create wealth for themselves and financial independence through the use of property. Because I know the subject backwards, it is really easy for me to help people do that.

So, if you just desire it, this property investing, if you just desire this wealth, this knowledge I am sharing won't help you *as much as it could*. It will still work for you. All you have to do is apply the skills I am teaching in this book. And if you want to, you can stay in the 'just desiring it' frame of mind. You can just go: "Yeah, I desire wealth. All I need to do is follow this, this and this, which he clearly says in his book is what I need to do – and which I know he's right about and I believe him – then I will get wealthy. All I have got to do is do that and, yep, I will be wealthy."

That is it. You have desired it. Brilliant. Yeah. It will still work for you and you will achieve your goal! Trust me, I will clearly state what you need to do so that you achieve wealth. So you will not need any of this goal-setting rubbish if all you want is wealth – but – there is a trade off. I can show you how easy it is to get wealthy – but only your passion can shorten the timeframe!

So, if you want this to happen fast, if you want to create wealth sooner rather than later, then you have got to get passionate about it. Understand? You have got to learn to love it. You know? You've got to really enjoy what you're doing.

Okay, let's get back to setting goals now. What would make you passionate? Is it seeing your family suffer? Would a personal crisis be enough to make you go, "Yeah, this is too much. This is wrong, I don't like my life at the moment." ?

I have got a friend I met recently who had that happen to him. It took a personal tragedy for him to change. The thing is, you look at a situation like that and you think: "Why do we have to wait for something horrible like that to happen for us to change?"

I know: This is the sort of stuff you keep in places in your mind where you don't like going. Well, I am sorry, but you will probably find your passion hidden in there as well, and that will help you BIG TIME with this.

So, why wait to see your family suffer? Why not have a think about it for a second and ask yourself, "What would change if a personal tragedy affected my life right now? How would I view my life right now? Would I look at it and think, yes, I'm living life to the fullest. Yeah." Would you? I doubt it.

I know I wouldn't, because I re-evaluate this sort of thing regularly, because it's part of my goal setting. I am having a fantastic life. I live an unreal life, as far as I am concerned. I have got everything so balanced and so in place. But there is still so much more I want to do and achieve, and to me that has to be balanced with everything else in my life.

But if seeing somebody in your family suffer would make you passionate about changing your life at the moment, then hold onto that thought. Use it. Use it to help yourself get wealthy.

Or is it seeing your friends suffer? Would seeing one of your friends go through a personal tragedy and real pain, be enough to motivate you into being passionate and change? Probably not. Probably not enough. It would change you a little bit, but it wouldn't change you as much as if you saw yourself suffer.

Would something like when the tsunami hit, not being able to give as much as you wanted to give because you are not wealthy? Yeah. Well, I was able to give quite a lot, as were my business partners, as were a lot of people I know. Some people could only give a little bit and they gave what they could. But, because I was in a position where I could give a fair bit of money, I did, because I chose to.

Just what will it take to make you passionate?

All right. You need to take some time out and write it down. You know? Take some time out from this. You are fired up at the moment, over this goal setting. Just get a pen, quickly, and write down your passions now. There are some pages at the back of the book or just write them on this page, but do it now. Just quickly write down what will get you passionate, because you need to know what it is.

Do you desire to become financially free? Or will you refuse to live without being financially free? Is that what would make you passionate? What would?

Okay, if you wrote them down your chance of success just rose by 500%. If you didn't, well, we will never know will we?

Which leads nicely into the biggest obstacle you have in your way right now. The biggest obstacle you need to overcome in order to achieve your goals is you! That's right! It is not the money. It is not the knowledge. It is you. You are the biggest obstacle standing in the way of your success.

The money can be found. The knowledge can be learned. The biggest obstacle is you, and the second biggest is your belief in you! You have to have a belief that you can do it. Right? I believe that success is going to happen. It is predictable. I believe that I will get to the end goal.

I was fortunate that from the age of 13, I was told that I would get there. If you have not been told you are going to get there, then you have to believe it yourself. Because if you believe it and it becomes your focus, your desire, your passion, then it will happen. You will make it happen. You have got to be structured. It has to be done in the right way. It is a case of, yes, I believe this is going to happen. Here is my goal of how it is going to happen.

Where you are right now in your life is a direct result of the choices you have made. They have all led you right to this point, right now. So, the very fact that you have picked up this book and you are reading this book and you have got to this point in it, means you have it within you to do it.

I think it was Anthony Robbins who said that less than 1% of all self-help books purchased are ever read through to the end. So, you are nearly in the one per cent just by getting to this point in the book. It is craziness to me, because so many people can choose wealth and so few do.

Attitude is everything. Whatever you really believe will become your reality. If you believe you are going to be wealthy, you will become rich. If you don't believe it, you will not. Right? It is your choice. Wealth is a matter of choice.

That word 'choice' has come up again. It is your choice whether you want to be rich and live a life of

116

limitless boundaries or you want to be restrained in a job, whatever. If you love your job, great. But why not, as <u>Rich Dad</u> says, have two careers? Have one for your job and one for your money, because that is what you should do – property gives you that.

I have lots of careers for my money. I have got my money split up and some of it is doing extremely well and is set for a fast return. Some of it is doing long-term returns. Some of it is doing mid-term. I have got different pots of money working in different areas all over the place. They all do the work for me so that I don't have to. I do not go to work for money. My money and other people's money go to work for me, my family and my friends. I do not get paid to go to work. I do not draw a salary. Literally, I do not get paid to go to work. I get paid in big chunks occasionally.

You attract into your life what you want and what you ask for. If you want to attract misery into your life, then you will do so. If you want to attract wealth and happiness into your life, then you will do it.

One of my personal thoughts is that I attract computer problems into my life. For some reason, I seem unable to get computers to work properly for me. I will try to do something and it will not work. Alison will come straight in and she will do exactly what I have just done and it will work for her. And I believe that I am attracting these sort of problems because I don't actually believe that it's *not* going to go wrong for me and, therefore, it goes wrong!

When I first wrote that 18 months ago, it felt like a changing point and since then I have focused on knowing I had done that. So I changed my thinking to, I know I will not experience computer problems. Guess what, I don't seem to experience them anymore...

But in property investing I not only believe, I absolutely know, that it is going to go right for me, and it does. In wealth creation, I absolutely know it is going to go right for me, and it does. I attract good things into my life the same way I attract into my life the problems I have with computers.

You can attract what you want into your life. If you want to attract rubbish and sh*t, as T. Harv Eker says, you will. By the way, his book, *The Secrets of the Millionaire Mind*, is excellent, first class, one of my top four and very easy to read.

You attract into your life whatever you want. And if you are thinking about sh*t and you are attracting sh*t into your life, you are going to get sh*t in your life. And when you stop thinking about that and you start trying to attract good things into your life and only think positively, you are still going to have some sh*t come to you. Do you know why? Because sh*t doesn't travel at the speed of light. It travels at the speed of sh*t!

But after a while, it will stop coming because you are not attracting it anymore. Yeah, it made me laugh, too. Brilliant line. I did a course once on attraction marketing and I believe so strongly in its impact that I am writing on it in the marketing section of my website www.AndyShaw.com

It is your choice where you go in life. Whatever your attitude is, whatever you want to do. I personally don't watch any negative TV. I watch the news because I want to know what's going on and I get a wonderful feel for the state of our country and other countries that affect us. But other than that, I don't watch any TV that is negative in any way, shape or form.

You know the kind of shows I am talking about! I don't watch series that focus on the grim side of life, shows like EastEnders, Brookside or Coronation Street. To me, they focus on desperate lives lived by people with no drive and no determination to change.

They inspire, if that is the right word, negative thoughts and I will not have that in my home. I watch escapism TV or funny TV & cartoons. I love TV that educates me. I love films. I love sci-fi and history programs. I want my head filled with ideas that reward my hard work and help me grow. I want that for my children too.

I really believe all this negative programming has an effect on us. It is minutia pumped out to keep you where you are. Why do you think that on Christmas Day, of all days, EastEnders shows a death or a suicide or somebody's overdosed or something like that? To make you feel better about your life the way it is. To make you think, hang on a minute, my life is not so bad after all; life's pretty good really, and you're right: it probably is, compared to that SH*TE!

The minute you say your life's pretty good after watching those shows, you have just swallowed the biggest sales line that is being dished out by the hidden-- Well, let us just call them The Hidden and leave it at that. I do not know why, but people eat this stuff up. And that is mostly why they do not get anywhere: the shows leave them too content with their lot to make the effort to change.

I have a very good friend who used to love Coronation Street; loved it! She is big in wealth creation and self-improvement too and a good friend. I used to try to stop her watching it, saying it was rubbish. And she would just say: "No, that's my one vice. I will watch Coronation Street." Then one day, halfway through an episode it hit her, what I had been saying, but more importantly what she already knew but did not want to accept. She went: "No, that's it. I am not watching it any more. It is junk. I am not filling my head with any more of this rubbish." And just like that, she stopped.

We never know when we are going to come to our senses about certain things in life. Just be thankful that we do and try to remember to avoid the rubbish in the future.

Now I am not telling you to stop watching that complete garbage. What I am telling you to do is this – the next time you are watching rubbish TV, look for the real message that is being sent to you. Then, think how your brain interprets it and places it into your life. Think about whether these messages are helping you with your goals or hindering you. Take a bit of paper and write down 'helps or hinders'. Then wait for the next message: from memory there are about six or eight in each half an hour, so this will not take long.

Phew, went a bit deep there. Sorry! But if I can save just one more person from a life wasted watching that cr*p, it will have been worth it. My wife used to watch Neighbours until she, too, came to the realisation that it was utter rubbish. If I came home for lunch when she had it on,

I would turn the channel over, saying: "I am not watching that rubbish. Why do you watch it?" Greg is amazed that I am still alive, as he thinks she should have stabbed me to death by now! But the message must have got through as it no longer retains a place on our TV screen!

Remember: whatever you choose to fill your head with will become your reality. What you think is who you are. I do not have any of those thoughts going around in my head. I do not think about people overdosing. I do not think about any of it because I do not need to, because I have got my head filled with so many good things, there is no space in there for that garbage!

So, you will attract into your life what you think about the most and you can make that whatever you want.

You are the biggest problem, remember. Unless you change, things will stay the same. Where you are now, reading this book is a direct result of everything you have done in your life up to this point. So you are doing something right. You have picked up a self-improvement book. Great. Right. Now, where do you go from here?

Is your future worth getting passionate about? Is it worth you taking some time out to think about what you want from your life (daring to dream a little is fun after all, and you don't need to admit to anyone else on the planet that you have done it)? Then, will you go that extra step and write down your dreams and goals - thereby putting your future life's plan into action?

13

Are You Ready To Change?

You have to change. You have to go outside your comfort zone. Yes, I know you do not like it out there. Well guess what? Tough! If you are passionate, you will find a way to enjoy it. I know that sounds a little sick, but that is how I cope with the things I do not want to do. You have to go, "Right, okay, yeah, I'm going to do that. I am going to take time out and I am going to write down my goals. I am going to actually do what he says to do. I do not really know where he is going with it, but I think he is right I do not really know what I want to do with it, but I am going to do it. I am going to move forward."

That is what you need to do because that will make a difference. It is what did it for me. I am now a multi-millionaire many times over and believe me, what I have achieved so far is bug**r all compared to what I have planned. Because I made a start somewhere; I actually took that first step. I stepped outside my comfort zone and I started to work out what I wanted. That is where it all starts. That's where wealth comes from: from inside you, from a plan. You obviously have some sort of plan to wealth, otherwise you would not be reading this. I am just trying to get you focused.

There is only one thing in this world you can completely control and it's the way you think. And there is no limit on the way you think. You can hear how passionate I am about this subject; how strongly I believe that you can move forward and grow and achieve and fill your head with the most wondrous things about whatever positive subject you choose to. You become an absolute expert on whichever subject you want very, very quickly. This is a real Zulu principle. We will come back to it a bit later.

There is no limit to how much better you can think. And as you get to each level, you think, crikey, can it get any better than this? Yes, it can because believe me, you cannot even conceive how good it can get. I cannot wait for the next stage of my education, the next big step forward, the next realisation of a truth. And I can tell you that knowing I still have so much to learn excites me!

The definition of insanity: doing the same thing and expecting a different result. What Einstein was saying was, if you do not change your life, then your life will stay the same. He also said that imagination is more important than facts. Going back to the fact of what you believe in your head, imagination is more important than facts. If you imagine you can achieve this, then you will.

The reason I bring up those two points should be obvious: if you are not willing to change, then you will not: but if you can imagine your life being different, then that will be enough to start the change that will eventually become fact.

When it comes to this sort of thing, to desire, passion, belief and attitude, you are working at the imagination stage. You have got to believe that you can do it to make it happen. You have got to believe that it is possible for you; you who does not know anything at all; you, whose friends will all think you are nuts when you tell them you are going to do this. You can do it. You can achieve it. If you want to. If you choose to. If *you* do not believe you can do it, who will?

A personal hero of mine, Winston Churchill, said: "Never give in. Never, never give in." As far as I am concerned, failure is simply never an option. Never, never, ever, ever an option. And when you truly believe this, you will realise that what the world will see as your failures are probably some of your greatest successes. That is a powerful statement, isn't it?

So, failure becomes a success? Yes it does. When you truly believe that you will achieve anything you are passionate about, your only way of viewing a failure is to see it as a step on the path to success. How can something that brings you closer to your goal be a failure? It cannot!

I am an expert in property, I never used to think of myself as an expert until I started to listen to the experts speak and I realised that their conclusions were all wrong. So now I am an expert in property and I am saying you can do this. If you have doubts, then you are basically telling me that I do not know my stuff! Your self-doubt is actually an insult to me! That's right!

I used to do the martial arts. When I was getting close to my black belt, the instructor turned to me and said: "Right. I think you are ready to take your next grade."

Now, I had been dodging taking this grade for ages. I mean, most people want to rush their way up there. I just wanted to understand why I was doing it in the first place. So I said: "No, no, no. I'm not ready. I don't really want to go ahead." And he said: "Are you telling me that I do not know what I am talking about?" And as I looked at him, he slipped back into a stance. I thought: "Oh, great, here we go." Because I was telling the expert that he did not know what he was talking about.

Well, I am an expert at creating money. I am an expert at buying the sort of properties I am going to tell you how to buy. And I am saying you can do this. You can do this really easily if you believe it and if you have the right attitude. And the right attitude starts with belief.

You are afraid of the unknown. And an expert is saying to you that it is not so bad. You will get through it because, if you have managed to be born, go through your childhood, go through puberty, go through adolescence, come out the other side and reached wherever you are in your life right now... If you have managed to do all that, I think you can manage to buy a bl***y property. It is not that hard. It's not so bad.

And I think you can manage to cope with what you have got to learn to handle, the tenants, among other things. This is not rocket science. This is not really, really clever stuff. This is basic. And if there is a fear inside you, I am going to try - with your help - to remove that fear and replace it with knowledge and confidence.

Yes, you will make mistakes. But *failure is merely an opportunity to begin again more intelligently – Henry Ford.* You have got to get it right. If it is the last money you have got, yeah, you have <u>really</u> got to get it right. So we will make sure that you get it right before we take that first step. But making mistakes is, and I will say it again, merely an opportunity to begin again more intelligently.

Yes, the deals you are going to find will not be as good as the deals that I would do. How can they be? You do not know what I know. But they will be good. You will not be buying the wrong property. You will not be buying a 16th century grade one listed building or a barn conversion. You will be buying the right sort of property. You will be buying in the right sort of area.

You will literally get rid of 98–99% of all the possible mistakes amateur property investors make, just by doing it the way I am going to tell you to do it. So, what I am saying is going to need a little bit of intelligence from you as well as faith, but I can help you with that as well.

You will make money. First up, you always make money in property. As long as you can cash flow it, you will always make money. Even if you have to sit on the damned property for ten years, you will make money. That is it. Even if you bought it at 100% over value, even if you got it that wrong!

But first off, do not worry about that: there are things in place to make sure you do not get it that wrong. For example, you have got the mortgage lender. He will not lend unless his valuer says it is worth the money. So that is a safety net, isn't it? The lender will not give you the money, which means you are protected from getting it wrong!

I mean, I bought a property once and I fell in love with this property. I desired it. I really wanted it. I thought, oh, yeah, that would be nice. A beautiful marina property. The bloke was trying to sell it for £250K. Well, I could not get it valued for more than £230K. I had three valuations done on it. None of them came up more than

£230K. Why do you think that was? That finally told me it was not worth more than £230K.

The problem is, it took me a while to realise it. I went through all the emotional headaches about property that you will go through as well *if you do not follow this strategy*, which is why I am gonna take them out of this book for you. By the end of it, you will go, "Bl***y hell. You know, all I have got to do is do that."

It is factual. It is not emotional. You will not have to think about it. People do not realise that you do not have to be superbly clever. You will make money on property, even if you get it wrong. Remember: As long as you can cash flow it, you will always make money from property. We will come back to why that works so powerfully later.

How you deal with those adversities when they come up will define you. How you deal with coping with the problems you have got at the moment is defining you now. I have got a friend who struggles with aches and pains like I have never seen anybody struggle with them. And she goes through immense pain regularly. And she is still happy. She is still jolly, even though most of the time she is in pain to some degree. Don't get me wrong, she is not the person who has got the most pain in the world, but she just deals with it. She deals with it far better than I would. I mean, come on, I am a bloke after all.

How you choose to perceive your place in life is your choice. If you choose to perceive yourself as nobody who's gonna get anywhere, then guess what? You are not gonna get anywhere.

I perceive myself as somebody who is a multi-millionaire. A multi-millionaire who is going to carry on helping people through self improvement, education and wealth creation, who will have a lot of people think that what he has got to say is worth listening to, who will have a lot of people say about him: "What he said to me changed my life." That is how I perceive myself.

Well, guess what? That is what's happened and is happening. It has taken people to show me that this could happen. Just like I am showing you now that you can do this. Other people are showing me that I can do things as well. I had no doubt that I was going to be a millionaire property investor. But I had no idea that I would be here to show other people how to do things, because why would anyone want to listen to me? After all, I am just here doing my own thing. I am just a normal bloke. You see? It is all about how you choose to perceive your place in life, it is your choice. Amazing how many times choice comes up, isn't it?

This is not an ability thing, what I am teaching you with property. This has nothing to do with ability at all. All you have got to do is choose to want to do it, learn how to do it, and then, the last but most important bit: apply what you've learned. That is it!

It is not about ability. You do not have to be really clever at this property game. You just have to know how to do the things I'm gonna write down in this book. It is written down. You can take it out on site if you want and you can sit there and tick them off as you do them. It is that simple. This is a tick list if you want it to be.

I have helped people who knew nothing. I help people who have no money or are in debt up to their eyeballs. And basically, I help them to create wealth and get out of debt. And it gives me a lot of pleasure to do it as well.

I have mentored people who are penniless, who are dead broke, who have and are looking like they are going to go bankrupt. I have saved them from the brink of bankruptcy. Not with giving them any money. Just by telling them how to do it and how to get out of it.

I have mentored people who earn millions of pounds a year. I can tell you, some of the penniless ones are far cleverer than the rich ones. Not all, mind! Some of them are as thick as they come. They are just nice and decent people, you know, because I only help nice and decent people.

But, wealth is not an intelligence thing. It is not an ability thing. It is making the right choices. The ones who achieve wealth are the ones who make the right choices at the right times.

I was chatting to a lady recently and she was saying to me about how she wished she had not sold and if she had only kept hold of the two flats that she and her husband had owned. She had one in Worthing and he had one in Horsham. They would be worth about £190k each now and they sold them for about £60k each.

So I said: "Yeah, you are right. You know, you should have kept hold of them." She said: "Well, we bought our house. And, you know, we have made about £180k for ourselves in equity. What I would really love to do, or I wish I had the gumption to do, is get up and go and live in Spain, which is what I want more than anything. I would sell up the house and use the equity to buy a bar or something over there."

And I said: "Well, why do you want to sell the house?" She said: "Well, I want my money." And I said: "Well, why not have the house and the money?" And she said: "Well, I don't want anyone living in my house." And I said: "Well, somebody's gonna live in it anyway when you sell it." And she said: "Well, yeah. But then I would have the money.'" I said: "Well, you can have the money and have the house. Why do you want to sell it?" And she said: "I just want to get hold of the money and it will be done."

So there she is, if she gets the gumption to move, she's about to make the same mistake that she made 12 years before, even though she said to me that she wished she had kept the two flats. She said it was a bad choice and she is about to make it again. Sometimes the blatantly obvious escapes people, and sometimes their own history is not even enough to get them to ask a simple question like: - How can I keep this house and own the bar in Spain as well, then I would have a fall back plan should the bar not work out?

Now, I can't tell her that because I am a strong believer that a prophet is never recognised in his own home. And those people know me as a person whose children are at school with their children. You know me as somebody who is here telling you about creating wealth.

Friends locally here have no idea how much money I have created or anything like that. They just do not know.

They just do not know how easy it is to do. If I told them how easy it was, they would not believe it. How can you believe it when that person's just living down the road from you.

So, I can't help her. I would love to. But, she does not want me to help her and it would create an uncomfortable situation. But I am able to tell you things in this book that I could not tell a neighbour of mine. That is one of the downsides of this knowledge; sometimes you have to put up with the fact that you cannot help the people you want to help the most.

You can choose to do anything or become anything you want. If you want wealth, follow the system. When you get stuck, ask a question. If I do not answer, the Internet will. There are plenty of resources out there. If you get stuck, if you want an answer from me and I do not answer, it is because I do not get time to get to it or something like that. But the Internet will always be there with the answer. One of the reasons I put my membership site together was to help the people who will follow the system written in this book. There is a forum where you can all work together to help each other to become wealthy using this and other systems; the idea being that as problems come up, others will help you overcome situations.

There are a few concepts in this book that I am writing about now that I have not seen anywhere else. But they are only concepts. When it comes to detail, the answer's out there. There is nothing new under the sun when it comes to this sort of stuff, apart from concepts. When it comes to, "How do I get around this particular problem?" you will always find that somebody's done it before.

A word of advice though, double or triple check the answers you are given by going to other places. You can get advice whenever you ask a question, but good advice or accurate advice can be very elusive.

So just remember, you can do anything or become anything you want to if you choose to want to. Look at the advice given and use your own ability to improvise, overcome and adapt. This is the 1% I was talking about. When you get stuck, look at a logical solution. Everything I do is logical.

Is it logical that a certain thing will happen? If it is not logical, I don't do it. I rely on logic to base my assumptions on. And if something is illogical, I will not go forward. So, when you are faced with a decision and you do not know what to do, look at the advice, think about it. I always take time out. I always slow myself down.

If somebody needs me to make a decision now, right now, then I will go to the loo. I will go and have a quick cup of coffee. I have just got to pop home for five minutes. It gives me time to think. Put the subject down. Think about it. I like to think about things over a day or so if it is a difficult decision, if it is involving a lot of money. I do not really want to think about it quickly. I like to make my decisions slowly. Sometimes I think about things for several months or even years.

You have got to use your own ability to improvise, overcome and adapt. By the way, I stole that line from

Clint Eastwood in Heartbreak Ridge.   Fantastic line.
Fantastic film.

14

The Best Investment You Ever Made

Do you know what the best investment you ever made was? Chances are it's the house you live in now. If you have owned your house for more than five to ten years, then I'm gonna give you a formula to have a go at.

In Robert Kiyosaki's book, *Rich Dad, Poor Dad,* he said that an asset is something that puts money into your pocket each month and a liability is something that takes money out of your pocket each month. I quite agree with that sentiment. Exactly the right way of looking at it from a certain point of view.

From another point of view, it is a case of an asset can take money out of your pocket each month as long as it is planned, but it can give you that money back and more, occasionally. If you do it correctly. But your own home should always be viewed as a liability. I quite agree with him on that.

So, do you know what the best investment you ever made was? If you have owned your house for five to ten years or more, how about this? I purchased the house in 1988, right at the wrong time as most would say. I disagree, as it is always a good time to buy property. No the mistake was that I paid too much, not when I bought. But thankfully my friend, Time, has stepped in and corrected my mistake for me. Here is an example of my own first property investment.

3-bed end of terrace in Worthing, West Sussex

- I purchased it in 1988 so I have
  owned it for (years)   18
- I paid   £65,000
- The cash I laid out was   £3,250
- I withdrew equity in 2000 to purchase
  my new home   £45,000
- I withdrew equity in 2001 to
  buy my first property with Greg   £33,000
- I withdrew equity in 2006
  because I could   £21,000
- The property was then worth   £195,000
- My first mortgage was   £61,750
- My current mortgage is   £160,750
- My equity is   £34,250
- The outstanding loan to
  value is   82.44%
- This one property has made me so far
                                                 £130,000
- I spent this many hours looking for it   30
- I spent this many hours negotiating it   ½
- I spent this many hours financing it   6
- Total hours to source my first property was   36½
- So for every hour of effort I put into this property I
  have made this much hourly so far   £3,561.64

So since I first purchased this property, I have made money over the LONG TERM despite the so-called bad times in the 90s

- For every year so far   £7,222
- For every month so far   £602
- For every day so far   £19.79
- For every hour so far   £0.82
- For every minute so far   £0.014
- So while I was asleep this one property has made me so far   £43,333
- While I was awake it has made me so far   £86,667

Your own property will show you a similar pattern, or if you did make the mistake of selling, why not look at what it would be worth now and see what a return you would have made.

Quite a revealing way of looking at property don't you think?

And remember that is tax free! So I get every penny of that equity withdrawal. And it stays tax free as long as I never do something silly like sell.

So, for every year since you purchased, you have made X amount. For every day since then, you have made X amount. For every hour, you have made X amount. Now, after you add all of the time up, have you earned that working for it? Probably! Well more importantly, have you retained it?

Asset building is a really easy skill to learn. The most important thing is to continue to build assets slowly and steadily. The point is, with the correct sort of assets, you build on a foundation that has already got structure. You put one asset in place and then you go and buy another one. And you add it to the other previous asset. Then you buy another one and you add it to the previous asset. That is all you've got to do. The secret is to never sell. And just carry on building assets.

The trouble is everyone will talk to you about when you should sell and how you should get out of the market before it crashes. Well, when you are listening to the advice from these people who have your best interests at heart, always stop and look logically at what they have said and remember this – The first rule of advice is, check out the person you are receiving advice from. Where does your friend live, how many properties do they currently own, what car do they drive, how do they present themselves, what sort of family life do they have, where do they holiday, what life experiences and knowledge make their advice worthwhile to you? These are some of the basics. If you stop and apply them, they will save you from yourself.

When the time comes, I hope those words will protect you from all your well-meaning friends. Judge their lives against mine and what I have created before listening to their advice rather than what I am saying to you. Do not misunderstand me, I am not great at everything I do, I just am at property!

In our old business I used to say, if all of the people who are trying to help me would just get out of the way, I could really get somewhere!

Now for the best bit! On your own home, all that money you have made; that was all tax free. I am going to go through it in more detail about tax later. You will probably find that if you take the equity you have made and divide it by the years it took to make it, that is more than most people earn. It is definitely more than all but a few people save.

You need to decide what you want, when you want it, what you are prepared to do to get it and what you have to get it with. Let us say you want £100k average per year for the rest of your life. Do you want it in your hand before tax, or do you want it in your hand after tax? – be specific, always, with yourself!

So, I will assume that you want £100k in your hand for the purpose of this point. The next question is, when do you want it? Starting in, say, five years? Then you have to have £300k of capital. If you have that capital, then there is no issue. Just use that capital, go and buy ten properties worth £100k each, with 85% mortgages on at full asking price and basically, you will have created that wealth. Nothing to it. You don't need me. Go and do it yourself now – goodbye!

If you do not have that capital or you need that explained a bit more or you do not want to risk that much capital to see if this idea I am telling you about works or any of a thousand other reasons, then you need to manipulate your goal to suit. You can raise the money through credit; you can raise the money by going through equity release; you can buy fewer houses or you can increase the time scale. It is just maths. You can decrease the amount you want at the end, because it is not really what you needed or wanted.

According to the Office of the Deputy Prime Minister's website, the housing market has gone up 11.74%

per year in the last 35 years. See for yourself at http://www.communities.gov.uk/housing/housingresearch/housingstatistics/housingstatisticsby/housingmarket/livetables/

There have only been a few years when the property market has gone down and it is a very minor percentage point. Over time, it has a constant curve upwards.

According to the Centre of Economic Business Research, the housing market will increase 6.24% per cent per year between 2002 & 2020. This was a very conservative figure, I thought at the time, and of course was proved right.

Currently the CEBR seem to be predicting that house prices will not rise or fall in 2007 (Well they got that wrong again didn't they ☺) and will remain pretty static until 2010 (and they will be getting this wrong too ☺). I think they are predicting this in a vain hope that this will bring their well-out-of-whack earlier predictions back into line. But what do I know, I am no economist - I just make a fortune from property.

So, between the Office of the Deputy Prime Minister which is showing it has increased by 11.74%, and the Centre of Economic Business Research showing that it will increase by 6.24% per cent a year, you get an idea of what the future holds. Personally, I think prices will raise over time at the historic rate of approximately 11.74%, but I decided to make my strategy one that did not rely on too much capital growth and I look for a very conservative 2.5% growth a year from the market as a whole. This provides me with a very substantial equity drawdown capability if I want it.

I look to be able to withdraw 2% of equity from my portfolio each year. So if you wanted £100k cash in your hand on a <u>very</u> conservative strategy then you would need a portfolio of 'easily financed' property worth £5 million. I will cover the sorts of property required to make sure they are easily financed later on as you can't just buy any old property to build up your portfolio and still be able to release equity.

History shows us that the housing market has traditionally gone up quite high. People who are predicting the property market realise this, so why do they fail to use long term history as even a basic indicator? After all, they quote it for the stock market whenever it suits them. (I discuss the property market at length on my website and various other economic points regarding it).

I think the problem with the economists who are so badly predicting the property market, is that they do not understand exactly the asset that they are trying to predict. So be very careful of who you trust when it comes to your financial future.

If you do not have the capital, then are you prepared to do what it takes to get it? In other words, do you want to refinance and pull the equity out of your house? Are you prepared to get it from credit cards or personal loans or any of the other sources? For example, are you prepared to borrow it from a relative?

If not, then revise your goal downward or look realistically at the sum you need annually to be financially free. Is £100k more than you need annually? What is the amount of money you are actually netting after going to work for a living, bearing in mind that, if you were going to work for a living, chances are that you would not need quite as much. So, what will you need to actually be financially free?

If you are prepared to do what it takes to raise that money, then there are plenty of resources. There are plenty of places available to get hold of whatever money you need. I will go into a great many of those later and I provide monthly updates of the best sources of funds out there that I have found.

So, let us assume that you have the capital or you can find it. Let us now turn it from a dream into a goal.

Write down, 'I want to have (total value of property you want) much property in (time it will take) amount of time, spending (Total capital invested inc cashflow safety) amount of capital.'

All right. Now, it is a desire. You have created a desire. Let us turn that desire into a passion.

I want you to write down, 'If I achieve this, then here is how my life will change.' And I want you to write down the top ten things about your life that will change.

Take time out now. Go to the back of the book. In the notes section, I want you to scribble them down as quickly as you can, the top ten things off the top of your head. Go on, go. Try and do it now in under two minutes. See if you can write ten things that will change your life for the better. Try not to take your pen off the paper.

Did you do it, or did you just carry on reading the next sentence? Most of you will have carried on reading the sentence. I used to do that too. Then I found that if I was not prepared to do it right then, I marked the page and came back to it. But I made sure I actually did that! The people who make a success for themselves from this book will be the ones who take action. However, the ones who have actually done it should go back to them now.

Look at that list again. What is the single biggest reason on it for you to actually do this? What is the single reason on that list that is so powerful that it will change your life dramatically just by achieving that? That's your prime goal. Now, put the rest of your goals in order of importance, and rewrite the list.

For me, it was proving I could do it. I did this because I wanted to prove to everyone else that there was more to me than people originally saw. It was not for my wife or my little boy or for what other people thought of me. It was for me to prove it to me.

People looked at what I did and thought, oh, yeah. There it is. He is being a bit of a show off and that sort of thing. No. It was for me. I had to prove it to myself. I had to prove that I was capable of this sort of thing. I knew I was capable of it. But I had to prove it to myself by going out and doing it. I thought I had to prove it to other people at the time. It was not that at all. It was just me proving it to me. And that was the biggest single thing. Took me quite a long time to realise that.

So when you are looking at your biggest single thing and the biggest single reason for you to do something, is that it? Or is it something else? Dig deep! Find your real reason. Because if you can find your passion, you will make this happen. If you cannot find your passion, it will just be a desire. If it is a desire, you can make it work, but passion will focus you. Passion will make it work fast and it will make you work hard. It is your true primary reason that you are looking for: the thing you are most passionate about.

What if your real reason is not passionate? You can still do this. It will just take a bit longer. So, let's read through your statement. Read it back to yourself. Read it out loud. You know, say it: I want to achieve this. And I am passionate about this point. And the other things that will change my life are these other nine things. And so, if I actually go out there and do this, my life is going to be so much better.

Now, you have got to sign and date the bottom of it. You want to basically take it wherever you go. Put it on your computer. Stick it on the wall. Stick it on the fridge. Do whatever you have got to do with it, but read it at least once a week to remind yourself what is going on and why you are doing it.

And if you have not actually done something, if you have not actually taken the steps forward, maybe that might drag you back because that is the only thing that will. It is only your desire and your passion that is going to make you do this. I can give you all the advice, the same as every other self-help book can. But unless you **do** something, you will not change a damned thing. Unless you actually go out there and do something, what you have always had is what you're always going to have. You have got to change. You've got to make something happen.

15

Property Is Easy And Success Is Predictable

Property is all about creating money. There are three ways you can get money, other than inherit it or win it. And we are not here to discuss luck, because you do not need luck in property and as luck doesn't exist then it would be difficult to get some of it.

You can earn it, you can make it, or you can create it. 'Earn money' means you go out and get a job. Basically, you work for somebody else and you trade your time for money. A lot of people have the illusion of their own business but they are in fact just working at their own job.

I was okay at a job. I would not say I was good at it. After I did my apprenticeship, I went on to various other companies for a three or four-year period. I was 23 before I started my first business. I had six years of working for other people and I did okay. My end job finished up with a reasonable salary for the time, about £30-£40k a year. It was not a bad job and I could have carried on with it.

I decided, though, that I would go and 'make money' myself and set up my own business. I was okay at it some of the time, but it was never enough. And it was really hard work running my own business. Those of you who have done it will know what I mean when I say it is really hard work, growing your own business especially with little knowledge of what business really is.

If you want to stay static and one size, it is no problem at all. However, if you want to grow it and you have got no money, then it is hard work. Especially in the first few years when you know absolutely bu***r all! I wanted to grow the business because I enjoyed it and I went into it to make money – making money is not a bad thing, remember, if you are giving the answer, 'because I want to do it'. And if the money reason is not supporting your good intentions, then you are going to run into trouble sooner or later.

Frankly, your answer should always be, I went in to make money first and then any and every other reason you want can follow that, if it makes you feel better. If your primary goal in business is not to 'make money', then I would say your future is going to involve the word failure. 'You are only in it for the money' bl***y British attitude probably causes more business failures than lack of education. What is more, if you are not focused on making money, you are not realistically looking at your business yet. But, don't worry. A few financial crises should sort that out for you.

Another way is to 'create money'. For example, at a car boot sale, you see an ornament for sale for £2 and you know that once cleaned and in a shop window, it would be worth £15. By presenting the same object in a different way, you have increased the item's value to the new buyer; you have, therefore, made or as I look at it you have created money. Some people would say you have made money here, I would say you created it.

Buying assets and having them go up in value automatically without you being there is making money, buying a prop for £100k and knowing it's worth £135k is creating money. So property investing actually features two of the ways to get money. You first create it by buying below market value (BMV) properties. And secondly you make money as they go up in value.

But to start with creating money is by far the easiest of the three. Creating money or seeing value in something that the current owner believes is worth less, is the simplest way I've found of producing considerable sustainable wealth with little effort.

Another one of my favourite books is *The Automatic Millionaire,* by David Bach. He says that becoming a millionaire is an automatic procedure and he is right. And the way he suggests doing it is very, very true. And will work!

This system I am showing you is not a fully automatic system of creating money in property investing. Unfortunately, you do have to actually take action occasionally. But the principle behind it is virtually the same as the one Bach outlines in his book.

He also recommends that you pay yourself first. This, as far as I'm concerned, is the greatest money creating method there is. I first read it in another fantastic book, *The Richest Man in Babylon,* by George S Clason. This is the secret to wealth but it is too simple for most to consider following.

By paying yourself first, you are basically creating money out of nothing. Mainly because it's giving you money from your own money, which you would normally just fritter away and lose by letting it slip through your fingers. This is a very, very powerful technique and one that is overlooked because of its simplicity. I cannot overstate the power of following the system from that book. I was already rich when I first read it and so when I applied it to my own cashflow, the results were simply staggering! They have made my system so strong now. What is more, it is so easy and so irritating that I didn't apply it years ago! I strongly advise that you buy the book, read it and put the system in place. It WILL transform your life, just as it did mine.

In fact, it is so important that it is worth mentioning again: I cannot emphasise actioning the words of wisdom in that book enough! As far as I am concerned, that is the secret to financial freedom and it is plain for all to read.

But let us get back to what we are doing here: I am showing you to how create money. As I say, it is the easiest way. I am really good at this bit. The other two – earning and making – yeah, I was okay at, but this bit I am really good at. And since learning how to create money I've actually now become excellent at making it as well, almost by accident.

And how me being good at creating money helps you is it means that you don't need to be. You do not need to be really good at it. You do not need to be fantastic at creating assets. You just need to actually do what I suggest and your own skills will develop as you need them to. Do what is written down and you will not need to be highly skilful. You do not need to be a star. You just need to do it. And you will create long-term wealth without any struggle at all. Create, not earn, not make; create.

At Passive Investments' Open Days, Greg comes out with this line: "What is all this magic?" And he asks people in the room, "How many people know somebody who had a £500k property in 1990?" <u>Nobody</u> puts up their hands. He says: "Who knows somebody who has a £500k property now?" And about 40–50% of the room put their hands up. Then he says: "And is it yours?" And most keep their hands up.

So, in 15 years, we have gone from nobody knowing anybody who had a £500k property to 40–50% of the room owning one. Isn't that amazing? Isn't it a wonderful magic trick?

What did all of them do? Did they just wake up one day and, as if by magic, their properties were worth £500k? No, there is no magic in it at all. It is because the property market goes up in value over time. It is that simple. It is not hard. It is not rocket science. That is what happens, people. That is the way it is, whether you like it or not!

Whether you believe in it or not, whether you want to or not, you will make money out of property. If you buy property, it will make money despite you. Of course, whether you make money out of it, is different! If you sell, then you may make money or you may lose money. Personally I look at selling as transferring your wealth to someone else, which in most people's eyes would be a bad thing, yet so many still do it because they do not understand what they are doing.

But if you just keep it and never ever sell, then it will make money, despite you. It does not need your help to do this; it will do it automatically. That is very powerful. And that can make you very wealthy when you put that power to work. After all, it is what funds the nation's debt, their increase of lifestyle, their bigger homes; it does it automatically, it does it despite us.

So all you have to do is put that little bit of work in at the start. And some time down the line, if you get a little problem or something, you have to deal with that little problem **without bl***y selling!** That is all you have to do. It is not a lot. This is not a 100% passive investment; it's about 95-98%. There are a lot of Passive Investments out there, none of which will return the man from the street these sorts of returns. I will show you one later, that is 99.5% Passive! But this is not a 100% passive investment. It's simple, probably too simple for you educated people reading this to grasp; but if you are like me and just a logical thinker, then we like simple and do not need to try and complicate a nearly perfect situation.

So, let us say you own a £500k property. Well, that is making £50,000 pounds a year forever on average. Fantastic! The only problem is, you cannot get at it all and cannot really use it properly because it is your own home and why would you want to release some of that equity to make you wealthy now and secure your financial future, when your plan is to get old and sell your big house and get something smaller?

Do people actually plan to do that? I mean, I live in a relatively big house and I can see a valid reason to have a small house if you cannot be bothered with the upkeep, but to sell so that you can live more comfortably, well, that is like thinking there is not going to be more money available. Simply put, if you own enough property and you can cash flow your borrowing, there will always be more money tomorrow than you have today. Why doesn't everyone get that?

Back to the point! Let us say you own a second prop that's worth £500k. And you are making your £50k a year from that. Forget the money you are making on your own home because it is irrelevant, because that is your own home.

If you want more than £50k a year to come out of your investments, what do you have to do? You have to buy more, don't you? Simple as that. And what if you cannot find the money to buy more? You go and raise the money to buy more. And what if you do not want to find the money to buy more? You wait until your property has gone up in value, pull the equity out of it and buy more then.

This is not hard, people. This is easy, all right? This is simple. Property investors have been doing it for years, most of them without any idea that they are even doing it. Or they are just doing it automatically. Or they know they are doing it, but they do not realise they are doing it so right and most of them don't use it to deliver its full power.

This is the simplest and easiest thing to do in property, you buy it and wait – if you do that and nothing else, you end up wealthy.

What I am saying is, if you realise this, you know it and you use it, you can increase the effectiveness of it, which is what I did. Which is why I went from putting no money in at the start, to owning over 200 properties in a very short space of time. This really is money for nothing and really is property for free. And I will explain exactly why it is for free shortly.

So, is it a really good idea? Well, it cannot be that simple, can it? It can't be. It cannot be as simple as I have just explained. Because if it was as simple as I just explained then we would all be doing it, no, no, it can't be. Forget it. Cannot be that simple.

Do you know what the problem is? Believing in it! That is the problem, because I had this problem as well. I have been there. I've been where you are. I had the problem of believing that it cannot be that simple, even after I had discovered that it really was. After all I had discovered, even after I had found ways of getting the money and all that sort of thing, I still had trouble believing it. You know, I could not get it into my head.

If it was that simple, after all, then the banks would be doing it. The banks have got all the money after all. Why are they not doing it? Why isn't every investment fund doing it instead of shares? If it's this good, why aren't they doing it?

Well, in my opinion, they just don't know it. And they just do not understand what they are actually lending money against. Or it may be that they just haven't looked at it. Because if they had, and they had really gone into it in depth in the way that I have, they would all be doing it a lot more.

I am all for diversification of money into the right areas. But, I am also keen on focus of money to create wealth in the greatest, easiest and quickest way. There is a lot to be said for diversification when you have created it, but focus when you are creating it.

But, the other reason is that they are just too busy, like I was. We wanted to get into property. When I bought my first property in 1988, the intention was buy the property, do it up and sell it. Of course, I bought it at the wrong time, which is what I used to say, but in truth I just paid too much for it. Anyway I did not make any bl***y money on it. So, that put paid to that idea. We were basically stuck in a negative equity trap, along with what seemed like the majority of the country at the time.

1992 came around and we saw a little flat, a little studio flat we knew was up for sale. At the peak it had been for sale for £45k. It was now for sale for just £10,000. I could not believe it. I thought to myself: "I have got to get into property investment. That is just so cheap. You can rent that." At the time you could rent it for £150/ month and that was a good deal. I thought, I can just take out a personal loan and buy it. That is what I was thinking. I would just take out a personal loan and buy it.

Well, I think I listened to some damn fool and I procrastinated for too long and it went to someone else. That £10k property is worth £105k today. £105,000! I recognised that it was a good deal when I saw it in 1992. I looked at it, I paused and looked at it and recognised a good deal. The property market could not have slumped 75% in 1992, I thought and I was right! It was a guess, but I was right.

It had gone down in value too much. This taught me a very valuable lesson. Do not put too much of your portfolio into studio flats, because studio flats can outperform the market in growth times, but they will also outperform if a market fall does come. They take the hit really badly. When I looked at that flat, I also looked at several other studios and saw a similar sort of thing happen to them.

So, I did not buy it because I listened to other people around me who knew absolutely nothing about buying property. I did not find an expert; I listened to uninformed people. Why is it in our nature to do that? Why did I go to people who were scared to death of the property market and ask their advice? Why didn't I seek out an expert or trust my own instincts? I listened to people who did not know anything and I took their advice. More fool me. Those people had my best interests at heart. They were trying to help – but all those best intentions cost me money. The fact that you are reading this book probably means a similar experience has happened to you. The question is, are you going to let someone's best intentions stop you again?

When you go for advice, don't go to people who don't know the answer. Go to an expert. Pay for that advice. People like me will charge for their time for you to come and listen. This is so you can say, what should I do? How should I do this? And they will give you advice on that. The problem is, the industry is not regulated like solicitors or doctors, so you don't know who to go to. What you need to do is listen to several of us so called experts and then decide who to trust and who you like. The chances are, if you can look objectively at it that way, you will have sought out good advice that can project you forward.

Go and pay for good advice. And I always advise not to take the first advice you get. Go and get at least two, if not three, even if you have to pay three times for it. Just make sure that you are getting value from the money you are spending.

So, back to the point - told you I drift off. I did not go into property then. 1995 came around. A friend of ours, a guy called Paul from Brighton came over to see us. He was a mortgage arranger. He came to see us and he was telling Greg and me about how he'd bought five properties and how we had to do this because it was such a good thing. He said he was making so much money on the rent because the properties were so cheap. With the money he was making on the rent, he was going to pay off all the mortgages within ten years. Then all five of those properties would be unencumbered and he would have enough rent to live on without going to work.

And we thought: "That's good. We've really got to look into doing that." We did not get around to it. Paul carried on. He ended up buying around 20 properties by the year 2000. I think it was with under 50% mortgages on them. We did not.

1997 came around. I got married to Alison, my long-term partner. We had been together for nine years at that stage. We went to St. Lucia on our honeymoon. We had a wonderful holiday there.

One day we went on a day trip to the Tobago Cays. We were on this boat, a big catamaran. And I was sitting next to this guy and his wife. We were chatting away. I was embarrassed at the time that I had done okay in business, so I always played down what I did for a living (typical British). Now, I don't care. You know, now I just tell people because I believe I can help them. Some people see it as bragging; to me, it is getting the message out, so that I can stop as many people as possible devoting their lives to a flawed system.

This guy said to me: "What do you do then?" And I said: "Oh, I fit building products and things like that." He said: "No, you don't. You run the company." And I said: "Sorry, what do you mean?" He said: "You own the business. How many people work for you?" And I said: "About 15 people work for me. How did you know?" He said:, "Oh, I can always spot a business owner straightaway."

We got chatting. I hit it off with him and his wife. Alison was feeling pretty ill that day, she had eaten some dodgy shellfish or something; either that, or the copious amounts of rich food and having too much alcohol in our systems. It wasn't really the day to be out on the high seas as the catamaran was going up and down, up and down. Anyway, that is another story.

So he said to me: "Well, I own several nightclubs and a few pubs and things like that in Yeovil. Do you buy property?" I said: "No, no, I don't." He said: "Well, you must do. You have got to get into it. You have got to get into it very quickly." I said: "What do you mean?" He said: "Property market's going to go through the roof in the next five to ten years. In the next two to three, it's going to really soar and you need to take **everything you've got** and stick it into property." He said: "That's my strongest advice. I cannot advise you any stronger than that. Get into property as quickly as possible." I find when someone is that focused, that they have something about them that just makes you know they are right.

So, after our honeymoon, I came back and had a meeting with Greg and told him what this guy had said. Greg and I said: "That sounds like a really good idea. We should definitely really think about doing that, this year!" However, at the same time, we were having no end of problems from the supplier of our products. So we looked at it and decided that we did not want to go into property. We would rather go into manufacturing and become our own supplier. So, we decided against property for the third time. We decided it was a good idea to go into manufacturing and a bad idea to go into property. Not our finest hour!

Obviously, time went by and we did not go into property. In the year 2000, we both moved houses. However, I managed to hang on to my first property.

In 2001, we decided we really wanted to go into property. We fully intended to do it that year, but it still might not have happened. The only thing that actually made us go into property was the fact that an employee came to me and said she was going to be kicked out of her home and she needed somewhere to live. She did not know what to do and asked if I could help.

Greg and I decided that we should just do it and then at least we would not regret missing out again. The plan could have fallen apart as it had before, except this time we decided we would go and buy that property. 1) Because someone needed our help, and 2) Because we were fed up regretting not doing it. So we did it.

Finally, after 11 years of procrastination we bought our first property. We finally bought it because we had to do it to help somebody! I have a saying that Mike gave me, 'No good deed goes unpunished.' And then he follows it up with, 'If you help someone, the pain is just around the corner'. It is uncanny how true these two statements are. But even though I know them to be true, there is something in me that wants to keep trying to help, even after my business mind has warned me against it. All of us – Greg, myself and Adrian – are drawn to help others when we can.

We thought, well, at least if we bought this property, we would **actually** have a property. We would **actually** have done it. We would not look back in 11 years time and think, I wish we had done that. So Greg had to put his hand in his pocket and I went and released some equity and we bought a property, our first one. That is the story of why we took so long to get into property.

Has it taken you as long or longer? It took us 11 years to actually do it. Even though I saw a fantastic deal when I was a lot younger, it still took 11 years. If it takes you 11 years to get into property, you can still make a fortune. So, it is up to you. But in my opinion, you want to get into property as soon as possible.

All right, you can stop reading now. I have told you enough. All you have got to do is go and buy a property. As I said, you don't need to be an expert. You just need to buy a property. If you have got £100k, then go and buy five properties and wait. That is all you need to do. Buy five properties and wait, £20k on each property and, basically, you will have £500k worth of property.

157

Even if you bought them at 20% over market value, it is only going to take two years to catch up. And then two years after that, you will have made £100k. Two years after that, you will have made another £100k. Do you get what I mean? It is that simple. No, it really is! You don't need to read any more!

£ £ £

Still here? Well, the other thing is, I am probably not teaching you anything you don't already know. If you have owned property, you know it goes up in value over time. Your problem, as I said right at the start, is believing it and believing it will continue. Oh, look at that. Believing it will continue. Why do we all find that so difficult to do? (A subject for another time I think).

Just think about it. If you stopped for a few minutes and decided that you believed it would continue, what positive effect would that have on your life? What would having knowledge of the future do for your life, and the lives of your husband/wife and children?

If you truly believed it as I do, and as Greg does and as all our clients do, then you would be like me, buying property like it is going out of fashion. So, you obviously don't believe it yet, because you are not. Or, you are scared because you do not know what to do. Or you are just doing your due diligence and checking out all these mass delusional people in the Property Investing sector.

Let me ask you a philosophical question – What is more logical, that the mass market is deluding itself or the minority market is deluding itself? The minority, right, as we all know about religious sects, brainwashes people. So, talking property investment only now: If we were able to look at the average wealth of the minority market and compare it against the average wealth of the mass market, is there any doubt in your mind which would be wealthier? This goes a long way to showing us why only 1% of the population will ever retire financially free. Do you need me to make this point any clearer? Herd mentality is invariably wrong.

There is an article on my website that covers the 1%, and it is very scary. Are you going to be the 1 in a 100 that gets through the 40 year plan and ends up financially free????

Or are you going to be in the 99% who fail in their life's work to become financially free. Yes, 99% of people will fail. The system we have been raised into fails 99% of the time, this means it really sucks! You have to do something different to get out of this 99% or you are doomed to failure. I have studied it and just five small properties are all it will take not to be on the wrong side of that dreadful statistic.

So, have I dealt with the belief that says, 'property goes up in value'? If not, then visit my website where I regularly update my info, which is taken from the Office of the Deputy Prime Minister's website. Look at the history of property value, just look at the past as a means of predicting **YOUR FUTURE.**

Do you believe it now? I can show you how to get out of the scared bit. That is easy. But I can't make you believe unless you want to actually get this and say to yourself: "Hang on a minute, **will** property go up in value over time?"

And if you still won't believe it, then the figures that the Centre of Economic Business Research gave out in 2002 predicting that property will rise at 6.24% minimum per year until 2020 should help you. Listen to and try and believe anybody out there in property who is a 'buy-and-hold' property investor: they know the truth. Try not to listen to a 'buy-and-flip', 'buy-and-sell' or 'buy-and-develop', whatever you want to call it, Property Investor. You don't have to listen to them. Because that is not the style of property investing I am advising you to get into.

Those people believe that it is better to grow a fruit tree, have it bear fruit and then cut it down and sell it for firewood. This is not my style. I do not believe in chopping up assets so that I can get all it has to give on one day. I prefer to take occasionally from the asset when, and only when, it bears enough fruit for me to take some surplus. The style of property investing you are getting into is a buy-and-hold system. So when you seek out others' advice, be sure to solicit advice from other buy-and-hold investors. When you are receiving advice you must know the style of property investor you are receiving advice from.

When people ask Warren Buffet his favourite holding period for shares, he says: "Forever." Why do you think he says that? Because if you bought a good share, it will go up in value over time. You will get paid dividends on it. This is what happens with property. My favourite holding period for property is "forever".

Do you believe it yet? If you do not believe it, go and do some blooming research! If I have not made it clear enough that this is what happens, and if you have not got it, I cannot help you. Stop reading now, because if I have not got that fundamental point over to you, I am not going to. You have got to get this, people. You have really got to get this. This will change your lives!!!! If you grasp this you will retire financially free, I have no doubt! Would you like that, is that enough, or do you want more?

After all, it's not going to cost you any money to be on the inside and wait and see.

16

Yes, It Really Is Free

Okay, now we come on to one of my favourite bits: why property is actually free. **This bit is just Sssoooo Coooooollll!**

Time is your enemy without assets and is your best friend with assets. Property goes up in value over time. The value of money comes down over time. Do you understand that? So, in other words, £1 today isn't worth as much as it was a year ago. It is not worth as much as it was 10 years ago. It is not worth as much as it was 20 years ago.

As an example, an average salary in 1984 was approximately £11k, I believe. I think the average salary today is £28k, generally across the country.

So, does money go down in value over time, then? Well, that is for you to answer. I mean, I am no economist. I cannot actually say: "Right, well, yes, this is how it works." But, from what I can see with my own eyes, money goes down in value over time, on average.

Inflation takes it up and it goes up at 1% or 2%. Personally, I believe that money down-values at a lot higher rate than that. That is my personal belief and I base it on property, not on the economy as a whole, because property is the market I'm in.

So, I only need to value the money going down to the value of the property at the time, so I relate the money to property. Yes, it is a bit of a leap of faith, that one, but I do not always let the facts stand in the way of my assumptions. That is a bit scary, I know, but as I said I am no economist and what I choose to work on is evidence that is presented to me, even if I am not qualified to put it in the correct language.

If you want the correct language, go to someone who doesn't make all of their money from property investing and just speculating. I am sure there are plenty of people about who can disprove what I am saying. At the end of the day, they get in their cars and drive home through the rush hour, whereas I get up from my desk, walk to the front door of the 5-bed detached bungalow we use as an office and walk next door to my home. If I was looking in from the outside I know who I'd believe.

All I will tell you, speaking generally, is that is how it works. I could get an economist in, one who shared my way of thinking and he could explain it and it would be very, very cleverly done, but we would still end up with the same assumption that I have already reached.

Likewise, I could more easily get an economist in who totally disagrees with my assumptions. And he could spend time showing you how it does not work and it would be a very clever statistic. And you would have to make the decision then.

I am telling you that I assume that money goes down in value over time at a reasonably high rate. If you do not agree with me and want to disprove it – and to all you economists out there – I would love to hear your

163

arguments one way or the other because I would like to use them in the future, so if you would like to send them to me, I would appreciate it and I will give you credit if and when I use them.

I am just going to keep on using my formula because it seems to be making me millions and it seems to be making my clients a lot of money as well. So I will carry on using that simple assumption until somebody absolutely proves to me otherwise – which of course they cannot, can they?

Now, why would you work when they give you all this money for free?

When we sold and got out of our old businesses we lost our salary. In 2003 we sold out to a major competitor. We had to give up our salary, which was not a bad salary. We gave it up because we knew we did not need it, because we had so much equity in our properties and we knew we would be able to re-mortgage these many times. They could produce something like ten times as much as needed. Since we knew we would always have plenty of money, we did not need a salary so we just lived off equity release. This made us professional property landlords.

The rent on properties is okay. They all make a profit, or thereabouts. But, it is not going to provide for me in the manner of lifestyle I've become accustomed to. My money comes from releasing equity from property. Out of every £100k I release, I get £15k to spend on me, £20k to put into savings or alternative investments and the rest goes back into property. At least, that was the plan. In the last 18 months I have re-mortgaged less to lower my loan-to-values a little, so I am spending more of the equity release on my lifestyle. But this is a short-term outlook and is only happening while we are in a consolidation period of our property investing.

Another great thing about the money that comes out – there is no tax to pay on it. Or to put it more correctly there is no tax YOU pay on it. The small amount of tax relief you lose on drawing down equity above the price you paid for the property or the value at which it went into the rental market can easily be covered from the equity released itself by understanding your property's actual cashflow.

So, let us introduce why it is free. Let's really get this down, before I drift off again. I will use an example of my parents' property in the next few pages.

For all of you out there who have owned property for more than five years, you should fill your own details in below, because nothing has so much of an effect as your own property showing you that it has been free.

But, before we do that, here is the one magic trick that I actually know how to do. I will bet I can tell you how much to the penny, everyone – who has owned a mortgage for more than five years – paid for their property. Bet I can tell each of you how much you have spent on your mortgage in your life. And it is not just the mortgage on your current house. That is the mortgage on your house before that and the one before that and the one before that, however many you have had. I will be able to name it to within £1 of how much money you have spent on your mortgage in your life.

Can you? Are you capable of telling me about your own property? I doubt it! But see if you can add it up. Go on. Because after all, I do not know you, do I? Don't know you from Adam. But I can tell you how much money you have spent on your property. Come on, give us a clue. How much? £10k, £20k, £30k, £50k, £100k, £200k? How much is it?

Okay, I will tell you how much it is. It's £0. You have never spent £1. Each month, your mortgage as you call it, is really just a way of paying into a savings plan. Each month, you put that money into a mortgage to pay it. And each month, on average, your property goes up in value more than you pay in.

So you've never actually paid a penny for your mortgage. Because it is worth a lot more than you have ever put in.

That means your property is free because, if you re-mortgage it now, you could pull out more money than you have ever put in, so it would not have cost you a £1. So that makes me a magician, yes? No, I am useless at magic tricks. But I am brilliant at spotting where the money is.

Just imagine for a second if your property valuation increase was a constant increase. Let's say you had £100k and were able to keep to a 100% mortgage and let's also assume you'd be paying say 8% on your mortgage, which is 0.666%/month or £666.67/month. But as history shows, the average increase is 11.74%/annum, or 0.978%/mth, which is £978.34/mth value increase.

So without even having a tenant in the property if there was a way you could create a constant value increase, sorry what am I saying, that's already been done by the market. What I should say is if there was a way you could prove it was real then in effect you'd pay your £666.66 and you'd receive cash for £978.34. So a profit of £311.68 without having a tenant in it (ask me now if I'm too worried about rental voids!)

Property is like your own cashpoint machine where once you own one you can go back occasionally and take money out and not pay tax on the capital released.

Here is an exact example of how this worked on my parents' property - a 3-bed centre terrace in Upper Beeding, West Sussex

- They purchased it in 1971 so have owned it for (years)   35
- They paid   £5,500
- Their deposit was   £750
- During 1971 – 1996 they
  paid in mortgages and capital repayment   £12,600
- The property was then worth   £70,000

So, did this property cost them any money, or was it just a savings plan, where they paid in £12,600 and made £57,400?

- Now in 2006 it is worth   £195,000

So did this property cost them any money, or was it just a savings plan, where they paid in £12,600 and made £182,400?

You can decide that!

You can do this. You have done it yourself with your own home already. Property is free! Right, so let us have a look, a closer look at it, then.

Add up every penny you have ever spent on your property, on your mortgage. Not on doing up the inside of it, because that is lifestyle choice and that is another subject which I am not going to cover in this book.

You add up every penny you have put into your mortgage, your £576.33 payment, for example. Add them all up. Get a total. Then take the value of your property, take off the existing mortgage, then take off all of your mortgage payments. Have you got more money than you started with?

For anyone who's owned a property for more than five years, the answer is yes, which means your property is free! That is right FREE! Nothing! Costs you zip, bug**r all, nada, nothing at all. It's Free.

ALL PROPERTY IS FRREEEEE!!!!

So, in this business, you get money for nothing and property for free.

Yes, it is a powerful piece of information! Somewhat life changing as I'm sure you will agree. I suggest you stop here and really think about it, as you want this to sink in into your bones. This concept wants to become part of you, as it will give you great power over money. Think about your own example and understand that you have never paid a penny for your home as it is worth more than you have paid, therefore it is free! If you do not understand or do not believe it, **do not move on**

until you do! Re-read this until you accept it at your core; it's a life changer when you do!

So it's all down to cashflow then, isn't it!!! And I'm going to come on to how to create that correctly.

Believing it, well, if you cannot add up, if you cannot put those sums on paper and if you cannot believe what is written in front of you right now, then you are not destined to be in property, because I do not know how to make it any simpler than that. Property is free. In this business, you get money for nothing and property for free.

How do I know that? **Because I know the real powers of property and this one is the backbone of why property is so good. This is the most powerful aspect of property and the most powerful CERTAIN wealth creation strategy there is!** Why do you think the banks do not mind lending on it?

Do you know what the funny thing is? They probably do not even know property is free. They probably do not even get it, because they have not broken it down. Only the really clever people out there, like Nicholas Van Hoogstraten and others like him will have really broken this one down.

Property is free. That means, it does not cost you any money. When I figured that out, it was like, 'oh, can I believe it?' you know. It is like the difference between repayment and interest-only mortgages. I mean, that subject's just been done to death.

I remember when I sussed it out and realised, why the hell did I want to pay off my mortgage with real money today when I could pay it off with false, free money from the future? Why had I fallen for that rubbish? Because like everyone else, I had been fed the dogma for years and it is easy to believe something that everyone else says is right. The hard bit is listening to a freak like me! One lesson that continues to be shown to me is that when the herd thinks one way the chances are they are probably wrong.

And it's more difficult to make money when you're trying to be the same as everyone else. To get a different result from the herd you have to become a contrarian thinker.

The day I first thought of only doing an interest only mortgage, I was like, oh, no, no, no. You need to have a repayment mortgage. Because, I had been brainwashed by the propaganda that is spouted at us. As supplied by the news, in the press, in education, everything, that you have to pay off your mortgage. **No, you don't! No, you don't! No, you don't!** What would you want to do that for? It is all just rubbish!

So, I looked to cutting my mortgage down. I had quite a big mortgage at the time. I think it was about £395k or something. And my mortgage payment each month was about £2.5k. That's quite a lot of money. By switching to interest-only, my mortgage payment dropped by £800 a month.

I thought, yeah, but I'm not paying off £800 a month on my mortgage. And I thought, well, no, but to get that £800 a month that I am paying off my mortgage, I am paying 40% tax on it.

What would be better is that I **do not** pay the £800 a month, or £9,600 a year plus the 40% tax I am paying on the earnings. What would be better is to eliminate the need to earn £16,000 a year to pay off my mortgage. Why should I use today's real money to pay off my mortgage? Why don't I re-mortgage just one of my properties each year and use that to clear off, say, £15,000 a year, because that is tax-free money. I have had to pay nothing to get hold of it and I can claim tax relief on some of the interest. So that is what I do now. Instead of paying my own capital off my own mortgage, I re-mortgage my rental properties and will use their equity to clear my own mortgage and I will get some tax relief on it.

I look at my own home as a big savings account, which I have a flexible facility on. At any moment I can draw out all the available mortgage I have on the property. The funds will simply appear in my bank account the next day.

Okay, back to the struggle I had with myself in switching over. I still thought it was scary. I did not know if I could go to this interest-only thing. Even I was struggling with it because I had been brainwashed so much. In the end, I got around my own programmed negative beliefs and convinced myself by saying, "I will try it for one year." And if, after one year, I don't like it, I will go back onto repayment. Yes, I had to trick my own brain into it as the brainwashing was so deep.

I switched it over and within a day, I got it. Yep, that is it! There is simply NO comparison. Interest only is the only way! All that work to get hold of a loan, what would you want to pay it back for when they want you to keep it????

People say to me now, what would you go for, repayment, endowment, pension or interest-only mortgage? There is no option here, people. It is interest-only mortgage, simple as that. What do you care about it? It is irrelevant to you. What do you want to pay it off for? The only reason to pay it off is the comfort factor or you haven't got the income to support it.

Let us say that you only owned one property for the rest of your life. Let us say that you only had a small mortgage on it and you only re-mortgaged it right at the start. You only had the mortgage you originally bought it for. And let us say that mortgage had gone down to 25% loan to value (LTV) of your home. And you only ever paid interest-only on it. And then every year from now, you went back and said I want another 5% of the equity out. And 5% will pay the mortgage for all time.

So, as long as the lender will let you have a mortgage right up until the day you die - what is the problem? The house pays for itself. After all, it is free, isn't it? We've already established that. So, what the hell do you want to pay the mortgage off for? The only reason to pay off a mortgage on your own home is the comfort factor and that I can fully understand and agree with.

But you must always keep a mortgage drawdown facility available to the maximum loan you can get on the house. Being able to get hold of £500k at one day's notice is very powerful and could come in handy when a real opportunity comes along.

But the only reason to clear it 100% and have no mortgage on it is comfort, or rather, perceived comfort.

You are not going to pay off the mortgage because you cannot afford it, because the house can afford it. The house pays for itself. Do you see what I mean? So you do not have to pay it off yourself, even if you have no income, as long as your lender is happy with that. In effect, the house pays for itself.

And people say: "Oh, well, that's spiralling into debt." No, your asset is growing faster than your debt. That's just good business.

And there you go. There you have it. That is the explanation of why property is free. Does it get any better than that? Well, no, frankly. That is the best bit about property. Property is free, so it does not matter what you buy. Over time, it will be free. Therefore, get your names on the deeds, people! That is what you have to do. Nothing harder than that. Property is free. All you have to do is wait. You do not wait to buy property. You buy property and wait. That is it.

It really is that simple. The problem is, we all have trouble believing a really simple concept because it is almost too simple to understand. But in you there is an element of belief and do you know why it is there? It is not thanks to my descriptive skills, because I am not that good at it. The reason there is an element of belief in you is that you knew this already. You just never stopped to think that it might be real. Well, it is real and boy, is it powerful!

A word of warning here: You may be believing it right now, but it won't be long before your conditioning starts to work on you, bringing you back into line. We all struggle with this. I had trouble with it myself, so I know that other people will have trouble with it, especially as you probably don't think as warped as I do.

So now, while you still know that property is costing you nothing and you know that you should only have an interest-only mortgage, let us cover the reasons why people sell property.

Why do people want to sell property if it's free? Do they really believe their property has peaked in value? After all that is so laughable!

It is because that is what they have been told they should be doing. That is what they have been trained to believe. If I have not made my feelings clear by now, that I think selling property is a bad thing, let me try again. It is a very negative thing, selling an asset. Especially after all the work you go through just to get hold of it in the first place, getting rid of it is just daft!

When you sell a property you are transferring your wealth to someone else, does that sound appealing?

There are times when people think they need to sell property, if they are in financial trouble and they need to get hold of money fast. Funny thing is, you can actually get more money by refinancing than you can by selling. And probably get hold of it faster too. I can prove that point a bit later.

So, why do people encourage you to sell? You tell me. I have not done that research. It is nearly certain that they do not know what they are talking about. Most likely they believe the rubbish that's spouted out. Understandable though if they are a developer.

I mean, if I was going to develop properties, there would be an element that I would want to sell, so it gave me cash flow. And I would not want an estate that's just fully a rented estate. I would want at least 75% ownership on it.

So, there are reasons to sell. It is just, if you really want to hang on and wait for the real money, you must wait for the future and delay your gratification.

Try looking at it this way: When you buy a property, you have planted a seed in the ground. By waiting the 18 months for it to go up in value so you can refinance it, you've let that seed grow into a fruit tree and it is now bearing its first fruit. So you can either take and eat all the fruit, or use the fruit to provide the seeds for more trees.

The following year or so, your first tree bears fruit again and your new tree bears its first fruit as well. So now you can either eat twice as much fruit or plant twice as many new fruit trees. Maybe you will have a fallow summer where it/they do not bear any fruit and maybe it will be the next year before it bears fruit. Or maybe you will have a bumper harvest for a few years. I want my orchard to stretch as far as the eye can see so that it bears fruit all the time. At any given time there are some trees that have ripened and I am able to take whatever fruit I need from them. In fact, I have so much fruit that I can keep more than I need for myself and still plant more trees.

But now, suppose I took that seed, planted it in the ground, waited until it got to the point that it was ready to bear fruit and then I chopped it down and sold it as firewood to somebody else. Then I took that money to buy more seeds to plant another tree, so I had to start from scratch again. I would not have any fruit if my tree was nothing but firewood. Seems a bit daft, if you ask me. But that is what is known as 'flipping properties'. Keep up the good work, people. After all I'm buying!

I think that selling property comes down to a complete lack of real understanding of how the system works. And in fairness I have read dozens of books on the subject and none have ever covered this in any way. Have all the experts just not found a way to explain it?

Most people have come into property ownership by mistake, most of the time, by accident. They do not structure their investing properly at the start. The people who do structure it are the banks, but they do not need to understand it to the level above, as that is not how they make their money.

This brings me on to why the banks lend money on property, but that is a whole other subject: the banks and why they loan you money. We will not be covering that in this book, either. So if it interests you, ask me the question via my website and I will put the answer in a blog article.

Okay, back to the point. So you need another property, right? And you are not going to do something daft like sell it? Okay! So all you need, if you want to have your cake and eat it, is property to the value of your own home. That is it.

If your own home is worth £1.2 million, for example, then you need £1.2 million of investment property. Then you will keep your own home forever and your investment properties will appreciate in value. As they go up, you will actually be able to have the money as if you were taking the money out of your own home. You are not, but you know what I mean, yes? In other words, to have your cake and eat it, you need to have twice as big a cake. And if you want more cake, make it bigger!

I am going to use an example of what you can do with property. My dad bought his house in 1971. He paid £5,200. He took out a 25-year endowment mortgage. He paid a total of £41 per month in mortgage interest and endowment payments. The £41 comprised £26 interest and £15 endowment payment.

In 1996, the endowment paid out and he paid off his mortgage. He was retired at the time. He had taken early retirement from teaching and he had been retired several years by then. He paid off that mortgage, which I believe was something like £5,000, when the endowment money came in.

At the time, he had at least £10,000 sitting in two or three of his bank accounts. That was just two or three of his accounts, plus his investments, his ISAs and PEPs, not to mention his shares. It was just sitting there. But the money came in from the endowment and he paid the mortgage off.

For every year from 1971 to about 1982-83, when I first went out to work, he struggled for money because when he first took the mortgage out, he was only bringing home something like £80/month. Over 50% of his income went on the mortgage payment.

So here he was, earning £80/month and having to pay £41. In 1984 he retired, fed up with the new enforced methods of teaching. By that time he was earning about £100/week, so about £430-£450/month. (You know, people actually used to live on this sort of money.)

So, at the start, the percentage of his income was enormous. But at the end, it was nothing at all. £40/month was now just 10% of what he took home, nothing at all. But, for all those years when he was paying that £15/month endowment policy, it really did hurt.

Now stop for a second and just imagine if he had not had an endowment policy and he had only had an interest-only payment mortgage. That would have meant several things.

1. He would not have had an endowment policy and therefore in 1996 he would not have paid off his mortgage.
2. He would still today have an outgoing of £26/month
3. He would have a track record stretching back 35 years of never missing a mortgage payment.
4. He would have not had those 8 to 10 years of really struggling financially, making a £15/month payment that was nearly 20% of his take home pay.

If he'd had an interest-only mortgage, he could have just written the cheque for that £5,000 and his mortgage would have been cleared. No years of struggling, no years of grief, you know? So he was sold the same poop that the rest of us have been, and all of you are today, who still have repayment mortgages. But who am I to say what you should do? I am not qualified to dispense financial advice – I just understand how property works.

Another thing my dad would have kept was his track record. You can't buy a track record! When my dad tried to re-mortgage in 2002 so that he could pull equity out and go and invest in property, they said: "Oh no, I am very sorry, Mr. Shaw. Because of your age, because you have not got a track record of mortgage payments, it could be very difficult for us to get you a mortgage." My dad owned his house 100%, his property was unencumbered and he held no personal debt and they would not give him a mortgage. It is craziness.

I managed to get around it another way, but it was frustrating. Even though my parents knew that it was a good idea, what I was telling them to do with their money, they were not allowed to get at the money in their own home. The only option they were given was this thing called a reversionary sale. They would sell their home to somebody at 35% of its value and they would have the privilege of living in it for the rest of their lives. That is what they would have to look forward to for all those years of struggle.

Then, when they moved into an old people's home or worse, they would give up their home for 35% of its value. Now, I understand why people would want to do reversionary property sales, and from a Property Investor's point of view I am glad they do, as it matches up two individuals who can solve each other's problems. But I do think there is a fairer way of doing it for the people who are trading their homes for less than 40% of their current value.

Reversionary might be all right for some people who do not really understand property, but the idea grated on me quite a lot. I was not going to let my parents do that.

179

It was not because I did not want my parents' money at any price. It was because they had struggled for years to get hold of that house. As far as I was concerned, they were damned well having every penny of that property.

What I managed to do was get them every penny of that property and a lot more besides. They have got a lot of property now because I used the power of property to really transform their financial lives for them. Maybe I will answer how I did that on my Blog. Maybe!

So, getting back to the point. My dad could have just written the cheque to pay off the mortgage or just carried on paying the £26/month if he had had an interest only mortgage. So, why the hell did he want to pay it off in an endowment policy over those years? Why the hell do we want to pay off our mortgages? Why the hell do we want to put a pension mortgage together? What are we doing this for? Why do we do it this way? Why don't we just keep our mortgages forever? What is this obsession we have for being out of debt? We know there are two types of debt, Good debt and Bad debt, so why do we want to be free of good debt? Good debt is a good thing!

We do it because we have been told that this is what we are supposed to do! Nothing more! But I am now telling you it is not real! It is just what we have been told we are supposed to do. We do not need to do it! Getting rid of good debt reduces our return on our investment! Why would anyone want to struggle to pay off good debt so that they can reduce their return on their investment? Surely I am not the only one who thinks this is madness?

In this business the less money you put in then the more money you make!

In 1996, my Dad's property was probably worth in the region of £85k. By the time he was finished paying for it, it had gone up in value about 16 times, over 1,500%. All that time while he was working for a living, he could have actually not worked at all! Probably he could have earned enough money just by re-mortgaging every year or two and enjoyed his life more. The money he was making at re-mortgage would have paid the mortgage and paid for his life. Is that too much of a whacky concept?

So here we are, all of us going to work for a living when our homes are earning and definitely retaining more than we are, by just being there!

I do not go to work for a living any more. I work through choice, because I love it. But nearly everyone else does, or everyone I see does. Why, when your house can be giving you more than you are earning! I am telling you, it will just carry on and on and on. It does not stop. It's perpetual. So all I am trying to say here is, for some, not all of you, you are putting undue pressure on yourself, when you do not need to.

And people say: "Oh, yeah, well, the market can go down as well as up." **Yes, it can.** **But it will always recover.** It is not like the stock market. It does not get wiped out. There will always be a demand.

What is the demand for Google shares, other than the fact that people want them, they desire them? On the other hand, people are passionate about having somewhere to live because you cannot do without it! So, are they as passionate about owning those Google shares? Not in the same way. You cannot compare the two. It is a completely different thing.

Have I convinced you that Property is easy?

Have I convinced you that anyone can make money out of Property?

Have I shown you things that subconsciously you felt you already knew?

Because, if you are not convinced by now that you already know what you need to know to go into property investing at a basic level, then I do not think I can help you. If you are not convinced by now that you are making money already if you own your own home, and you are making more than it ever needs, then I do not think I can help you. If you are not convinced by now that property is free, then I don't know what to say to you, really, other than sorry, you have wasted your money on this book.

To the rest of you, though, there are two lots of you left. If you are convinced, then you are going to love the rest of this stuff. And if you are still on the fence, then the rest of this stuff will convince you by the end.

The property market does not matter to you if there is none of your money in it. I will explain that in a second.

17

Don't Wait To Buy Property. Buy Property And Wait.

Who cares about the property market, whether it is going up, down or dead flat? There, now you can argue: "Well, I do care if it is going down, I care if it's going up and I care if it is dead flat." Positive, negative, in the middle! It is irrelevant to me, I do care but only because the strategy alters slightly. It is always a good time to buy and hold property. Thankfully I seem to be able to predict the market better than anyone I have found so far, so it makes it rather easy to know what play to make.

You do not wait to buy property. You buy property and wait.

If the market is going down, you have got to be a bit clever about it. You have got to do a little bit more research and you have got to know a little bit more. But it is still a very good time to buy.

If the market's flat, fine. Buy all the property you can. If the market's going up, fine, definitely buy all the property you can.

Who cares what the market is doing? Just buy property all the time and don't wait!

If the property you buy hasn't cost you anything, then it does not matter if it is going down in value because property recovers over time. And the further that it goes down, as long as you bought as it was going down, then it is going to out perform later.

Do people stop buying shares when they go down? No, the savvy investors get in when they are going down, just before they get to the bottom. Or they trade them on the way down.

So, does it matter then when it is going up, because you could say: "Well, the savvy investor definitely would not buy when it is going up. They would only buy when it is going down," which is a lot of what traditional property investors do.

I, on the other hand, decide to buy all the time because I don't really care what is going on with the property market. I used to care a lot, as I explained earlier. That was my strategy. Now my strategy is, who cares what the property market is doing? Let everybody else invest in the property market.

I invest in **a** property that is in **a** block of flats, that is in **a** street, that is in an area of **a** town next to **a** school, that is next to **a** railway station, that is within **a** certain district, that is within **a** certain town, that is within **a** larger group of towns, that is within **a** county, that is within **a** certain area of the country which is located within **the** property market.

I invest in **a property**. I do not invest in **the** property market. As with nearly all Property Investors, I focus on **a** and do not waste time generalising with **the**. That property might be in the property market somewhere, but I am not investing in the property market. I am investing in **a property**. And I make **a** decision, **a** small decision, on **a** single property. Buying property because the market is going up is just gambling or speculating at best; not investing.

There are four types of property buying; First there is gambling, which is a case of speculating, if you like, on the property market going up. Or you are buying at a low price and you are speculating it is going up because you are buying it at a low price, at whatever the market value is and you are speculating that it is going up. Basically, it is gambling, right?

Second is investing for no-money down within a year. Some people call this, 'No money down eventually.' This is what I do and we do for our clients. I buy a property. I get the builders in to refurbish it, hopefully prior to completion; if not, then immediately after completion. And I get the valuer in there within a month. So, I am looking to refinance that property out within three months.

So, from buying to refinance in three months is what I am looking for. If it takes six months, that is okay. If it takes a little bit longer, I get a little bit peeved. But basically, I look for a no-money down deal within the first year. In other words, the money is out and the money comes back comfortably within a year. The money is out, the money comes back. In other words, what I am looking to get is my whole property purchase, from the start, 105% funded.

The third one is buying with what is known as a daylight bridge. This is achieved when you can buy a property at least 18% below market value and you can get the re-valuation figure you want prior to actually purchasing the property. This can be a very quick way of acquiring a lot of property but has its own set of problems attached. But the big upside is you will need very little money to build a substantial portfolio. I am not going to be covering this strategy in depth in this book.

The fourth one is another investing for no-money – down-eventually. This is the easiest way for you to do it, if you are patient. This is the way that anyone can do it. This is the way that any damned fool can get into property investing and win forever.

Let's say you have £200k and you want to get into the property market and you want to buy properties that are valued at £100k each. You can go out there with £200k and your money will buy you about 10 to 12 properties comfortably. So, you could literally go, well, I am going to invest my £200k and buy 12 properties. Then you would acquire £1.2 million worth of property.

You then sit there and wait! You can carry on with your life because, if that £200k is spare to you and it does not matter and you do not need it back, you do not need to learn all the semi-clever stuff. You just need to buy the property and give it to a managing agent, make sure you have done your due diligence on him and get him to rent it out. And you need to wait. You need to wait two, three, four, five years.

Five years comes up and you go: "I would like to revalue all my properties, please, and re-mortgage them to a cheaper lender." And they go: "What are the properties worth?" And you go: "I don't know," because you do not care! Because you have not looked at them!

You go to an estate agent, who says: "Oh yes, that is worth X, X, and X and all of those properties have gone up in value roughly 30, 40 or 50%. So, you re-mortgage them and you get your £200k back. You probably get another £200k, £300k, or £400k as well that you can do what you want with for free, interest-free (to you personally) and with no capital gains tax due. We will come back to that later – yes I know I keep saying it but we will.

There you go. What the hell do you need to become a property expert for? That is it. If you have got £200k, go and get rich. I am not stopping you. It is easy. And there are no catches in this book that say, "Oh, you should not have rushed out and done that." Yes, you should have rushed out and done that! It is a good idea!

But there are better ways of doing it. You can earn more from your buck! But, that could be considered greedy because, after all, you will then have a property portfolio worth £2.5 million+ that goes up in value £250k+ a year. So, every year you are making your £200k back. And you have had to know nothing about property, other than going to an estate agent and going: "How much is this property, please?" And they go, "£100K." And you go, "I will have it for £100k please!"

That is it. That is the level of skill you need to have in property investing the fourth way. You do not need to know anything about it. You just need to know, will it rent?

Why does that matter? Well, first off, the lender will not let you buy it unless it will rent, so that is a level of protection for you even if you are completely dumb. You will not be paying too much for it, as I said earlier, because they will not let you buy it unless you put more of a deposit in. That's the warning sign, people, just in case you do not know. If the property does not value for the price they are asking, then it is not worth what you have agreed to pay. Go and re-negotiate it downward! This is a good way of protecting you from mistakes, although it does not work every time.

You know, the protection's already there for you. You do not have to even know about it. You just have to think with common sense. Can you do that?

So, the quick guide of all you need to know is number four, investing for no-money-down-eventually. This is the easiest way for you to do it if you are patient. There is not a simpler way and it will work, full stop. Any damn fool can get this one right if they have the cash required to do so. There is only one thing they can really do wrong… if they break the one golden rule.

And what is the golden rule?

Don't bl*y sell!**

However, the full guide in this book directs you towards number two, and this way is good fun and creates sooooo much money! This way, to me, is just the best. I love what I do. I love making money for people. I love making money for me. I love buying property. I love negotiating the deal. I really do enjoy it. I get to play monopoly for real! It is great fun!

Well, how could I not enjoy it even when I was getting bored with it? I started looking at it. I thought, "I'm bored with that," and I was fortunate enough to read a book. I can't remember which one it was, but it said, when you get good at investing, investing becomes boring. When you get good at something, it gets boring, and when it is boring, that is when you are really in the zone. And it got boring for me. It got really, really boring.

But now, I have learned to pick the best bits out of it - the bits I really enjoy that I never, ever get bored with. And I never get bored negotiating a deal. I never get bored finding a property. And I never get bored, never, ever, ever get bored receiving £20,166.07 from my solicitor, as I did earlier this week, or however much the next mortgage payout is.

I never get bored with that. I remember when I did not earn that amount of money in some of my best years ever. And that is just one re-mortgage that has come out in the last three months; just one. It is not the only one. It is just one. You can see that it affords me quite a nice lifestyle. I am not saying this to boast, I am saying it, because it can happen for you as well if you desire it. In the fantastic book *Think and Grow Rich* by Napoleon Hill, the formula to create great wealth is **clearly** written down. I myself used this formula without knowing. However, the technique requires a significant level of faith, which is why so few still achieve great wealth. My purpose is to take financial freedom to far more than 1% of the population. What I am going to show you here in this book is a technique that just requires following to achieve a level of financial freedom, and if YOU want, then it can provide great wealth.

As I have said, the property market goes up in value over time. And if you go back to 1966, you will see that it averages at 11.74%. Before that time, it went up at a slightly lower average. But in 1965 the Rent Act was introduced and this seems to have been the catalyst that changed the rate of growth.

Anyway, the important thing for us is that it has remained at the 11.74% constant since then. So it is reasonable to assume that over time, the market will continue along this trend or thereabouts. This is without considering the strong upward price pressure on the market. In actual fact because of a number of other facts, which include the government stopping building council houses in 1989 and the planning restrictions (which restrict the building of the right number of homes in more importantly the right areas) this 11.74% trend has considerable upward pressure.

But let's stick at 11.74% for now, so if we project it forward at its long-term rate, and overlay the rate predicted by Centre of Economic and Business Research (CEBR) in 2002 of 6.24% you will see that if they were right, the trend would take a shift that is completely out of whack? That's probably why they increased their 20 year prediction to 7.6% last year. The CEBR predicted that the average house price in 2002 of £101,164 would raise by 2020 to £300,643. Well, the average price at the start of 2006 was well on the way having achieved 50% of the raise in just four years so it is looking too good for this particular prediction. However, it is looking very rosy indeed for all property owners!

So if you feel more comfortable taking this conservative look at it, then take that as your trend. I personally like to use a conservative prediction to my clients of 8.5% increase annually. And as a property owner I look to withdraw no more than 2% value in equity release each year for my own personal use. So if you want £20k a year tax free and want that with as much certainty as you can get in life, then you need a £1 million pound portfolio. I'll cover this in more detail a bit further on.

The main point is, **the Property Market as a whole just goes up in value over time, whether you want it to or not!**

If you do not believe me, and I mean really do not believe it in your soul, then this is not for you and you are wasting your time by reading this book. If you do not believe property goes up in value over time, then you are not in the right business, because this book is about making money out of property over the long-term. This is not a get rich quick strategy. It can be if you want to be mad like me, but it is, more importantly and pay very close attention to this, **it is a get rich CERTAINLY strategy.**

If you're not reading this book with a highlighter pen then you should be. But if you're not then I suggest you go and get one as you'll want to re-read the last few pages and especially highlight those last two points. Until you make it your purpose in life to become a life long property investor, then you are leaving your real wealth on the table as I did myself for years.

The lottery has a catchphrase, 'you've got to be in it to win it.' The catch phrase is accurate but if they were more truthful then it would be, 'you've got to be in it to have a 1 in 10,000,000 chance of winning it.' Well in this business we can use their catch phrase in the form they use it, and with full honesty. Basically if you're in it then you win, full stop!

I am in this for life. I am in this for the long-term. I am not in this for 5, 10 or 25 years, on a 2-year strategy, a 3-year strategy. I am in this until I die. And then my children get all my property. And they are in this until they die. And then their children get all their property. That is it. We just buy property. That is all we need to do. We need to just keep buying more of it. We are in this for as long term as it gets. Being clever in Property Investing is investing forever; ask The Duke of Westminster.

I am not going to be covering inheritance tax in this book, as I'm sure you've guessed I have found a doosey of a way to avoid as much of that as possible. It will be covered on my site though and in another book to be released next year.

There is a risk though, and the risk is cash flow. You are only at risk if you cannot cash flow the property. I am going to cover that in detail later, but that is the only risk you have got. You must not ever over-extend yourself, because that's the only time you put all of this wondrous free money at risk, by over-extending yourself.

Do not over-extend yourself. Do not chase the bl***y deal. Do not go for a deal that is too big, too out of your ballpark. If the market goes down, and you aren't sure of what to do then you sit and wait, just like we did in the 90s.

The only people who lost money in the 90s were the ones who sold or got repossessed. They got repossessed because they could not cash flow it and they sold because they thought they had to.

The rest of us, the ones who sat and waited, are all sitting back at the moment now, all living in £300k plus houses because the property market goes up in value over time. And because we sat and waited and were able to 'cashflow' it then it all worked out for us.

This is not like the stock market. If it were that fortunate then the FTSE 100 market should recover to where it was in the year 2000. I mean, it does make me laugh, the stock market, actually. I mean, don't get me wrong. I like stock trading, but the stock market is, in my opinion, a bit of a joke. You know, you have got the FTSE at the end of 2000, it was about 6,500 or something like that. Well, we are in 2006, and it is not up at that level now – no comparison – end of story!

So how can these people even compare that to the property market? You know, they are not worthy to even be in the same room talking about the property market and comparing the stock market to it. The property market is just so strong, so good and when used properly is simply unbelievable! Why do you think the banks will not lend to as many people and as much money on shares? They will lend to complete beginners in the Property Market as long as they have a pulse. This is not rocket science, people!

Long-term vs. short-term. You are not in this for the short-term. I think I have made that point crystal-clear. Anyone who thinks they are in this just for the money you can make by using the techniques I am going to show you to buy property and to get it to be worth more just to sell it are basically in it for chump change. What the hell do you want to do that for?

All that work you put into buying a property to then go and sell it. What is wrong with people who do that? Do you know what I mean? Have they got some burning need to be a salesman?

I would rather have everybody think I am an idiot and have all the money. The estate agents used to look at us and go: "Well, why are they keeping all that property? When are they going to start selling some of it?" Now, they do not say anything any more.

You know, we have got a deep-rooted respect now from a lot of the people. We have got some people who still have a lot of animosity and a lot of jealousy, as well. But, on the whole, they just think: "We do not know really what he is doing, but he seems to be doing something right."

What amazes me is, if I had somebody like me around me in my industry, I would try and buy me lunch! I would take me to lunch and I would go: "Right, what am I doing wrong? What can I do better? How can I get something of what you have got?"

Is that just the way people who go into personal development think, and other people just do not think that way? Because to me, it's a case of, whenever I am sitting next to an expert, I try and gain as much of their expertise as I can, because they have done it before. It is a case of, this bloke's got the map, best I ask him for directions!

I have got the map to create wealth in property easily. I am giving it to you. I am giving you, in this book, two distinct ways you can do it. If you have already got money, then you can do it one way easily. If you have not got lots of money, then you can do it my way. It is a little harder, but it is still a lot easier than working for a living.

I do not understand, if you have got an expert around you, why you do not go and listen to them. Go and chat to them. Go and find out what makes them tick. Go and find out how they do things. I know I do.

Okay, back to the point. You are in this for the long-term. When the market goes up, which it will, that's a bonus. You cannot bank on more than 2% of the money coming in each year, but you nearly can, well as much as you can bank on having your job next year.

You cannot bank on the fact that next summer you are going to refinance and pull out £250k and then you will be laughing for the rest of your life. Unless of course you have a large enough portfolio, and then there may be a change in the mortgage market meaning that you can't get at it.

You have to wait. You have to delay that gratification until the property is ready to bear its fruit. That is it. You have to wait for it. You are not in control of it. After you have done your bit where you have forced appreciation, which I will come onto in a little while, after you have done that bit, you cannot do anymore. You are out of it. It is not in your hands. It is in somebody else's hands. It is in the property market as a whole. You have just got to wait. Your property is now in the speculation phase of its life cycle, and it will remain there forever. You just do not really want any of your own money in a speculation.

It is in the hands of the estate agents. Until they realise that the property market in their town has gone up in value, yours will not go up. They do not value property by going: "Oh, let's value the bricks and mortar." They go, "What do you reckon I could sell that for," in the same way every product on the market today is valued and sold.

Do you think Bic Razors go: "We are going to sell our Bic Razor for £3.55" and just pull the figure out of the air? No, they look at the market around them and they go: "How much is our competition selling their razors for? Is our razor worth more than theirs? Can we sell our razor for a bit more?" Then they look at ways of manufacturing and retaining their margin.

Estate agents look at other property to find out what their vendors' property is worth. So, until prices start going up from other properties, the property market will not move in your town. This is why you can ride a wave of price rises in a boom time if you pick your market carefully. But that is another subject for another time.

I have proved to myself how the market is valued. I have proved it to my business partners. I have proved it to my clients. Only you know if I have proved it to you.

All you need to do, if you want to have your cake and eat it, is buy property investments to the same value of your own home and you will regularly receive lumps of money. Sometimes you will get lots. Sometimes you will get two or three properties re-mortgaged at a time. Sometimes just one!

So, there are only two things you need to get rich. One is cash flow and the other is time. You must never over-extend yourself, as I have said clearly. If you have got plenty of surplus, then great, get on with it. You do not need to learn anything clever if you want to do it efficiently.

You can learn from this clever stuff but, apart from that, you do not actually need it. You are already there. You have already got what you need in front of you.

If you already own £2,000,000 worth of property and all you want is £40k/year income for the rest of your life, do not be scared to re-mortgage and pull that money out, as you are making nearly £240k and you are safe to draw up to 2% of the portfolio to live on. It will go up in value over time and you can have the money. There is no need to struggle through your life, as my dad did. You can have the money right now if you have already got it. You have done it, so why not enjoy a better life with the fruits of your labour.

Now, that will give you nice problems to have. A nice problem to have is how to mitigate as much of your tax as possible. Property can really help with this.

The government is an ineffective provider of housing, very ineffective since they stopped building any. And the government wants you, as landlords, to provide housing for people.

Therefore, it gives you as many tax benefits as are reasonable to give, without making the market unstable. And so, you have got to take advantage of every tax break the government offers you on this because you can mitigate virtually all of your tax over time and it should become a case of you only have to pay tax if you want to. As a business man said to me once: "We view tax as a Flexible Expense!" and he was right. You need to take good professional advice on this, and I will be covering a lot more clever tax advice on my website.

18

The Only Thing You Need To Worry About

The title here says it all. Pay very close attention to this chapter as it is the only one you need to worry about.

My golden rule on the cash flow part is you only ever invest 66% of what you borrow or have available to borrow. So in other words, if you've got £100k of equity on drawdown from your house, you are only going to go and invest £66k of that. The other £34k sits around as spare cash flow. If you have £50k of credit card availability and you are prepared to use it in conjunction with the equity drawdown, then you can invest the £100k as you do not go past your 66% invested i.e. your total is £150k, so you are only using 66% of your available funds.

If you have got it in a drawdown mortgage, it means it is just available, which means you are not paying interest on it. In other words, only spend 66% of the amount you borrow. Do not go: "I need to buy a car for £20k so I'll borrow £20k," because you have the insurance and the payments on the loan and lots of different things that are going to mean spending more than £20k. The reason most people struggle when they borrow money is that they have not borrowed enough to correctly integrate it into their life. Yes, they have enough to buy the car but all the extras have put them into their overdraft and that is where they will now stay or more likely go backwards. Do not put yourself under pressure.

When you are investing, you do not put yourself under any pressure at all, as pressure makes you make bad decisions, like selling property in a panic to raise cash. Let other people do that sort of silly stuff and capitalise on it when they do by being there to take their property off their hands when they need the money fast. This is not you being horrible, this is you helping them out of trouble and believe me, they are grateful or they would not sell you the property.

You make this as relaxing and as pressure-free as possible. And you do that by always borrowing more than you need! If you have got to borrow it from high-interest credit cards and loans and things then do so, just never go past 66% of your money tied up. If you want me to go deeper into detail here, then ask the question on my website.

Okay, let us put it this way. What is the cheapest borrowing you can get in the conventional world? Mortgages? Cheap rate loans? Or is it free credit? And where is the only place you can get 0% ? Credit cards!

According to society and popular opinion, credit cards are the most expensive borrowing there is, but when used correctly they can be the cheapest as no one else gives you money for free. It's funny how all the sheep think they are the most expensive form of borrowing. The sheep are correct, of course, if they are mismanaged.

I think they are the cheapest thing to borrow from on a short-term basis. Where they are not cheap is for hard-core debt. They are very cheap for short-term – less than six month borrowing terms (occasionally up to twelve months). You might have to pay a drawdown fee, but they are still cheap if you can get it at 0%, or anything less than the bank base rate. Because you have got to remember that you are paying a lot more than that on your interest rate for your mortgage.

So, if you can borrow on credit cards at 2, 3 or 4% and you're paying 4, 5, or 6% interest on the mortgage, then you are actually borrowing cheaper on your credit cards than on your mortgage, even though a mortgage is traditionally considered the cheapest way of borrowing money.

Remember the 66% rule and never leave yourself short, otherwise you can mess this up real quick. And if you see yourself going short, by doing your cash flow and working out where you are going to be, you have to go and raise more money to make sure that you are not going to go short.

Do not wait until the last minute. That is where people go wrong.

Here is a golden rule that you must never forget,
<u>You must never, ever miss a payment on anything.</u>

You have to protect your credit file as if it was the Holy Grail. Your credit file is everything to you. It is your statement to the world. When done well, your credit file should say to all potential, conventional lenders that you are a good risk!

On the whole, when you are in the sort of position to borrow the way we are borrowing, when you have got banks that share information, credit cards that share information, you have to protect your credit file and you have to make sure you make all your payments. **This is not negotiable!** If you want to be in property then you have to pay your bills on time every time.

Because if you miss just one payment on one little mortgage, you can be out of the borrowing game for six months minimum and in reality probably longer.

In property, the business you are in is the **'borrowing business'** so you cannot ever over-extend yourself and get it wrong. You have to pay promptly without fail!

There was an article in *The Guardian* recently about how buy-to-let landlords are considered now the best risk, better than first-time buyers, because so few of the buy-to-let landlords are in mortgage arrears. Too right, because buy-to-let landlords should bl***y well know better. I have been saying we were a far better risk than 1st time buyers for years. Now finally the Mortgage company Actuaries have recognised it. This will ease borrowing requirements in the future and has the potential to lower interest rates.

And I can tell you this much. The landlords who are in mortgage arrears are the idiots: they are the ones who are screwing it up, because they will not be able to go out and do more borrowing. All of the rest of us, everybody else gets it. Everybody else gets the fact that, "Hang on a minute, we do not want to have mortgage arrears because if we have mortgage arrears, we cannot borrow more money. If we cannot borrow more money, we cannot get given all this money for free!!!" Whereas first-time buyers, well, you know, they over-extend themselves at times, so they are going to have mortgage arrears occasionally. I did in the

90s! I'm sure most people have done. This comes from a severe lack of financial education.

If I get time then I am going to start a small mission to help first time buyers get on the ladder, as I think it is important for them and it is important for me to help. I know that by doing it, it will actually be damaging my own market slightly, but I cannot bear to hear the rubbish on TV about how first time buyers cannot get on the property ladder, because they can't afford it. This statement is a joke, as you all must agree, because property is free and anyone can afford that!

The real problem is raising the deposit and not over-extending themselves. That is easy to fix and I can show them how to do that. One of my personal goals is to get younger people into property sooner and get them to use financial intelligence to construct a better life.

A point to remember is that interest rates are just one of the pitfalls of doing business. You'll make more money, more quickly when they are lower, but when they are higher your expenses may be higher, but there will be a lot more opportunities around. But when the rates are higher your mistakes are not so easily forgiven by your portfolio. So all higher interest rates mean is that you need to be more diligent when making decisions.

Drifted off again! Anyway, if you are short of money, stop borrowing to spend. Start borrowing to invest. You have got to stop borrowing to spend, full stop! This is seeking gratification now, which you can have in small amounts, whereas if you delay that gratification and put your reserves into property, when the time is right you can have large amounts to enjoy and blow!

You do not borrow to spend money. I am talking credit cards and loans. I borrow to invest money. I spend money that I have made through investing, through borrowing to invest. In other words, I live off the children of my investments.

It is not that hard. It is like weaning yourself off an addiction. Basically, it is called "delayed gratification," and everyone can do this. I mean, when I first started coming up with this and we started getting the cheques coming back to us, well, they were not even cheques. It was just CHAPS payments, which is money straight into our bank account.

I would go online to the bank account and more money would keep turning up. I would be looking at it going, "Hmm, this is nice," and I did not go out and spend it. In the end, I did, yeah, I bought a Lamborghini, but I bought most of it on finance, only putting down 25%. I now disagree with finance, but I had not learned my own rules on delayed gratification at the time, so it cost me a lot of real money, well 'realish' money.

Then the following year, I bought some more cars and I should not have bought them. They were a mistake - not because I over-extended myself, but because they took up too much of my time and caused me immense grief. Just imagine how you would feel on a Sunday afternoon when you wanted to take one out – at the time there were six super cars stored at my home (there were always three in garages) – and not one of them would start! As my friend Pete described them, "Andy buys supercars as tarmac covers."

A boyhood dream turned into reality and then realising it was not real, but an illusion created by my own opinions and attitudes based around what the media is telling you what things are like. But that is another story!

So, now we are going to look at getting hold of the money. Well, any damned fool can get hold of the money, right? Any idiot can get hold of it, but you have to think outside the box. Do not think: "Oh, can I get hold of it in my own name if I've got bad credit?" Well, no, you cannot, so how do you get hold of it? Is there somebody you trust? Have you got a partner? Have you got a friend? Have you got somebody who, no matter what, if you're broken down, you are at Dumfries bus depot, will come and get you? Because that's the person you go and talk to if they have got a good credit rating.

If you have got bad credit then you need to start rebuilding it and in under 18 months you can do that with as little as £1,000 using my crossfiring techniques and tools which are available on the website. People describe the cross firing techniques as the most powerful tool I've ever created. And I have also had complaints from people telling me that I shouldn't teach Men of Straw how to look like Men of Substance (their words). But as far as I'm concerned, you want to know how I did it. Well this is a key element to my fund raising and as such I would not be giving you all of the info if I held back on this. It is down to you to use the info responsibly...consider yourself warned (and there is zero hype in this!).

Asking a friend or relative for money is a taboo for most people so we've now entered the world where you do not feel comfortable. We are outside your zone of feeling safe. Well, your feelings are normal. It is not natural to be here, believe me, but if you have nowhere else to go for the money and you have a solid proposition, it is one of the easiest places to go to raise money. People often ask me how I can find people with money and I say it is simple, become an expert at finding property investment deals and they will find you. There is an abundance of money out there! And most people who have it have not got what you will have, time and expertise.

One day I was at work and I could not help getting annoyed at all the deals I kept missing in the paper. I was frustrated that there were two or three I was going to have to pass by. I got up and went out into the yard where all the fitters were having their coffee. And I said to them, 'Has anybody got £40k they can lend me for a few months?'

One of them said, 'How long do you want it for? I said four to eight months, but I told him not to worry because I would give him a good return on it. He said, 'Will a cheque be okay?' I said, 'Yeah that will be fine. Can I have it in, say, four weeks?' He said, 'You can have it today if you want. Can I ask what it is being spent on?' I said, 'I do not know yet, I will just go and find out!' Moral of the story – If you don't ask, you don't get!

If you don't know anyone who has a good credit rating, then you have to do sweat equity deals. You have to go and find the deals. You will have to become a bit of an expert to find these. The only reason I was trusted with this guy's money was a) He knew me very well, b) He knew I was an expert, c) He knew when I said I would give him a good return that he would actually get one, and most importantly, d) He knew he would get his money back!

There are always ways to get hold of money. There are people out there, as a lot of you soon will be, who may be sitting with £50, £100, £200, £300, £400, £500k of equity and lots more in their property.

Just because you have no money, don't assume the people you know don't have money. One thing I have learned since I created a little wealth is there is always someone else out there with more money, and usually a lot more!

They may also have £200, £300, £400k worth of savings and investments and don't know what to do with the money. Many of them are desperate to be matched up with somebody who is keen, somebody who is diligent, somebody who will go out there and find deals and work with them for a share of the profits, because all they want to do is place their money with someone they can trust.

We now do joint ventures with people where they provide every penny of funding for 25% of the gain. They have the equity not working properly for them, we have the skills, the system and above all, the integrity to deliver on our promises. Not surprisingly we do not find it hard finding JV partners, but we can always place more funds.

So, there are loads of different people out there with money. You have got to become an expert if you haven't got the money. You have to become what those people need and they will come to you. It will not take long. If you get a good reputation, if you get a good result, make one deal work, then brag about it. Show how you got it to work and somebody else will come to you. The rule in this part of the game is 110% integrity, 110% diligence when making payments, 100% efficiency in adhering to

207

timescales. Simply, someone else's money is far more important than yours. If you want to be in this for the long term, you have to get an impeccable reputation.

I think those three points deserve covering in a little more detail:-

Integrity: If this is not at your core, then do not even think about borrowing money. Never borrow what you can't pay back. You should be aware of all the pitfalls and all the possibilities of problems before ever spending someone else's money. You have to protect their money as if it were your first born child. Their money is far more important than yours! Them winning on the deal is far more important than you winning. You do not ever employ the line that they should not have lent the money. If you even think like that, then you are just conning people and you are a conman.

If you are in the property business, and you decide to play the long-term game with a short-term outlook, you will fail! I will only do deals with integrity; even if it costs me more money than the original agreement. This bears fruit time and again. I am always offered more money than I need to do deals, because my integrity is so high.

Diligence: Never miss a payment or be late with a payment, when paying back all or part of the loan someone has given you. Make sure you write down at the start all the details of your agreement and both sign to make sure that you both understand the basics of your deal. Make sure it includes the timescale for repayment and the payment amounts.

Set up a standard payment by standing order to the lender, and make sure there is always enough money to meet the payment. There should not be any doubt about meeting the payment because you have only spent 66% of the amount you borrowed, right?

But, if there is a doubt, diarise to check that the payment will go through three days before it is due. The day it is due, check that it has gone, and maybe make a call to the lender to check they received it three days later. This attention to detail may seem excessive, but it reassures the lender of your diligence and attention to detail when it comes to them being paid. I suggest checking that the money is sent for the first three months and every month, check that there is enough money in the account.

Efficiency: This comes into play when it is time to pay the loan back. The first rule is to set up a timescale for borrowing at the outset that is easy to adhere to. For example, if you are going to need money for three months, borrow it for six. If you need money for eight months, borrow it for 12. Build in a deal-overrun period. It is very important that you pay the money back on time, every time. So be efficient with the final loan repayment. Build your extra borrowing costs into the deal and make sure the deal still works for you before borrowing the money.

It will take time to establish trust. If you are starting from the very, very bottom of the ladder, you are not even on the first rung. If you have got a good credit file and you can go and borrow, then you are on the first rung of the ladder. If you have got equity, you are way up the ladder.

Debt can be such a good thing, but there is a difference, as I think Robert Kiyosaki says, between good debt and bad debt. We should all know what bad debt is. But just in case, for clarity's sake, bad debt is the debt that is sitting on our credit cards, that was spent on non-income or capital producing assets. That means we spent money on things we should not have spent money on, right?

Good debt is a mortgage debt on an investment property in which the interest is being paid by the tenant of that property. Good debt can be a debt on a credit card that is a short-term debt where the interest payment is being made by the equity release of the property you have just refinanced.

So, some credit card debt can even be good debt, can't it? Okay, that is a bit contentious as well. That goes against the grain, but it is a fact, you know? Even credit card debt can be a really good thing if it is producing more than it is costing! But be careful, because 18% a year is expensive!

How much mortgage should be on your property? I always advise re-mortgaging to the maximum. Let's say you have a £500k house. You are allowed an 80% mortgage, which is £400k. You want to get hold of £50k and your properties are unencumbered. You re-mortgage to 80%. You draw down the £400k and you pay £350k back in. To do this, you go to a mortgage lender who will allow you to do what is called a drawdown facility or similar. From then on, you can write a cheque at any time for the rest of the term of that mortgage for up to £350k. Pretty neat eh? And very useful.

Why would you want to go through all of that? Well, do you think that by having the flexibility of that money available, opportunities will come to you? You bet they will. Opportunities will come and stare you in the face, because you are ready for them. You have probably passed by countless opportunities so far in life, because you did not have the funding in place, ready to capitalise on them when they came to you.

The point is, there is a lot more chance of you making money on a good investment if you have the money required ready to jump in when needed. I am not saying, rush in. I am saying be ready to rush in when the opportunity turns up. Only rush in when you have done your due diligence.

I always have the maximum mortgage available on every property I can. I do not always have the money drawn down on all of them, just waiting for a deal to drop in my lap. I only draw all the money down on some of them when I need to. But, I always, always have it all available.

So, you always, always, always re-mortgage to the full amount you can get, because you never know when you are going to need it and it is always better to have it available. There are plenty of mortgage lenders out there that will let you do this and let you call it down.

For example, let's say you are earning £60k a year and have a great job. You own a £500k property that's got a £100k mortgage on it. You don't re-mortgage as I'm advising and all of a sudden you lose your job. Just how much of the £300k you could have got on a re-mortgage do you think you'd be able to get now. Yes zero!

It pays to be prepared. Let's say you did re-mortgage and you did lose your job then you could probably survive on the £300k of equity for ten years while you are looking for a job. Isn't it just plain common sense to keep the maximum drawdown in place on your property? Just this could save you immense problems in your life, but we are never taught this because we are all taught to pay off our mortgage. And why do you think that is? Remember the government work on a much longer timescale than you do and they know that one day they will be paid from your estate, and obviously it is in their interest if you have spent your hard earned cash on clearing debt rather than holidays.

When I first had one of these mortgages on this house, I could not really believe it. I had re-mortgaged this house and got another £200k. And I thought, 'Yeah, I don't believe that I can actually get that money actually into my bank', because at the time, I had never had £200k in cash all in one place at one time. So I thought, 'let's wait and see what happens,' because you don't really believe it until it's there.

So, I phoned up my lender and I said, 'Hello, yes, my policy number is X blah, blah, blah and I've got a draw-down facility on my account for X', and she said, 'Yes, you have £220,000 (approx) available, how much of the £220,000 do you want, please?' So I said, 'Well, when will I have the money?' She said, 'When you tell me how much you want, I'll press transfer. That will go to this number bank account, and it should be in there tomorrow morning.'

I went, 'I will have £200,000 please.' And so she said, 'Certainly.' And next morning I went online and there it was, £200,000 sitting in my account on a draw-down facility. The next day I paid it back because I only wanted to see if it was working as I did not really believe it!

Remember, all you want to do is end up owning the property and have it cost you nothing to do so. This alone will ensure an infinite return on your investment.

So, once you have pulled back out of any property you buy, all of your money, every penny you put in, every bit of money you make from it thereafter is providing you an infinite return on your investment.

You are in the buy-and-wait game. If you are looking for a cash return up front within three months of buying, then you will need to become a real expert and this book skims these subjects. We specialise in getting cash up front on 99% of all deals; sometimes lots of it. But, you will have to become an expert in order to do that and until you have done your first few deals this will prove difficult at best – but not impossible!

But you don't need to do this to make money from property. You only need to become an expert if you want to get very clever like that and be able to build portfolios very quickly in that way. You do not need to learn it to get rich in property.

So, there are two lessons I am trying to give here. One way is how to do it and do it really fast, and the other way is the easy way. And the easy way is the real point of this book: it is understanding what you have already got and learning how to use it positively. The real point is, as the title says, <u>Money For Nothing and Your Property for Free</u>. That is the point of this book.

So, if you could just buy property for 103% mortgages, then there would never be any property for sale, would there? Sorry, you would have property for sale in the short-term because you would get the idiots who would sell it. But, as you were getting 103% mortgage, you'd just buy everything you could, wouldn't you? That is if I hadn't bought it first!

I mean, without going to any specialised lenders, I could probably get hold of another £30 million in my name and £30 million in my wife's name without any trouble at all. And so, if I could get 103% mortgages, I would go and buy another £60 million worth of property now, today. I would not care about whether it was going up in value or not! As long as I could cash flow it, I would go and buy it!

So, there would not be any property for sale if they would offer 103% mortgages to buy to let landlords. But they only offer that sort of thing to trusted borrowers, and in small doses, because the lenders want to see that you take part of the risk with them. Banks consider 65 – 75% no-risk funding. Even if the property market goes down, then they have a large safety net at that level.

At 85%, the bank's only risking a small bit, but the banks also knows that, if they really want to, they can sit there with the property for a while. They don't, because that is not how they make their money, but they could do. What is more, they usually make you take out an insurance premium called higher level borrowing insurance to protect their interests over 75% anyway. So it is no risk to them.

I can't remember which book I read it in, but I read it somewhere that if you have £1,000,000 of debt, in seven years you will have £1,000,000 million pounds of net. That is because the debt will still be there but the property will be worth £2,000,000.

Took me a while to really understand what they were banging on about but when I got it, it was like, 'Oh, yeah, yeah, of course. I am already doing that.' I already understood it; it was just a different way of explaining the same thing.

There are different ways of explaining the same thing I have gone through in this book already, and I will carry on going over them, because I am trying to get it through to you. Because different things hit different people's buttons and one thing that works for me definitely will not work for other people because I am just a weirdo, anyway.

It may only take three years or it may take 11 years, but on average, it will take seven years for your properties to double in value. That is it. That is what you have got to do. So, you might have to wait 11 years. You might have to go out with your £200k, buy your 15 properties now, or £300k, whatever it takes, and you might have to sit there for 11 years before you get paid out.

If you get paid out in 11 years, wouldn't it be nice to get paid another £200, £300, £400 or £500k? Tax free? I thought so, that's why I did it. Do this enough and it will definitely be more than you earn when you put the tax you're not paying on top of it; much, much more.

As Rich Dad said, there's good debt and there's bad debt, and mortgage debt is good debt as long as you've got income, positive income coming from it. Is he right?

Hang on. There is something controversial coming.

Instead of saving to pay off your debts, why not borrow more, invest it wisely and wait for it to clear the debt for you?

Oh, dear. I should not have said that, should I? I am going to get slated for that. Because of the so-called debt crisis in this country where credit card debt is rising at a so-called alarming, rate – am I advocating borrowing more? Well yes and no, and I think I should cover this debt crisis a little before moving on.

Because of the relaxation of credit in our country, credit has become easily attainable and even easier to use and lose control of. Debt per head is the highest it has ever been, which of course it would be, and it will in all likelihood get worse every year. And we all know why that is, don't we? Money goes down in value, therefore debt figures rise. Obvious, really, isn't it! So why do they make such a fuss of it.

But the economists out there are, at this moment, going but, but, but. And they are right, as there are many other factors to take in. I am not going to cover all of them here, and I am now going to generalise. So on one hand we have large credit debt per person, and on the other hand we have large equity per person.

The figures I would like to see displayed are the figures that show what a person's real wealth is now, adjusted over time, compared to people from, say, 1970 with virtually nil debt in comparison to today, and with only reasonable equity. Compare that to today, with relatively high levels of debt and very high levels of equity. I think these figures would be a lot less newsworthy as there's not much news worthiness in telling the general public how well it is actually doing and how, on a balance sheet basis, we are actually so much better off.

Still, it would be nice to see that one proved. But then that would kill off all their headlines and people would get even further into debt. So they better not do that, because if they did, they would also have to bash out some financial education, which would mean not having a population that is virtually illiterate when it comes to creating money and financial intelligence.

I will just step down off my soapbox now, I am feeling much better! Please put the white coats away, I promise to take my medication.

Back to the point, however contentious it is, of getting someone in debt to borrow more to invest and then have the investment pay off their debt over time. This is not just a theory. I have actually done this for people and I am doing it for people now, people who came to me when they were in debt, spiralling debt in fact!

What I have done is I have turned their credit file around. I have made it so that they have a perfect credit history over a six – 12 month period. I have then gone out and borrowed on their credit and raised them mortgages and extra credit. I have then bought them properties below market value that are near instantly re-mortgaged to release the equity. This was the money we put into it, from the raising of credit. Then they can buy another one. They need about two or three to get them out of debt and basically put them into positive cash flow for the rest of their lives. It takes about two – five years, depending on the level of debt. It took me longer when I first tried, but now I have the system down pat.

I had never heard that one before, not from anywhere or from anyone.

And all this rubbish about student loan debts being a bad thing: How can a virtually interest-free loan be such a bad thing? This is a good debt; they have invested in their future in order to produce a greater return on their investment, i.e. they will be paid more. Isn't it amazing how the word 'debt' can turn a positive thing into a negative, and then compound that with the public's lack of financial intelligence and everyone looks at this as if it is wrong to charge for students' extra education. I think the government has it about right here and I think it is fair and reasonable to ask for a contribution towards further education. I think it is the government's responsibility to subsidise it the way they do. Anyway, that is it. I am going to put the soap box into the cupboard and I will be back…

I just turned people's credit files around because I could and because I thought it was madness, encouraging people to pay off their debt, when they were going backwards each week. They were out of control and needed real help, not tired rhetoric telling them to cut their spending and in 7-10 years, if they are lucky, they will be at zero! Especially when there is another way, if they are prepared to learn and conform.

When I was in debt up to my eyeballs back in 1991-92, I paid off every single pound. It took me about 18 months. I set myself a target, a goal of two years, and I chose to delay any gratification from the money I was earning. I basically sat in, spent no money and paid off my debts. And I paid off every penny of debt. In today's world, in all that time, I have never yet met anybody else who paid off all their debts when they were in that much debt.

I had £15,000 of debt, which is nothing in today's world. You know, you hear £40-£60,000 of credit and loan debt is nothing at all. But I was £15,000 pounds in debt and that was at the higher end of personal debt levels back in the early '90s, and I paid off every penny without entering into any 10% deals with my creditors either.

When I finished paying off the debt, I swore that I would never get into debt again and that I would have my mortgage paid off by the year 2000. This was when I didn't know what a life-long friend debt was going to become to me.

The problem is that the very word 'debt' has such a negative vibe and bad association about it that it puts people off. I do not know of a way to help people come to terms with the problem of associating debt with the thought of 'bad thing'. What I do know is what a friend my debt is to me, and how much I respect and look after him, and how – in return for me looking after him – he provides so wonderfully for me.

My debt, because I look after him so well, provides me with so much money that it takes a lot of my time just deciding where the best place is to put all of the surplus cash that is created. Still, it is not a bad problem to have, thanks to my friend Mr. Debt!

People I help today don't pay off every penny. I don't advise them to pay off every penny. I advise them to get good credit, keep up with their payments, borrow more money, invest that money into capital producing assets, refinance that money, give the money back that they borrowed. Then do it again. Then do it again. Five properties is all they need for the future, anyway. So at the end of seven years of doing it my way, they are not only out of debt but they have their future finances secured as well, and within a few short years will be financially free.

I will say it again: Five small properties are all you need to secure your financial future. Three of them gets you out of debt and puts you into your own home. The other two provide the security that there is always going to be more money. That is it. Takes a little time, but that is from debt to home ownership and financial security. It takes about four to six years to buy the others and sort it out fully. During that time they have to live very frugally and if I am sure they will do that and I want to help, then of course I help. If I have the time! But, at the end of four to seven years their asset base will be created and the foundation of their future financial life is set. So, it is a bit controversial but it works and I can prove it!

A scary concept. And it is just a taste of how aggressive you can be with this property investment strategy, because these are people who were already in debt and were out of control. I have had people who were going backwards by £200 a week and were £45,000 in debt and I have stopped the rot. I am sorry, I have slowed the rot, then I have stopped it, then I have turned it around so it is at least balanced, not going any further. Then, I have shifted the debts around, got them onto low interest rates while maintaining a good credit rating for them and then I have gone out and borrowed more money for them, to have credit availability.

And these people are still succeeding. And now, on a balance sheet basis, the people I have helped are about break-even and we are about two years into the people I am helping. I reckon there are another two to three years to go before it is done, finished, fixed.

So, you have got to get rid of this fear of borrowing. Borrowing is a good thing – borrowing bad debt is a bad thing and using it for consumables is a very bad thing. I read somewhere recently, that years ago when you ran out of money and you got to zero, that was it. You went bankrupt.

These days, you can whistle past zero like it's not even there. You can get into debt up to your eyeballs very, very quickly. But, if you are in control of it, if you don't fear it, if you respect it, and if you look after it, it can be very powerful and it can give you an ability to go out and do things you simply could not do without it.

Do you think most rich people made their money with their own money? No, it is from borrowed money. Everything I have done, 100% of everything I have done with assets in my life is from borrowed money; 100%. I have not put any of my own money into it, ever. And I have only put very little money into my own mortgages, very little money, and this was just to cashflow them (even though I did not know it at the time). I have had that money back many times over already, and now I can say that I have none of my own money in my investments; my investments now provide me the money to pay for my investments, whenever needed.

So, you have got to learn to control your fear of debt. Debt is a big, scary monster, right! Sometimes it can be really scary. But then, there are other times when you have the debt – equity – revenue balance just right, when all you want to do is get more and more debt, more and more equity and more and more revenue.

You look at people. My goal is to acquire debt, because the more debt I acquire, the more money I make on other people's money. That is what debt is: other people's money. That is fantastic, because I make 11% a year on other people's money and I pay nothing for that because my tenant covers my interest for me. Well, that is not bad, is it? That is not bad at all. So, it costs me nothing and I make 11% a year on having a debt.

So I ask you: Is debt a good thing or a bad thing? Well, when it is the correct sort of debt, it is a very, very good thing, all right? Love to hear your thoughts on that one, because I have said something very controversial there and I would love to hear some feedback from people, so please feel free to email me on feedback@andyshaw.com

You have got to control your fear. It is natural to be a little bit afraid. Don't get me wrong. Occasionally in places I don't like to go very often in my mind, I think to myself when I see the figures on the page at the bottom of my balance sheet, , 'That is unreal. That is just so much money.' Because it is not fictional money, where I am going to win the lottery or something like that. It is real money. That is in my name. That is mine. Yeah, that debt's also mine. Look at the size of all that debt!

As a friend of mine, Pete Halm used to say, 'When I die, I want small African countries to go to the wall!' It is just a figure of speech, but it is very funny because basically, he is right in saying he wants to acquire as much debt as possible.

But you always have to, always, always, always respect that debt, control your fear around it and, above all, respect your lenders. They are the ones, after all, giving you the money. Without them, you haven't got any, so you have to respect them because they are your best friends.

Never, ever, ever miss a payment, right? Golden rule. You never miss a payment, all right? Your credit file is your statement to the world of conventional lending, and it states that you are a 'Good Risk!' If yours does not state that, then this will be pointing to the root of your problems.

The lenders that you are going to go to with this sort of strategy want you to have a good credit file. They will check your credit file. Therefore, you must have a good credit file! If you haven't got a good credit file, start making a good credit file. The sooner you start doing it right, the sooner it will take effect and work in your favour. I suggest you use the crossfiring techniques on my site to re-build your credit rating and raise extra funding for investment.

If you can't make your payments, borrow more money so that you can make your payments. Maintain your payments. This is not a try to, this is a MUST DO! Controlling your spending is another MUST! All of this stuff is available to learn about and it is done by other people all over the place on the Net.

Learn to control your spending. If you have got a spending issue, you have to control that before you can get into this. If you don't control that spending problem, if you are not in control around money, this is going to give you access to huge sums of money and then you won't go bankrupt for a little bit of money - you will go bankrupt for a hell of a lot of money. The chance of ever recovering from going bankrupt from a lot of money is very slim unless you have learned to control money in the first place. So you must respect your debt, respect your lenders and never miss a credit payment, never ever!

I think debt is a good thing and I will be in debt until the day I die. So will my wife. So will my parents. So will my children. Why not make money on other people's money?

I am going to try and explain it in a more basic format now. Let's say you buy £100k property and you take out a £50k mortgage on that property. So, you've put £50k of your own capital into it. If that property goes up in value by 10%, you have made £10k. So, what is your return on investment on that 10% gain you made? Is it 10%? Is it 100%? Is it 110%? Is it 50%? Is it 20%? What percentage is it?

Well, first off, your total investment was £100k, which is the mortgage lender's money as well, so you would have a 10% return on total investment.

But, since the total investment was not all your money, I 'choose' not to count that. What I count as the return on investment is the amount of money I have to put into something. So, if you have had to put £50k into it and you have made £10k, then you have had a 20% return on investment. This means that the property has gone up in value 10%, but you have made 20%.

Now, if you put £10k into that property and you take a £90k mortgage and we do the same thing, the same thing happens. The property goes up in value 10%. What is your return on investment now? It is 100%. You have just made 100% return on investment! Not too shabby!

So, instead of just making a ridiculously low 20%, you have made 100%. Instead of making £10k for your £50k invested, you have made £10k for your £10k invested. That is very powerful and that is one of the most powerful things in property. Sorry if it was a little basic for some people, but I think this one is a really important point that people need to grasp to really create wealth.

In conclusion, the less you put in the greater the return on your investment.

19

Q: Where Can I Get Money From?
A: From Wherever It Is Right Now!

Where there's a will, there's a way. There are always ways to find money. There are always ways to get hold of it. And there is an abundance of money out there.

But you don't need to believe that you can get hold of it because if you believe you can't then you'll be right. This in no small part is down to the law of attraction, but don't have that as your main focus. Just believe that all this money is out there and all you need to have is a good enough 'reason why' people should lend it to you, and then you will find they will and it is available.

Okay, I'm not going to go on too much about ways to get hold of the money, because I have primarily written this book for people who already have equity in their property, and they can just release it from there. And it is, frankly, the easiest way to obtain the money butut I am going to cover it briefly.

First off, as I just said, the easiest way is through equity release. Any good mortgage advisor can help you do this and can help you to release more. There is a wide variety of different products available that will suit you in different ways. You just have to decide what you want first.

My advice still holds: re-mortgage to the max, put back in what you don't need. Then you have always got it available whenever a deal walks your way, which it will do. When you have the money available, it is amazing how many opportunities come past your door when you are ready to go.

Anyone that is not too old can get hold of 75% mortgage to the value of their property. Anyone can do that. There are dozens of lenders out there that will loan just on the value of the property. You don't have to have huge proofs of income or anything like that. You can get hold of 75% of your property. Don't get me wrong, they will probably send out a valuer who is very favourable to their situation, so you might not get a true 75% value. You might only get 65%. But you should get, according to their criteria, about 75%. There is a broker I now recommend as well as the current best mortgage deals that I am using for my investments; I update this monthly in the mortgages section.

And for those of you who consider themselves to be too old and have just seen me saying that and want to use it as an excuse so that you don't have to go and get wealthy now: There are now several mainstream lenders who will lend people money on property irrespective of age. This year a 102-year-old man took out a 25 year interest only mortgage, so that excuse isn't going to wash. You may just have a limited supply of lenders, that's all, but it's still possible. If your broker doesn't know of mortgages like this, then it is probably time to change your broker!

If a standard equity release re-mortgage cannot help you, then the second-charge loan people can. Personally I do not like this way of borrowing. It is too adversarial. I don't use it myself, but I have friends who have used it and raised big lumps of money over and above their 80-85% mortgages. So, it does work. In fact, it is really easy and most of the companies that offer it seem to be very good. I avoid 2nd charge loans, but if I needed the money and had no other way to raise it, then I would use them. The only problem with them is that they use the same calculations as your original mortgage lenders do to loan you money. So if you've borrowed to the maximum of your income then you may not be able to get at any more despite having equity available.

In my opinion, your credit file reads as if you have had to go to that particular lender to get a second-charge loan because you are in debt up to your eyeballs and cannot find any other way to clear out your debts. That is my impression of it. I don't know if that is how it looks at all. That is just my impression. And yes, maybe that's rubbish I am saying and there is nothing wrong with them at all.

All right, there are plenty of easy places to get hold of cheap money. But there is a system to ensuring the maximum chance of success. This includes going to lenders who have money to lend at the right time, which is why I monthly update my list of recommended credit cards based on who I think is in what I call a lending frenzy. The quickest way to damage your credit file is by going to lenders who are not taking on new applicants at the time!

Different lenders will give you different credit cards. Some credit card companies love me. Other credit card companies will not let me have a mere £200 credit card (not that I would want one, of course). I do not know what their criteria are. But you need to think logically and try to put yourself in the lender's shoes. When answering questions, don't volunteer any information that they haven't requested. And do think carefully before answering each one by thinking, will the lender like that about me? If the opportunity presents itself then answer the question in the most favourable way you can. None of those things are breaking the rules. I cover this in a lot more detail on the site as this book really isn't for this subject but just doing those things will probably double your chance of success.

As I have said, credit cards are probably the cheapest form of borrowing there is, over the short term. I include on my site, various tips on dealing with specific credit card companies, but obviously, they change their criteria all the time so these tips are just guidelines.

Personal loans are another excellent way of raising up to £25k very quickly. These are close to interest rates, and are therefore very cheap. If it was not for the capital repayment portion of the monthly commitment, they would, by far, be my favourite way of raising cheap, small level funding.

If you can get hold of the personal loans over a 10 year period then obviously the monthly expenditure is a lot less. After all, you can repay the money any time you want, so the last thing you really want to be doing is making a capital repayment. I also recommend my top five personal loans each month on the site because again, there is no point applying if the lender is not lending.

Bank account overdrafts are particularly good for quick funding. If you have a good relationship with your bank, there is no reason why any of the major banks won't give you a £10k overdraft, but I have found up to £30k is easily obtained once you have a track record.

This brings up track record and this is something that can't be bought so this has to be developed. Well, I came up with a way of developing one of these in record time and manipulating the bank's own system.

It's called cross-firing and if the banks know you do it then their shutters will come down real fast and you won't be lent £1, so this must be done the right way (again you've been warned!) But if you do it successfully then you can take a poor credit history and turn it into a reasonable one in three to six months. Or you can take a superb one and become a star!

It is all about moving money between bank accounts in a pattern that makes the bank's computers think that you have more money than you have. Creating the pattern and repeating it monthly is the essential ingredient. After running this system, at times you'll find the banks offering to increase your overdrafts and give you credit cards and loans just by you circulating a mere £1,000 in the correct way.

I'm not going to cover it in detail here as I've done that on the site, but if you imagine for a second, paying £1,000 into your account on the first of the month. Then paying it from your first account to a second account with another bank the next week. Then paying it from the second back to the first the next week. In fact repeating it say three times in one month. Then instead of your bank seeing you with an income of just £1,000, they both see that you have an income of £3,000. This is all done with just £1,000.

Well, I ran £30,000 through eight banks and created a wonderful track record with each that got me unrivalled credit capacity by designing a tool to help me manage it each month. That tool is available on the site and I would say that use of this will significantly help you to create credit facilities. If you have poor credit it will first help you rebuild this credit and then help you create credit. I could write a book on this subject as it is at the core of credit raising.

You will also need a good high interest savings account because there are times when you will want a place for money you have raised which is waiting to be invested. This mitigates most of its cost to you by earning interest.

You should have all of the above in place and growing. This is so that, when you need them, when an opportunity comes your way, you can take advantage of them.

The reason I give my top few each month, is so that everyone can see the ones I recommend and also discuss the benefits of each one with other people on the forum. In this way we can all benefit together on learning the personal funding game.

The banks share information after all so why can't we?

In your early years, you want to be adding extra credit cards and overdrafts etc., to your availability as these will produce track records that will enable you to arrange higher levels of funding later.

And for the few people who think it's wrong of me to take advantage of the banks' systems then remember: if they do not get that money out onto the street, they are in trouble themselves because they make money from lending money. This is a win-win deal.

The idea is that together with regularly updating the best deals available on the website and the forum, we can all share information regarding credit raising and work together at making sure we take advantage of all good opportunities presented when cheap credit is available. I expect this element of the site alone to produce enormous wealth with none of your own money down deals. And you should be able to mitigate the monthly membership fee, just from interest savings on credit!

There is a little story on the web page regarding a time when I found a credit card company that was paying out. I won't tell you who they were, except to say you dunk soldiers in them. Anyway, it is quite an amusing story. Check it out if you have the time – I think you'll see the benefit of it.

Credit cards are the easiest borrowing in my opinion because you only have to repay the interest each month and a small amount of capital, which you can take back immediately anyway. The actual outstanding loan you do not have to pay; whereas with a personal loan, you have to pay back a portion of it along with your interest monthly.

So, it is a lot more of a drain on your cash flow. But beware, I have not got the exact figures to hand, but I believe the average timescale to repay a credit card debt is 37 years. So these are short term funding strategies that you use equity withdrawal from your investment portfolio to clear. You can re-use it, but clearing it regularly looks much better on your credit file.

And when you are doing short-term funding, credit cards are much better for it. If you need £15k to complete a property, then just pull it off your credit card. If you need another £5k to do the refurb, pull it off another credit card. Make the payments to both cards with credit card cheques from a third card. Re-finance your property and pay all three back, that's it! It is virtually free lending and it has not actually taken a bean from your own pocket - just some of the profit from the deal. So in my opinion, no cash outlay is a great deal.

You can only use that strategy if you know the money is coming back to you. If you do not know the money is coming back to you, then you cannot use credit cards because you are going to be into hardcore borrowing very, very quickly, up to 18% as an average of long-term credit card debt, all right? So, that strategy is only useful to you if you're going to be getting your money back. You do not use credit cards to acquire debt and leave it sitting there, because that is just ridiculous.

So the best place, as I said, is probably my website to get a good idea of different credit cards available because I find out which ones are trying to lend. But if you just go onto the Net and search credit cards, you will get lots and lots of different ideas of where to go for credit cards. The problem is, there are so many to choose from and when you are starting out, you want the simple ones. You do not want too many hits and fails on your credit file so the idea is that, by putting the ones that are most likely to pay out on my site, you increase your hit/win rate.

Here are some other really good places to get hold of money quickly, easily and cheaply. Mum and dad. They are always great. They are always there for you – at least mine have been and I am very grateful for that. Basically, your mum and dad will have money because they are a lot older than you are (unless they have screwed it up, in which case they are no use to you at all financially.) But, if your mum and dad have got money and would like to help you, you can show them a way. Your job is to convince them that you are not going to fritter it away; that you are going to invest it and you are going to make sure that it gives both you and them a good return, if you want to do it that way.

Usually, you will find that your mum and dad have got plenty of equity and plenty of savings, but not very much income. What you can do is provide them with a bit of income in return for their equity or credit availability.

So let us say you borrowed £50k equity off your mum and dad and you covered the loan interest payment on it and you went out and invested that. Let us say you also gave them, I don't know, £200 a month extra income. Just gave it to them. It is under the tax threshold, because you are allowed to give away £3k a year.

Now, all of a sudden, your mum and dad have a bit of extra income And you have the capital you need to go and invest in property. Of the £50k they gave you, you can go and invest 66%. The remainder will pay any loan interest while you have got your money exposed in a property deal.

'That was easy, wasn't it?' You can do exactly the same thing for other relatives as well. You look around. Your Aunt Gladys, she is sitting on huge amounts of equity but she is living sparingly because her pension is so small and she has got no way of getting hold of money. She's no income. She can't go to work. But she has you. You can change her life by giving her £300 a month while she gives you her property as security, or something like that. You have changed her life for the better and she has changed yours.

Now you have got to be absolutely 100% certain you are doing the right thing when you do this, because this is scary stuff. You get this wrong and you are affecting other people's lives, so you must not get it wrong.

If you really want to go down this road, which was the one I went down, you will never feel such responsibility in your life. Of course, I went on to deliver on all my promises and so their trust in me was borne out.

This is definitely NOT for the faint-hearted. You're risking other people's money now and they are not just any people. It is not the bank's money. It is not people you don't know. It is the people who brought you up, your family! Be certain of your success, before venturing down this road! Once you take the plunge, however, you will find that it can be the best win-win deal you will ever do!

Friends are the same. Friends will always look at this sort of thing as well. That includes good friends or just acquaintances. They are all particularly good. You can do exactly the same thing. Find out what their button is and push that. You can say, 'Oh, hang on a minute, you are exploiting situations here. This is not good.' But this is a very good thing you are doing for people, as long as you are honest and true. Anyone with even a small amount of money is always open to ways that they can increase their return by making the money work a little harder. You have to be sure you have diligently protected their money and you have to fully understand that it is your responsibility to pay it back, or pay them their income when you need to.

If you are helping other people out, as I did because my mum and dad did not have much of an income, this is a good thing. My mum and dad were not badly off, but I have some other relatives who did not have an income and I sorted things out for them too.

As long as you know what you are doing, as long as you do not over-extend yourself, you can protect yourself cleverly by not spending too much and by borrowing enough. The biggest problem is that people do not borrow enough.

Yes I know I'm repeating myself, but I learned a long time ago that repetition is a master skill that you should practise. I also know that most people need to hear things at least three times before it sinks in and countless times before they take action.

One last, often overlooked, area of raising capital is other people's credit. You'll be amazed at how many of your friends and family have five, ten, twenty or more thousand pounds of credit available on credit cards. You simply pay the bills and give them a fixed return for the use of their cards.

Anyway the point is to look for what other people need and how you can help them and the money will come.

You can trade money for services. It is called having your own business, actually, but let us look at it from another point of view. You can help people get into property. You can go and source the deals and get paid a commission to raise your money, raise your stake capital. You can offer to help your friends do it for a cut of their profits.

So you have none of your own money at risk and, basically, you are not going to actually get any revenue for the next two, three, four years. But in two, three, four year's time, you start getting payments. It is called delayed gratification. And if you haven't got any money to start with, it is another good way of getting your foot on the ladder.

What you have got to think is this: what have you got lots of that the people with money have not? Mostly people with the money have no time. As I said, it is my most valuable asset. You have lots of energy. If you haven't, get some and get it quick! Changing your diet will seriously help with a lack of energy! You have lots of persistence. If you haven't, get some and get it quick! And you have lots of knowledge, or you are getting that now!

If you are going to do this with other people's money, you need to become a bit of an expert. There is no good going down the easy route. You have to learn about it. You have to understand how property works and you have to make sure that for every deal you do, you know what you are going to get before you actually say yes to buying it.

Before you spend anybody's money, you have to know the outcome. In Passive, I know the outcome as close as I can to the penny. The software we have designed adjusts to each deal as it comes to fruition and evaluates how accurate our prediction was and then makes adjustments to the whole system from the start to adjust the efficiency of it. Clever, eh?(Yes I am bragging here!)

Every time we refinance a property, the system adjusts again. So, if we are making a prediction that a property's going to be worth £100k when it comes out and it is only worth 98.5% of that, the system is corrected to cover that error in all new predictions, policing our methods automatically.

Sorry, I drifted off there for a second! My point is you must know what the end result is going to be before you spend any money at all. You really want to know what the end result is going to be before you put an offer in, and that takes knowledge, which takes time to learn. If I tell you that I know what the end result will be before I even leave my seat to view the property, then would you believe me? Well, better than that, I'm saying that you will too when you've bought your first handful of property. You probably won't trust that judgement for a while but in time you'll find it to be correct.

This won't take much time to learn fortunately, if you have the right tools and support. You have this book and there will be further support on the site.

We are planning to do a one-off seminar that will be recorded next year. But there are also a lot of other people offering courses. All you need to do is watch out for conflicting and therefore, confusing information. When in doubt about who is right I always use logic to try and sort the wheat from the chaff.

I do recommend attending things like the Wealth Creation Conference and other similar seminars which will give you insight into how to use the knowledge to do this with success.

You have GOT to go to seminars; they will make you a lot of money if you go to them and if you know how to apply what is learned, without wasting a fortune on the wrong products for you. I am not saying don't buy the products, just decide what you want before you go and then stick to it.

They can cost a bit, yes, but the benefits far outweigh the expense. I sometimes have to force myself to go to them, but I make sure I do at least four events a year. I never, ever fail to increase my wealth substantially by attending them. The benefits come from angles you cannot possibly see. I will do a piece on my site about the benefits of going to these things and give you examples of plenty of seminars I have been to and the amazing deals I have struck up from attending them.

Property seminars are probably the best for you to start with - except for the fact that I'm going against what most say. But a good grounding in wealth creation in my opinion is best. I am not going to cover full wealth creation here, but I do go into it in depth on my website.

Not all property courses deliver everything that you want them to, but all of them deliver something of value and I have yet to go on a course where I did not learn something to mitigate the cost of attending. In addition, I have retained the skill and used it over and over again, at no cost. I have never been on a course that I have thought, 'No, this is not good value for money!'

The problem is, if you don't utilise what they are teaching you, then you won't value it for a lot of money. I went on a property course once, thinking I was the Credit Card King. What they showed me about credit cards was incredible. I went away from that weekend and raised a further £250k in the following six weeks, thanks to the knowledge they taught me. That £250k went on to be invested. I invested about £170k of it and created so much money that the value of that knowledge is now incalculable.

Do you see what I mean? I used what they taught me and I leveraged it against the skills I already had to produce an incredible result. So, even though I was already an expert before I went on that course, I learned something new that increased my efficiency dramatically. You know, serious money! I mean, I would say I have made an absolute minimum of £500k thanks to going on that one course when I already owned over 150 properties! So we invested £2k plus accommodation and made easily that sort of money.

20

The Only Thing That Matters

The next point is a very simple one and I'm going to cover it quite quickly in just a few pages, but I felt that it was such an important point that it needed its own chapter!

Very early on in business I was taught THE business Golden Rule, that cash flow is King. And in business I don't think I could agree more. But, when you are in property, cash flow isn't king! **Cash flow is the only thing!** It is the only thing that matters. All you have to do is get your cash flow right, make sure you have got plenty of it and that is it.

Nothing else matters!

Cash flow is the only thing that matters in Property Investing!

People often forget this when they are learning how to do deals or how to handle the builders. Or, more commonly, when they are busy building a portfolio at speed which their cashflow cannot handle.

I know this because I was one of those people and if I hadn't been able to literally (for lack of a better word) invent money, then I wouldn't be here writing a book on property investing acting as if I was the big ' I am'. Instead I'd be in court trying not to feel too stupid and trying to stop the repossession of some, if not all, of my portfolio. Then in the evenings I'd probably be trying to stop my family from falling apart as I scre**d it up so badly. These things to me are a scary place that I don't like to even go and having that scary place gives me a <u>very</u> healthy respect for my cashflow.

I tell you this to try to ensure that you respect your cashflow above all else. Never forget that what you are getting into can eat you alive!

Right, that's enough doom and gloom but it is very healthy to be a little overly concerned about this area of your property business and if it is causing you too much concern then back off a little until you are comfortable with it.

Why is it the only thing that matters? Well, because even if you have got it completely wrong and you can cash flow it for 20 years, it will make you money, won't it? (I recently wrote an article in our Passive Investments newsletter, where I was able to show one of our clients how a bad investment she had made would be repaid overtime. You can find it on my site www.AndyShaw.com)

Now I know that this might sound scary as well, and it is. But you can lose all that money and still have the property sort it out for you, if you can cash flow it. You can lose it all and still have it work. Is that cool or what?

I don't understand why property investors choose to lose money in property. The only reason they can lose is if they haven't got enough cash reserves, or they are just plain stupid and they have not cash-flowed it properly in the first place. That is the only reason they can lose it in property; unless they sell, of course, and that is just silly, as we have already explained.

You know, everyone always has a good reason for selling, right? I'm sure it was a fantastic reason at the time. But, if you can find a way around it, do so, because it is very good to get round it. Dolf de Roos said in his book *Real Estate Riches*, 'I'm tempted to say never sell.' But what the hell! Yeah, stuff it, I am saying never sell. Never sell, right? Go out of your way to never sell any property, ever!

And if you have protected and understood your cashflow, then you will never need to sell. However, you may be bringing some baggage with you into your new business. Someone I spoke to recently had four high value properties that produced around 3% yield. These made up 100% of his portfolio; simply he did not have the cashflow to retain them.

If he'd had those four properties and another 36 small properties producing a rental profit, then he would have been able to retain them. However, he didn't have a balanced portfolio so I advised him to sell to protect his cashflow.

The only time there is a justifiable reason to sell is when you are doing so to protect your cashflow, as that is more important than you creating wealth!

21

The Mechanical Advantage Over Other Ways To Get Rich

If compound interest is the eighth wonder of the world, then leverage is the ninth. Leverage is your best friend. And so is time!

Here we go. This is one of **the best**, I would like to say **the best thing** there is out there in property, but there are so many great things. This is right up there close to the top though.

Traditional property investors do not leverage their property portfolio as much as they can because, simply, they prefer safety, security; they prefer to get cheaper funding from the banks because they can take lesser loan to values.

Right, I want to make my feelings clear on mortgages. They are wonderful things. There are wonderful banks and building societies with absolutely delightful customers who are lovely, truly wondrous people. They put their money into their bank and building society accounts to earn their interest. Those banks and building societies want to loan that money to people and secure those loans onto their preferred security, which is property. And little old me and you want to buy property with their money. So we get to meet those wondrous people in the middle with the most fantastic win-win deal ever created. And it happens everyday! Do not be afraid of the term mortgage. Learn to love and adore it, as it is a wonderful thing!

Quick term for what a mortgage is. The word mortgage seems to scare people. It should not scare people at all. The term 'mortgage' is a French term which means "unto death." Basically, a mortgage is a loan that is attached to a property. So you have a property loan unto death, right? And 'unto death' means either the term on the loan or until you die.

A mortgage is nothing to be scared of. If you don't like the word mortgage, use the word loan because that's all it is. It is a loan. You have taken out a loan. You have agreed to pay so much. You have got to pay so much, but it is attached to a property, which is a very secure loan from the bank's point of view.

Let us recap our standard procedure. This is the easy way, if you don't want to try too hard. You buy a flat with an 85% mortgage. So, on a £100k purchase you put £15k in and by the time the deal closes it's gone up £10k in value. You have made 66%. That is pretty unbelievable, isn't it? Not really. Any idiot can get that. Anyone can get 66% return on their money. But 66% return is not bad at all for doing nothing other than going "I will have it, here is £15k," and then you just sit back and wait. Time again.

Now, let us buy it well and refinance it and make it so that all the money comes back. So we buy it with an 85% mortgage. First off, instead of buying it for £100k, we pay £75k (I will come back to how you do that later). After purchase we re-value it for £110k. We get an 85% mortgage on the new value, which gives us a loan of £93.5k.

You have had your £75k back. You might have spent a bit on refurb and you might have run into £1.5k for the fees to get the property in the first place. So, let's call it £85k. You now have a loan of £93.5k on it, so you have £8.5k in your hand. Simple eh!....What do you mean it's not that simple? No, you are right: it is simple for me, but you need to learn it. Don't worry: we will go over the details one bit at a time.

Back to our example. All of a sudden you have added in clever buying and you have leveraged your return to an infinite return and you have got a load of cash. Now you have the whole thing funded for a very cheap amount because you have also tied the mortgage into a three-year discounted rate. And, basically, your tenant is paying the rent for you. Done. You sit back and wait. Time is your friend, time and leverage.

You have leveraged it to the hilt. You have got all the money. You have now got £8.5k you can do with what you want. Let us say you have gone out and run up a credit card bill that was too high and you have not been able to pay it off. Let us say you had bought a holiday. Let us say you paid for your daughter's wedding. Let us say whatever. Who cares? Spend it on whatever you want. It is yours to do with as you wish, NICE! On my website, I give you clear direction of how I best use this money to make more and still enjoy some of it.

So it has given you an infinite return and that is what I get for myself and all my clients – well I would like to say 100% of the time, but I can only say 99% of the time.

I really like the word "infinite." Sort of like has no boundaries, you know. And really, that is how I see money. Money has no boundaries other than the limitations that my own mind puts on it.

The power that leverage gives you is the power to have infinite returns. If I did not leverage this example, I would only consider this an okay return. It probably wouldn't be an acceptable return and it definitely would not be a good return, not from my point of view.

From anybody else's point of view, 66% ROI ain't blooming bad at all. You know, if you go out there and you talk to 100 investors and one of them says to you, 'I get 66% return on my investment!', you start thinking, 'Nutter!' You don'[t believe him. But now that I have shown you how 100% ROI a year is for amateurs, you are just not impressed with his statement. Anyway, yeah, he is one in 100. There is probably one in 10,000, maybe one in 100,000 that gets what I get, and I get infinite as standard 99% of the time for myself and all my clients.

Quick sidetrack on my worst ever investment in property. It was for a client I'm afraid! And we only achieved just over an 1,800% return on their investment. This was because we couldn't get the valuation to work at the time and we decided to accept leaving about £2,000 tied up in the property.

Within two months we were achieving the vals of course, but by then the client was tied into a two year deal, otherwise I'd be able to say we had a 100% all money out success rate! Still it's not bad when a company can feature their worst investment ever and put it in a book too.

Back to how a 66% return is better than virtually anyone can do, but any damned fool can do this in property, so you don't have to be very clever.

Now, if you have done it the clever way, you have none of your own money at risk, right? So, what happens if the property market goes up or down? **What do you care?**

What do you care, because you have locked that property into a deal for three years minimum, five years preferably (depending on what's going on at the time).

You do not care. You're going to revisit that property in five years time. It is rented out, is it not? Tenant pays the rent, managing agent pays you. What's the issue? Why do you want to know about that property again? **What do you care?** All you have had to do is buy it, get all your money back, get another load of cash as well and sit there. Sit and wait. And while that one is just sitting over there planted, waiting to bear another crop of fruit, you are using the same money to go and do it again.

This is not hard. That property is now free. It has cost you nothing, you know. It does not owe you any money! It is giving you loads of money, so you can't ever say it's cost you any money, can you? Because you have got more out than you ever put in. And the money you put in was only for a very short period of time.

I mean, some people fund their deposits on credit cards. I do. I do it all the time. I do not do it on every single one, you know. Most of the time I am in a fortunate enough position to get the bank to fund the deposit for me, but that is only because I have a very good track record.

You know, getting a real no-money-down deal can take a lot of time, a lot of track record with the bank, unless you can go to vendor loans and things like that. And that is really getting leverage to work for you. But I am not here to talk about that sort of thing and daylight bridging loans are one for the website as well. I am focusing on just one strategy here. And believe me, those deals can be a lot more complicated to get to work in this country than they are in the States.

For those who don't know, a Daylight Bridging Loan is when you have bought a property for at least 18% below market value and have an instant re-finance set up for the day you complete. This will mean that you have bought the property for no money down.

Even though they can look like the easy route, they come with their own inbuilt set of problems. If you can get them to work though and you have the infa-structure to handle a rapid growth portfolio then they can be another fantastic way to build wealth.

But Daylight Bridging Loans come with an Andy health warning - as something that can also damage your wealth if you have an addictive personality. I regularly receive emails from people who have overstretched their cashflow because this was an easy way for them to get started. And I have received emails from people who have lost it all because of over committing themselves because they took these to be the Holy Grail.

When I started to do them it was at a time when solicitors didn't even understand they were possible and if they had worked as well then as they do now, then I believe that I would have gone bust! If you use these, then use them with care and protect your cashflow at all costs.

There are many reasons why I do it my way. The main one is that I make more money, but there are times when a daylight bridge works very well for me too.

Back to the point. Leverage is the backbone. This is where your strength comes from in property. Property works for you. Property going up in value over time is the biggest of the lot but leverage is the backbone that supports time and together they become an incredible wealth creating tool that really works for you.

Property is an <u>other people's money</u> business.

You have just leveraged other people's money to get what you want and those people's money is tied up in ISAs, PEPs, TESSAs, savings accounts, whatever, who cares? It is tied up in this, that and the other. It is put in their bank account, whatever. That money is being given to you to go and buy property. Great. To all you non-believers out there, thank you and keep up the good work!

See, other people's money always sounds bad to me because I always look at it and think, 'Oh, that does sound bad,' but it is not bad at all and I use it all the time. I am making a living, thanks to other people's money invested in my properties for me.

Wow! And they are happy to do it because I'm paying them a good return on that money. Well, they think it's a good return, anyway. They're happy with it. It's a no-risk venture for them and a lot of people want a no-risk venture, or to use the correct term, a low-risk venture.

I have got a risk. There is a risk attached to what I am telling you to do here. What is the risk? The risk is that you run out of cash and you cannot cashflow the property. That's it. That's the risk. Let's not look at if the tenant trashes the property because, if the tenant trashes the property, the property will have to pay for it for you. You may need to cashflow it though. That is cashflow, right? Greg came up with a great analogy, to make it really crystal clear how little this really happens. He says it at our company open days and it makes me laugh everytime I hear it so I won't spoil it for you. It's also available on my website.

But, the property will always give you the money back, won't it? You just have to wait a bit longer. And it is not as if you are going to have one tenant trash it, the next tenant trash it, the next tenant trash it, the next tenant trash it and so on. You might get one in – well, we have probably had one in 500, maybe two in 500 trashed. That's it. So if you say a total of £14k spent to fully re-furb those two, then average that over say, 200 properties, that's £70 per property. I can live with that, but then I nail the tenants to the wall along with the managing agents.

It is all about the banks. Other people's money is all about the banks. The banks want to loan you this money because they make their money from paying Bill, Fred, Sue and Angela at a rate of 2-3% and they charge you 5.5- 6%. So, they make their margin in the middle.

So, if you imagine the amount of money they lend against the amount of those 2-3%s coming in each year, it is monstrous and that is how the banks make their money. And believe me, they are welcome to it. And I am really pleased to pay that money to them because they provide me with a service that is just simply the best. So, they are welcome to their cut of the action. And the people who get their 2-3%, believe me, they are welcome to it.

Other people's resources. This is using other people's skills and experiences to help leverage your progress using their resources. You have paid for this. If you have bought this book, you have paid for what is being shown to you.

What this book will show you first is how to use the right language and get to meet the right people because everything you get into has its own dialect and you need to become an expert in saying the right words.

As an example, I use the word "props" all the time. I used to call them "houses" and everyone used to get confused when I was talking about a flat, because I was calling them houses. Now, I call them all "props." Yeah, I have got this prop down here, I have got this prop here, I have got those four props in that block.

Everything about this has its own language. You will get to know it and, by using the right language, you will bump into people who know what you are talking about and they will understand your language instantly. There's a property language page on my website. They will be talking to you about things so you will glean information from them. So that is one way you are using other people's skills and resources.

It is like using an estate agent's skills to help negotiate the deal. That could still be considered other people's efforts as well, and it is one of the great ones.

This is a lot more opportunistic, which means you can make gains by stepping in at the right time and be the solution to their problems.

What that means is somebody else has done all the work on something. This is just one way of looking at other people's efforts. And I am only giving you one way to look at each of these, you know. There are hundreds of ways to look at each of them. Somebody else has gone out there, created it, done the deal, got the property at the right price, basically, then failed to complete.

That's when you step in at the right point. They have already had the price of £82k, for argument's sake. You go, 'Yeah, I will mend this chain, but I will only mend it for £78k.' And they go, 'Oh, can't you pay a little bit more, please?' And we go, 'Well, all right then, £78.25k.' And they go, 'Well, we were thinking more like £79k.' And you go, 'I will tell you what. I will meet you in the middle at £78.5k.' And they go, 'That's not in the middle.' Then it is a case of, well, that is as far as I am willing to go. And they go, 'All right, then.' That is it.

I have used other people's efforts to get the original price down to the £82k. I have used other people's efforts to tie everything up for the six months it has taken to get to the stage where they have pulled it away from the other person. You are not exploiting a situation here. You are matching up. You are a solution to their problem. If they didn't want to do the deal, they would not do the deal. And you know, you can't do a deal without two people being happy. You have got to have a win-win situation. This is not a matter of unethically exploiting a situation. You are helping to solve their problem.

Other people's time. Well, this is just so powerful, this one. Where to start, really? Other people's time. I use other people's time every day. Starting in the morning, I use my wife's time. She makes my breakfast and a cup of coffee. And her time keeps our house clean, (She will not let me hire a cleaner, someone to do the washing and ironing, honestly!) And then I go to work and I get Lindsay, my wonderful personal assistant, to do all my work for me, using her time. I compensate her for that. And I use other people's time in the excellent people who work with me. Then I use the estate agent's time. He gets compensated for it, of course, by being paid his standard fee. I use the managing agent, I use the solicitors, I use other people's time, all the time. It's hard work to get rich on your own efforts and time, so I always try to use other people's.

This is just another way of describing other people's services. I try to do as little as I can myself, which leaves me able to focus on bigger things. Planning in marketing and innovation is where I currently focus my main body of time. But for me, this changes regularly to suit the time of year and the opportunities and my own interests.

My way of working is one of construction. I first learn how to do it, then I practice doing it, learning more as I go and making plenty of mistakes along the way. Then, when I have got it right, I systemise it and set up key performance indicators. I also make my system as self-policing as possible. Then I hand it over to someone to run. I monitor their progress carefully until I am confident with their results. Then I back away and monitor it from a distance using the key performance indicators. Then I monitor it less regularly, like once a month. At that point the task is constructed and I only need to monitor it monthly, stepping in occasionally if there is an improvement needed to the system.

What I do is leverage my knowledge and use their time to apply it. When I am into helping somebody, I help them through buying them a property. It is all their time. They have to do all the legwork and they get to speak to me a bit. And basically, when they speak to me, I may give them a little bit, but the reward I am getting is quite a lot. So, I have leveraged their time to generate the reward.

They do not always pay me; mostly they share the profits. So I have put a little bit of time into it, they have put a lot of time into it and we both get a big reward because I have leveraged other people's time.

You basically pay other people to do everything you can. And this is why I set up my company, Passive Investments, in the first place. I didn't want to do anything myself in property investing other than get paid. Anyway, I will do a bit more on Passive later.

You are already doing this, so just do it more. You are already using people, so just do it more. Try and think, 'Well, do I need to do this job or can I get somebody else to do it? Can I systemise it so that somebody else will take this job away from me?'

Refurbishment is really the best way to save time. Do you want to know how to get builders to jump when you want them to? It's quite simple, really.

How to get builders to jump when you want them to. This is simple. Builder tells you the job's going to be £3k and he wants a 20% deposit. So, you give him £600, if you know and already trust him. Then what happens is he finishes the job. The job's done. You get in your car, you go around, you walk around the job, you okay it and you write him a cheque there and then for the balance. Simple eh?

I will tell you what. Man, you would be amazed, and I mean amazed, how quickly a builder will turn up on-site if I say, 'Can you do this for me?' They are there. I don't know why. Maybe it is because I am paying them when they're due. Builders are builders. They get paid to build. They are not money-chasers. They hate that bit. So, give the builder what he wants, and what he wants is his money. If you are getting properties done on a regular basis and you pay on the button, you will be their favourite customer. And what you want to be is their favourite customer.

Now when I decide to buy a deal, I spend a total of two minutes on average agreeing a property purchase. Then I spend a maximum of 10 minutes on due diligence, checking all the details after we have agreed to purchase to make sure that no-one has made any mistakes.

So, for approximately 10 minutes work from me each time, we are expecting to buy between 150 – 200 properties this year. In total, back to back, this is under a week's work for me in a year to buy 200 props, each one making approx £25k. Wow! Is that leverage, or what? Under one week's work for me a year and we create all that lovely money for us and our clients.

Now, each of those properties makes about £25k, right? Not for me, most of it for clients and that is after everything. So, have you done the maths? 150 or 200 times

£25k = £3.75 - £5 million. Let us say I broke a sweat and did two weeks work a year…

No, only joking. The infrastructure will take a fair while to grow to handle taking on more than 100 new clients a year, but when it does, I should still be able to do my little bit! But as I write this, the software is actually being written that will eventually remove this small task from me. When that is finished we will have completed a project that I started in 2002, which was to create my own property-buying machine. Of course, it will take three years of development on the software before I will have zero time invested in it. But by the end of it, there will be zero time invested by me to produce any number of deals. Then, because there is no time involved in it at all, and because we have got bigger and more effective at it and our buying power continues to increase, basically more deals will be done in less and less time.

Back to the now, where that small amount of time is producing that huge amount of profit for me, my clients, my family, my friends. All of those clients and all of my business partners and everything, they have no time involvement in the purchasing of property at all. I do that bit of it. I leverage time for myself, incredibly. I try and systemise everything I do. When I have broken it down to the absolute bare stuff that I can do, I then try and systemise that.

When we started to get good, I think it was about early 2004, every four doors we walked through we bought one. You could view this as a success. I viewed it as 75% of our viewing time wasted walking through the wrong doors. Now people say, 'You managed to walk through four doors, and every fourth one you bought?' Yes!

Of course, Julian had to do a lot of research to just get those four doors. He probably looked up, I don't know, 500 properties to get us to walk through four doors, from which we bought one. Do you get what I mean?

But then, Julian's time was leveraged as well because of the way he views the properties. Instantly, you can dismiss 98% of all properties in a blink of an eye. So, that left 2% he had to do a little work on to track down whether those properties were going to be suitable. He probably tracked down a mere eight properties that were suitable. Then, out of those eight, he got on the phone and he honed that down to four properties. Then we got off our backsides and walked through the doors of four and bought one.

I like other people. They are so good to me and they like me. Basically, people offer me deals all the time, so I have to look at people who say things like, 'Oh, I don't like meeting other people.' I love it! I love meeting other people. You never know when opportunity is going to present itself, and if you are ready and watching then, oh look…opportunity! Opportunity is everywhere when you learn to open your eyes. The problem then is getting down to choosing the ones that produce the biggest and best result – in other words, the biggest improvement to your current situation.

I had a meeting with a guy yesterday. I was putting in place an insurance policy for my parents. If they ever have to go in to have medical care in their old age, I want an insurance policy to cover the majority of the expense.

I researched and got nowhere. Then I spoke to a few contacts and got them to recommend somebody. The guy came to see me and I was really rushed because, unfortunately, Lindsay was ill yesterday. Luckily, she had phoned me from her sickbed to tell me I had a meeting, otherwise, I would have completely forgotten it. That's how much she looks after me.

Anyway, the guy turned up and he was really friendly and we got chatting. Basically, he was only going to be with me for an hour or so, but by the end of the afternoon he was still there. Meetings with me tend to drag on because I like chatting to people in the comfortable surroundings of where I work. By the end of the afternoon, he was coming to an Open Day. He has become an introducer. He is bringing two clients along. He is introducing somebody to me who will basically want to do joint venture property deals with me.

He wants my help on the Internet to help his business. He wants to have a stand at an exhibition we are organising in the future. He wants to give us a commission for marketing his products. And of course, once I have tested what he does, I will be happy to market it.

If I did not like meeting other people, that meeting would have never taken place. Oh, and he offered me a property deal in Cyprus, an unbelievable deal: a friend of his – a client, one of the people coming to our Open Day at the weekend – owns 47 properties and he's selling the lot off. And basically, you know, he did not pitch me. He was just telling me about it and I thought, 'That's a good deal.'

So, what came out of that meeting? I went in there to get an insurance policy. I mean, is that boring or what?

And what has come out of it is a number of lucrative business ventures.

Make everyone your friend. You never know when a gem like that is going to appear. You never know. I mean, we have lots of friends in the village where we live. You never know when all of a sudden, one of them will turn out to have access to something that works for you. For example: Greg was friends with somebody, and it turns out that he is in charge of high-level funding in property investment for a main bank that only deals with loans above £50 million and below £250 million.

Well, how would we ever get to meet those people, do you know what I mean? And if Greg had not been friendly and chatted to his friend, he would have never found out that connection because it is not the sort of thing you talk about when you're at a party. 'Oh, I deal with property investment lines, blah, blah, blah,' you know?

So, unless you make everyone your friend, unless you get to chat to people, you do not know what opportunities are there. If you don't do this, if you don't start enjoying meeting people and trying to learn from everyone you meet, then you are walking away from opportunities all the time. When you sit at a party quietly in the corner, you don't know what you're missing.

Go to various open days, there are plenty that are free, but they can really be worth paying for. Network, find and meet more people. Don't get me wrong; you are going to meet a lot of – what is a nice way of saying morons. You are going to meet a lot of nice, friendly morons. But, you are also going to meet a lot of fantastic people, and that is why you are going there. And believe me, the morons are less than 5% of the people you will meet. When you become good at this, the percentage will be even less than that. So, just sort out the wheat from the chaff. You will find good ones, no, really good ones.

So going back to what I was talking about. Let's remember, time is your best friend. But, what you have to do is actually do something. You actually have to take action. Once you own the first property, you are on your way. That's it! If you already own your own home and, frankly, this book is more written towards people who have already got equity than people who are starting from a standing start, once you own your own property, you are on your way anyway.

I am not really teaching you much new here in the way of how property works. You already know this stuff. You probably just do not realise you do and you are more than likely not leveraging it properly. I am just confirming it and I am just saying to you, 'Yes, that is real, it really does happen. Yes, if you had bought one at the same time you bought this one, you would have two of them now. Yes, wouldn't that have been a good idea?'

Well, it would be a good idea to do it today because the same thing is happening. The universe has not changed all of a sudden. We have not shifted dimensions or anything. If you want to know the future, look at the past. That is all this is about.

You have got to follow this action through. You have just got to do it. You have got to buy one. You do not need to learn to be an expert like me. You do not need to pay somebody like me a lot of money to do this sort of thing for you. You do not need to learn too much. You just need to do something. You just need to take action.

I spoke to a lady recently who just stumbled across her properties. You know, somebody said, 'Oh, this property's for sale,' or she was talking to somebody or a friend was selling it. And she said, 'Oh, I'll buy it off you,' and that sort of thing because she had a bit of money sitting in her account at the time and she heard a friend was having trouble selling a property. So, she bought the properties from them, just from socialising over coffee (she had coffee mornings and things like that) and she built her property portfolio of about 10 props that way.

You can just let this happen, as long as you are open to it. This book is about changing your attitude toward property investment and toward all investments. There are some really good ones out there. I mean, I was talking to the guy about tax planning yesterday and there are some things that I should be doing that I am not. And so, I am looking at it now. It was one of my goals this year to sit down and properly plan tax and properly plan inheritance tax. But I just have not got around to it.

I have only created my wealth in the last three, four years. You know, give me a chance. I am going to get to everything, one after another, they are all on my life goal plan; they just need prioritising at the moment. You know, the biggest thing I had to solve in the last six months was my weight and that is well on the way to being done now, as I have lost all of it - nearly 10 stone. Yes I was a fat bars***d, now I'm just a bars***d. But the real work begins now which is managing the loss.

When you have done it, when you have just let it happen and when it is finished and it has done its cycle and you have had your five years, then you have to tickle it. You just tickle it a little. You go back, go in, 'Hi, how's it going, Mr. Property? Have you gone up in value?' Mr. Property goes, 'Why Mr. Owner, I don't know. Why don't you send Mrs. Valuer around?' Mrs. Valuer goes around and she goes, 'Yes, Mr. Property's gone up in value.' And you go, 'Great. Can I have some money, please, Mr. Lender?' And Mr. lender goes, 'Certainly, here's some money.'

So, you have to tickle it, just a little bit. It is not a 100% passive investment. It is close. It is very close, but you do have to do something.

Do not mess around with your properties too much when you get them, right? You know, these people I see on TV, 'Oh, I think that wall would look good as, you know, having stars on it, or...'**no**, **no**, **no**, **no**, **NO**! Neutral, neutral, neutral, right? The three key words in refurbishment are neutral, neutral, neutral. It's not up for debate!

There are times when you want to be flash, flash, flash, but do not mess around with them, what I mean by mess around, is structurally. You don't want to knock walls around. You want to get in there, you want to refurb it. If somebody has lived in it before, then there is a good chance somebody will live in it again, so why mess around with it? If you mess around with it, on small properties, 99 times out of a 100 it does not add value. You mess around with it like hell if it will add value. But, do not think it will add value - know it will add value.

I do not do anything to a property without knowing what the end result will be. I do not go, 'Oh, I think that will work.' No, I know it will work when I do it. Just knocking a wall out does not add value. There are things you can spend money on and there are things you cannot, and I will cover that in the refurbishment.

A £185 light fitting does not add a penny of value to the property unless you have gone for a particular style and you have decided to spend £3.5k to create something that's added £15k of value. A light fitting on its own will not make a blind bit of difference. There is little to no point in spending £5k to add £6k of value, because you are in this to create money, not earn it or make it.

The sooner you start this, the sooner you'll have made all the money. It is that simple. Property market lift, property market drop, property market flat, who cares? Just buy property and make lots of money out of it. It is that simple. So, the sooner you get doing it, the quicker time will help you. Because, as they say in the lottery, 'If you're not in it, you cannot win it.' When it comes to the lottery, I am not in it.

You know, there was a euro, millions jackpot the other day, and the draw was too much. I just had to spend £1 on a ticket and, despite the fact that I knew the chance of me winning was like a billion to one or something, I had to spend that £1. What a punter! I just could not stop myself and I have to admit to blowing that money!

Lindsay bought £1s worth as well, right? And I said to her, I said, 'You could not stop either?' And she said, 'No, I could not,' because it was too much money, you know? It was what they said, 'you have got to be in it to win it.' If you do not own the property, you cannot win when it goes up in value. But, if you do own the property and you have got no money in it, you cannot lose when it goes down in value, either! In property, success is predictable.

22

You Must Have a Strategy

You must have a strategy, but that is easy. My favourite way to invest is in the small ones, because the small ones are more juicy. This is my favourite way to look at it and the technique was given to me by my business mentor, Mike Grimes, words that guide me to the best deals. He said, 'Andy, always look for the small deals. The small ones are more juicy!' He was saying it about business deals but it applies perfectly to property.

This is where you spend £75k to create a further £30-£40k, by getting it to value for £110-£120k. Not bad, is it? And bear in mind that we are not spending our own £75k. We are actually spending about £13-£14k. So, I am spending £13-£14k to gain £35k. Then I get my money back too! And some equity and hopefully some cash. Well even that's not really true. What you are actually doing is moving either equity, or cash or other borrowed money from one place to another. It is not spent; the only thing that gets spent is solicitors' fees, valuation fees, loan arrangement fees. So to buy a £75,000 property and make a £35k gain, all you've actually spent is £1,200 - £1,600. Even better now isn't it?

You know, these small ones are so juicy, Mike's advice is so true. I do other property deals where it is a case of, I bought a property for £1.05 million and it was worth £1.6 million, plus I had the freehold and everything else that went with it. That is a good deal, is it not?

On the face of it, yes, but it is a pain. It is hard work. I would have been better off doing 16 small deals and making the same amount of money or less, to avoid the pain. The small ones are more juicy and if you systemise what you do, they will be very easy too.

The deal with the 16 flats completed in January 2005 and finished nearly 30 months later. It cost us a good relationship with a bank. It made all the money and more than I'd predicted but it took five times as long to happen and caused immense stress It looked for a while like the bank were going to call the loan in. If we had spent the same time doing small deals I estimate we would have done 25 to 30 of them without any stress and made a lot more money. But when I first saw it, it looked like a short cut to wealth. It was a juicy deal, but the smaller ones would have been more juicy.

There are all kinds of strategies. You can have a strategy for houses. You can have a strategy for flats, a strategy for shops, offices, small factories, large factories, buying off plan, buying off plan abroad, redeveloping, developing, HMOs, students' rents, even buying banks!

Do you get the point? You can have a strategy for absolutely every type of property. And you can even break it down from there. So, houses can be two-bed houses, three-bed houses, four-bed houses. They can be bungalows, they can be detached, they can be semi-attached, they can be terrace, end of terrace, they can be houses with potential to convert.

There are too many to mention. The strategies you can have are just endless. Finding a strategy is easy, finding the right one too, is even easier, because I am telling you to do 1 & 2 bedroom flats. However, your area may be more suitable to two bedroom terraces and flats may not be the desired property. That usually happens when an area has a lower average house price. So you know your own area's property or you will do soon.

But if in doubt, an expert is telling you what to do. Do you know what this is? This... is... opportunity... that... you... are... reading... right... now!!!!! You know that thing that keeps passing you by? You know that thing that you keep wishing you could find that would make all the difference to your life? This is IT!

I can't make it any clearer or simpler than this. Go to your calendar and write this page number down on the calendar for you to re-read in twelve months time, as if it was somebody's birthday. Make this day a day you remember each year! Make this day the day that you re-read this page, so that in one year or two years or five or ten or fifteen, it actually inspires you to get on with it. This is opportunity; it is happening now, people, and it is yours to take and make your own. I have no ulterior motive here. My goal is to inspire you to do it, to make it happen at some point in your life. Or you could just go, 'Stuff it!' and do it now! Start today, and you will be on your way to becoming financially free at some point in your life.

Do you know why I now call myself an expert? I never used to. Even after I had purchased over 200 hundred properties I did not consider myself an expert. But one day when I was listening to one of the many so-called experts and I was fed up listening to them getting it wrong as they just kept reaching the wrong conclusions, I finally realised that I was an expert. So it was thanks to their lack of expertise that I finally realised I could call myself an expert. To all those so-called experts that I can never name, thank you for showing me that I'm an expert.

Bit big headed really isn't it? But it doesn't matter really does it, because me saying it doesn't make it so, only it being real does. And then my expertise is only to the level I have done. Who is to say that there is not a real expert out there saying that what I've done is wrong and it should be done another way.

There are ways you can combine your strategies. You can do houses in this location or houses in that location. Or you can do two-bedroom houses in this location or have two-bedroom houses in that location. You can do flats in this or that location. You can go; I want to buy flats in this particular block.

I have one friend who focuses the strategy she created with her husband on flats in a lovely development in Shoreham, which is on the south coast. These flats were built just before the last property crash in the '90s. And of course, they were top dollar then. After that, they dropped down to reasonable prices.

So my friends have been buying them over the years. They bought one. When it went up in value enough, they re-mortgaged it, pulled the money out and bought another one. When that went up in value, they re-mortgaged it, bought another one. Now, they've got 11 of them in just one block. That is their strategy and it works really well. It is stress-free, you see? It is fantastic. Excellent strategy. Nothing wrong with that at all.

You can have a strategy that takes in this road or even that block. There are different ways to fund each of them and there are different ways to buy each of them. There are different ways to hold or flip each of them. The combinations you can do on strategies are endless. Then, you can combine them with income or capital strategy or tax efficient strategies.

The truth is, there are literally thousands, if not hundreds of thousands of different ways. No wonder people struggle to come up with a strategy. Because, when people start to look at what different strategies there are, where do you start? There are just so many.

All I am going to discuss in this book is the only one you need to know right now. And if you want wealth without effort, just do this. It is that simple.

And you know the one I recommend. I recommend the small ones because the small ones are more juicy, because they are easy to rent and in high demand. They are easy to refurbish. They do not cost a lot if there is a problem. In fact they do not cost a lot at all. They do not cost a lot, get it? If you are going to make mistakes, make small ones!

They are quick. You are in and out in no time. You have not got a lot of money at risk. And when you have got your money at risk, it is not at risk for very long. So, hardly any money at risk and, even when it is at risk, it is only at risk for a short period of time.

People say to me, 'But what if the property market crashes?' I say, 'The Stock market crashes, the property market slows down!' The only time a crash occurs in value is if you have paid too much for it! So don't do that.

So, if your money is only exposed for six months you are at very little risk in a market that only slows, not crashes. That is, unless you're a complete idiot and the western world is saying do not buy property and you do anyway. If you go ahead without reading the press or visiting my website for regular updates. If you pay no attention when the interest rates start going up, or you did not notice when it started 18 months before.

When I say that it is easy, that it is simple, I am not saying you don't have to do your homework. Changes are obvious if you do your research. There are always clear indicators that tell you when rates are going to go up and that they are going to raise them every two or three months. If you do your research, you will be able to spot this sort of thing before it happens.

If you can't spot it before it happens, then you just have to put your trust in one of the many predictors out there. You know who I mean, the newspapers, the house price crash merchants, the city's wise men. But before you decide to put your trust in one of these experts, whoever you decide to put your future in the hands of, do your homework on them. Why not spend three or four hours, reading what they write? Why not try and find out a little about them? Why not find out whether they make their money out of selling newspapers or writing predictions, or spouting clever statistics that are diligently prepared to prove that their point is correct when it's clearly wrong to anyone with a modicum of common sense?

As a sensible alternative, you could listen to someone who has made and continues to make the VAST majority of his wealth by creating wealth in property for himself, his family, his friends and – last, but by no means least – his clients. Therefore, if he predicts it wrong he has a lot to lose. Common sense really, but why is it human nature to listen to just anyone talking about a subject we are interested in?

There are a few people out there who know what they are talking about, not just me. But I have to say that the majority of the people who make all the predictions either don't walk their talk or, worse than that – no, much worse than that – they do not actually understand the market that they are advising others on!

My predictions have consistently been right regarding house prices, governments, changes in the budget, interest rates and many other things to do with the economy. I am no economist and really I don't understand half the stuff they talk about, but I know what's logical and what is not. I know how to spot trends and how to maximise returns from them. I cannot always say why the price is wrong, I just seem to instinctively know that it is.

When I first started to predict – no, that story is for another time. Ask me on my website to tell the story of my first accountant and the predictions he used to solicit from me.   Also, ask me about how I used to believe my predictive skills were like a sixth sense until a friend called Brian Hughes showed me how they were really based on a lot of calculations. If you want to, that is!

Anyway, when you decide to take someone's advice, at least get them to show you a result they have had in the past where they actually got it right at least once. And I am not talking about a ¼ point fall in interest rates. I am talking about a big audacious prediction where they got it right. As I have plenty of those, so should they! Stand up and be counted boys!!!!

Again, sorry back to the point!

So, your money is not at risk for very long because the property market is only slowing down. You know, the property market has not dropped off the edge of the cliff. It has just slowed! It is important not to buy high at the wrong time of the year, as well, when the market in your area may be slowing. Time of year is so important to the property market. I know when the best time is to arrange to purchase a property. While that time is any time, you will get the best deals when people are desperate to sell. So think about the person who is selling, find out what their motivation is and you will find the best time to buy from them. Buying from a landlord is great if there is no tenant in the property. Why? Because he knows he is losing money on the rent, so he wants to sell now!

If it is coming up to Christmas and you are buying from a couple, they will be feeling that the year is closing in on them and they just want to go into the new year feeling that they have removed what they consider a millstone around their necks. So the best time to buy from them is just before Christmas, say 18th or 19th of December. Do not leave it till between Christmas and New Year, as they will have resigned themselves to the fact that it will not sell for a while. You want to get in there so that you can get them to appreciate all the consolidation benefits of the feel good factor, of having sold the prop.

Their feeling good about the deal is essential to the deal completing. You help them by buying before Christmas, it means they feel good going into Christmas, they feel they are moving forward in life, they now have time to plan their Christmas without the worry of having to sell their prop. They think you are a wonderful person and the little they had to give you by way of a concession in the price is a small price to pay for this wonderful Christmas and great feeling they now are enjoying. And all they had to do to enjoy this was give up a mere £5k by dropping their minimum figure!

Do you see how powerful it can be to choose your timing and understand the emotions of the people you are buying from? Is this unethical? What, giving someone that much inner peace and enjoyment at a time when they need and want it the most, is it unethical? Well if you really think that, then you will not get to help as many people as I do in life, as there have to be two happy parties in a good deal. They got what they wanted and you got what you wanted, a match made through timing!

I know the best time to arrange to sell a property. Not that I want to do that sort of silly thing, of course. But if you really want to know, your property wants to be new to the market and in the property papers the week before Easter. No more on that in here, as selling an asset is just too negative for this book.

I know when the best time is to put a silly offer in. Do you want to know when that is? Then I will tell you: it is the time when the vendor is willing to take a silly offer, of course! But seriously, put in silly offers in November, because not many people are buying then. You can also do this if the property's been on the market over four months without an offer. This is not rocket science, people, this is logical common sense. I know when the best time is to pay full or near the full asking price. I mean, I never pay the

274
- www.AndyShaw.com -

full asking price any more, but I know when the best time is to pay a fair amount for a property: it is when the vendor has put the property up for a realistic price to sell it now in the first place, and if the time of year is right, and there are too many other fishermen around, if you know what I mean!

Timing is very, very important for this particular strategy, for my particular strategy. It is not important if you are going to just buy property to wait for it to go up. You buy any time.

If I get it wrong and I am doing 10 small deals and I could take the fall on one, the rest cover me. Not that it has happened of course, but if it did. If you sink all your money into one big deal and you have hold-ups, you are in trouble. I have a friend at the moment who is developing about a dozen flats. Basically, he had the plot of land and decided to go into development and he got it wrong, very wrong. We advised him to stop, to go to a main contractor to get all the development works done because, I mean, I know how to develop property and I would not take that job on! Why would I want to use my time when this is an other people's efforts business?

I said, 'You pay somebody else to do it.' He would have had to pay an extra 10% so rather than do that, he decided to do it himself. So he saved his 10%, or so he thought, because he did not have anything else to do! He didn't have a job because he had closed the business down, as it used to be on the site where the flats were being developed.

Well, it ran over. Everything ran over. Costs spiralled. Everything cost more than expected. It also took a lot longer. As of this July, it will have taken two years longer and he is still not out of it. A fixed price contract tied to money and time would have been really cheap, now wouldn't it?

He has got no profit in it at all. He has lost all the money that they had in the original value of the land. And all because he went for that big score! Instead of being happy making £45k less, he has lost 10-15 times that, and two years of his life. Who says greed is good now, eh? He didn't pay that 10% extra to have somebody do it all for him. Not only was he greedy but he was cheap as well and forgot one of the primary powers of property. Property is an 'other people's efforts' business as well.

Why do you want to learn to become an expert on big deals? Make your mistakes on a small one. Get it wrong on a small one. It is less painful.

There's no need to rush it. Just do one. Make a few mistakes. Recover from them. Don't make the same exact mistakes again. Then do another one. Make a few more mistakes. Don't make those mistakes on the next one. Do another one. Make fewer mistakes. Make fewer mistakes. Get it?

I made loads of mistakes on my first 20-30 properties. I made a hell of a lot less on my next 20-30 and a hell of a lot less on my next 20-30. Virtually none ever since. And now, a mistake is a rare thing, because I have bought plenty of these properties before. I have become an expert at it. So, mistakes don't happen for me in these sorts of properties very often any more. Did I go broke making all the mistakes I made? No! Did it kill me? No! Am I stronger for making mistakes? Yes! Would I change any of them? No!

So, let us just say we buy 99 and one does not return all of the money. It is not as if we have got all our money in it. And it is not as if it did not return ANY of the money. We have had one that left approx £2k in the property in the last 12 months. And that one is producing a very hefty rental profit which will cover that capital within eight months anyway. So, do you see what I mean?

Even when you get it wrong, you still have a way of recovering in property. I consider that we got this property wrong, and it still returned several thousand percent return on investment! So, if I am doing 10 deals and I get one wrong, the other nine are okay. They are still infinite return deals.

My definition of wrong isn't so bad. Ask yourself, would you be happy if, when you got it wrong, you only made several thousand percent return on your investment? Am I bragging? Yes, and why not? Isn't that a good thing, should we not as people be proud of what we can do and what we can do for others? Should we not continue to strive to make our lives and the lives of people we know, better – especially when we can do it so, so easily in property. Maybe bragging is not the right word, maybe it is pride.

Went off again there, didn't I?

So, go for the small deals. I make cash in no time at all on them, and so can you. So, my first cash is very quick and it comes out fast too. The yield is highest on them. Stats to show that one-beds are the highest yielding properties are available online at the ODPM website amongst others.

There we have it then. On the small ones, you will make the most cash. You will make it fast and the yield is highest on them.

Big concept coming now!

I am only really buying to get hold of the debt. That is it. That is all I am doing. All I want to do is acquire debt. I do not consider myself a conventional property investor because I do not want to flip properties. I never want to sell any of them, as it is so negative and unless the point is rational, why would I ever do something that silly? I just want to buy and hold. As Warren Buffet says, 'My favourite holding period is forever!' Well, me too!

So, I don't consider myself a conventional property investor who buys it, holds it for a period of time, then sells it when the yield is not working properly or something daft like that. Selling property is nowhere near as tax efficient as holding it forever. And there is no such thing as the top of the market, unless it is for a short period of time. Now I'm only in this for the long term so the top of the market will be when I die. So my exit strategy is the same in property as it is in life…death! ☺

Some people want to sell because they have entered the market on one of the other infinite number of strategies there are. As far as I'm concerned those selling are great. Sell them to me, or to you. I buy property all the time from landlords. All the time! Because they think the market is at the top or something. Whatever, cut your fruit tree down, give me the fruit and then do what you want with the firewood. Brilliant, if that is your strategy and it is working for you, who am I to say you are wrong. After all, your strategy supports mine. Keep it coming, guys. You are my best friends and I will buy your properties because I want to and because you want me too as well. Nice!

Most of the conventional property guys think I am nuts (I wonder, could they be right?) They like and want my results, but they think that basically, 'whatever he is doing, yeah, he is nuts. But bl***y hell, he has had a result! I still do not know what he is doing exactly, though!'

If I was one of them and I was respected, (because I do respect them, as their achievements go to prove how virtually any strategy in property works, even one as silly as one that gets rid of the appreciating asset) I would want to know what I was doing. I would like to come and chat to me. I would want to take me out to lunch. I would say, is there any business we can do together? But, they do not seem to want to talk to me, which is fair enough. Maybe my nuttiness would rub off, or maybe they would have to question themselves, or maybe they have got to a point in life where they are content and wish to go no further.

I was at a bank evening 'do' in the middle of last year. It was a property investment bank. They took us all out, gave us a great meal and evening. At the tables was the Who's Who of property development in the area. I was sitting there and there were some people who apparently do not like me and some who really like me and some people I had never met before.

And you know, buying as many properties as I've bought in such a short timeframe, more or less everybody got to hear our name. I mean, solicitors used to say my name was at the bottom of every tenth property chain in our area. We were buying so many times. And it was not just one solicitor who said that. Lots of solicitors were saying it.

Anyway, this guy came up to me halfway through the evening and he said, 'Hey, you're Andy Shaw, aren't you?' And I went, 'Yeah, last time I looked.' And I am thinking to myself, great, he is going to smack me in the mouth. I have obviously done something to offend him! I was readying myself thinking, crumbs, I am going to get a whack here for something. I do not even know what. And he said, 'I would just like to shake your hand.' And I was a bit shocked. I said, 'Certainly,' and shook his hand. I said, 'Can I ask why?' He said, 'I am a surveyor. I have a valuation company and I have been valuing property in Worthing for 15 years now. I have been in property development for a long, long time. And I watched as you came into the market just a few years ago. We all looked at you and we all thought, yeah, yeah, young upstart, does not know what he is doing. We all sort of scoffed and thought you were a bit of a flash in the pan, and you proved us all wrong.'

He said, 'When I saw you here, I just thought I would like to come over and say hello and say I wanted to shake your hand for doing such a fantastic job in the last few years. You have helped establish the area, because rents have come up in the area, because you have pushed them up. The standard of your properties in certain areas has raised everyone else's standards too. I think you've done a really good job and made yourself a fortune as well and I wanted to shake your hand and say well done!'

I was blown away. I was not expecting that. You could have knocked me down with a feather. I said, 'Wow, thanks very much. I do not know what to say to you.' Then we got to chatting and I said, 'I bet there are some guys at this table who would curse me and hate my guts.' He said, 'Yeah, there are but, I do not think there is anybody at this table who does not respect what you do.'

Blew me away! I had no idea. I had no idea I had become accepted. You know, I just thought I was still looked at as this young upstart. I say young figuratively as I get to open the door to 40 within the next 12 months.

So these very clever property investors who do extremely large deals from my point of view, had come to respect me in spite of the fact that the biggest deal I have done is about £1.5 million and these guys are doing £10-£15 million pound deals all the time.

I am happy that the majority of them still think I am nuts and do not understand what I do. Even though they respect what I do, I am very happy that they think I am nuts because it keeps them out of my market. I do not want guys with that sort of money coming into my market because that is where I make my money.

I like simple strategies. My strategy is far too simple for most people to understand. That is why the only people who seem to understand it are people I can teach it to from a fresh start.

What actually surprised me at our open days was how many property investors signed up. We never intended our Passive Investments product to be interesting to property investors because we just thought, well, property investors know what they are doing. Why the hell do they want to pay us to do it for them?

It turns out over 50% of our clients were property investors before becoming our clients. I do not know what their number of properties is, but I would imagine it is an average of four, and some of them have a lot more. Because we did not understand what we actually did for people at the start, we did not realise that we were doing the whole job for them. They told us that. We did not notice it! Anyway, more on that later.

I love simple strategies. It has got to be simple for me to understand it. If it is too complicated, it takes too much time. If it takes too much time, I am not interested. I have got literally hundreds of different strategies on the go all the time. I have got strategies for blocks where I am trying to acquire the whole block at a time. For example, I started buying one block of flats. There are 20 flats in the block. I first bought a flat there in January 2003. Currently, I own 14 in that block. But, I'm still buying them at the price I was paying in January 2003. And they are worth a lot more than that now!

I have got strategies in roads. I have got strategies in areas for the different types of flats. I look for an area that's, in my opinion, about to start turning around. And I go in and I start buying in that area. And because I am buying a lot of properties, I am able to turn an area quite quickly, as well.

My main one, though, is to keep buying as many properties as I can throughout my entire life. That is my main strategy. I keep to the small ones, being juicier, but I will also do the bigger deals. You know, not too big. I am not clever enough for big deals. All I want is to keep buying small amounts of property that rent easily, that basically do not use too much of my borrowed money or do not expose my borrowed money for too long. Nice!

I will never stop buying property. Why would I want to when property is free? Why would I want to stop buying? After all, I get money for nothing and property for free! So, why would I ever, ever want to stop buying?

Yes, I could get and will get better deals. And often, I do buy bigger properties. And yes, I can ferret around and find bigger deals. I mean, basically, I have just bought a block of flats that's got five flats in it and paid £400k for it. And the flats are done, finished. And I think the block is worth about £630k as it stands. Not bad, makes me sound clever, or fortunate. Some would say we were lucky with that one, but I don't believe in luck.

The best bit about that deal is there are hidden profits in it, because there is a development opportunity at the rear, and, because I own the prop next door it could be worth an extra £250k. So, you know, it is a quick turn. Basically, it is a good deal. So, they are out there. We do buy good ones when they are particularly sweet like that one.

I had the bank on the phone. I e-mailed the bank manager and said, 'You have not comeback and offered me the loan on this property.' He said, 'We are having a bit of trouble with this one. I should have it sorted today, but we are having a bit of trouble.'

And I said, 'Why is that?' And he said, 'Well, because the purchase price is so much less than the valuation.' We just don't get those sorts of deals come along very often.' And I wrote an e-mail back saying, 'I am so sorry that I have bought so well.' Right? And it is the truth.

Actually, it is not the truth. I am not sorry at all. That is my job. His job is to lend me the money on the banks terms; unfortunately banks often move the goal posts when they find out that their terms are favouring you a little too much.

The advantage with this sort of bank is they loan on valuation, not on purchase price. So of course, they are looking at it going, he wants how much? But I am only paying this much for it, because I am basically getting a cash out deal.

But forget these superb deals, they are not what will make you rich. To try and get hold of this sort of deal at your first attempt is a waste of time. Do the small deals and these will fall in your lap as they do mine! The strategy that I have been showing you is the easiest strategy I have found. And it is without a shadow of a doubt the easiest strategy for a beginner to start with.

This is the one you want. Just buy the little ones. When you want to venture out and go and start buying property abroad and speculating instead of investing, that is fine. Yeah, it is good. I do it. I spend money on property abroad, but I know it is gambling. I am speculating on a market rise because it is a desire for me to own villas abroad. It is not, in my opinion, a good investment. It is an enjoyable speculation at best. It feeds part of my inner need but I recognise it for what it is. The only reason I was able to purchase property abroad recently, was that it was a good income strategy and would return my capital within a reasonable timeframe.

23

Investment Vs Speculation

What I am showing you in this book has two parts. The first part is investment - where you know what return you are going to make before you part with your money and you know when you will get all your money back. So at the end of the first part, you have equity, but no money at risk. The investment part has now finished.

The second part now begins, and this is speculation. You sit back and wait for a market rise. Notice how this part is what you do with foreign property or off plan property from the start, making that purely speculation or gambling! But it is worse than that, not only are you gambling, but your money is on the line as well! Interesting eh?

So why do I buy property abroad? Because I want to. I just understand that what I am doing is speculating, not investing. If you understand that and you are happy tying up money that could double itself every year by investing it instead, then carry on. I use a small amount of my 'real' money to buy abroad, because that way it doesn't affect my strategy over here!

I am actually doing research with the property we have bought in Cyprus and I think I have found a way to turn foreign property speculation into foreign property investing. But that is going to take me a few years to prove. I've been discussing my plans for this in depth on the site, but it is still in its early stages right now.

Know what you are doing, and know that if you are buying a property in your town, you will at least know what it is like there. You probably know how much it will value for. You know what you're paying for it now and you know what it is worth. And you know you are buying it at 10-20% less than you think it is worth. Yes I know I make it sound easy, but I will be showing you shortly how to find what is hidden in plain sight. I am first making sure you are going to go and find the right thing. You are investing because you know you are in a good deal. You know it is a good investment. You know what your returns are.

Complex strategies are for people who like to stay poor and keep busy. I can have hundreds of those sorts of complex strategies if I want to, but mine are all simple. And I keep to the simple way. My way is for the lazy man. Believe me, that is me. I might look like a hard worker and things like that on the outside and, yeah, I have put in the hard work. But, I want my hard work to create an asset that basically produces money for me in the future.

This is the strategy I have set up for Passive and it is so clever. If I had known I was being clever, I would have probably messed it up. There it was, the one moment in my life I was really clever; it was not just me. Greg and I built the product, with help from people who work with us. Do you want to know why it was so clever?

When we designed it, I said, 'I want our product to be so good that I would want to buy it myself!'

So, I am a lazy man and it is a lazy man who takes the greatest pains and finds the easiest ways. And I have found the easiest way to do this quickly and easily.

Here is another problem you are going to have. Over-thinking the strategy! Don't over-think what I am telling you! Just get on with it and bl***y well do it. All right? It does not need to be complicated. Just keep it simple. After all, this is supposed to be easy.

Okay. So, the strategy I am advising you on is one and two-bedroom flats. All right? That's it. One and two-bedroom flats. Have you got that, no matter what other examples I cite in this book, the clear and present strategy for you is One and Two Bedroom Flats! Got it? Good! The only deviation from this is in areas where two bed terraces are predominant. And if I was in one of those areas then they would be what I was buying, but my areas are the flats, so I'll be talking about them.

You want to pick properties that are in a good rental area within the town. Within five to ten minutes walk from a station is always a must in my opinion. Close to the town centre, within five or ten minutes of the town centre is always good as well. See how simple it is? If you drifted off in the last twenty seconds, you will have missed it.

That is a particular strategy of mine that has worked very well. I also employ a strategy of buying in the catchment area of good schools, which again are in good rental areas. But, that strategy goes more towards the three-bedroom terraces and things like that. The flats; stick to the centre of towns.

You can buy the occasional studio flat because they are really, really, really juicy. But unfortunately, they can take a bit of a hit in a property market down time. So you are a lot more at risk in a studio than you are in a one-bedroom flat. They do not rent as quickly, either.

So, even though you can make it on the capital, you can lose it on the income side. You can go into loss on rental income with them a lot quicker than you can with a one-bedroom flat. But they produce a hell of a lot of cash. Some of my best cash-outs have been from studios. I have had over £20k cash out from studios before now, which is not bad for an investment of less than £12K. That is all my money back, plus £20k in cash out, plus 15% equity left in the prop.

You can pick up the occasional three-bed flat, two-bed house or three-bed house but they are not your mainstream. If they are a particularly good deal, yeah, pick them up. Have a go. See if you enjoy the time it takes to rent them. See if you enjoy the bit longer that it takes, the extra wait, the extra ten days. But my advice is just try the flats first – trust me you will like them a lot more.

If you do not buy leasehold properties, then you don't have maintenance costs or ground rent. But they are a small cost so that you can make a huge profit. You see, to me, because you have the maintenance and the ground rent, that is a damn good thing. Because after I own 40 percent of a block, I get to buy the freehold. And then I get half the freehold for everybody else in the block because you control it. By law, you are allowed to buy the freehold once you control 40% of the block. But, that is another strategy and that is not what we are here to talk about.

Anything that is not a one or two-bedroom flat should not be bought at the start; only when the deal is superb and after you have started with a flat.

Let's say you go, oh, yes, this is not a one or two-bedroom flat, but it is a superb deal. Well, first off, make sure it is a superb deal. If it is and there is nothing else to buy, then buy it. But your strategy should stick at one or two-bedroom flats first and don't buy until you find one.

Now, here is something contentious. Buying, well, it does not even matter. It is not really contentious any more because I have told you about it before. You just buy and wait. That is it. Buy a property and wait; nothing else.

When to buy and when not to buy, that is the question. Always buy. That is the answer!

On your first few, it is simple. If the math works or even comes close, just buy the bl***y thing. Work it out to see if the maths starts to work, which you will see here because I am going to show you how to calculate it yourself, or you can use my 'Can You Buy It' tool on my website. This tool is a hybrid of the spreadsheets I created which went on to help me buy my first few hundred properties.

I still use this tool myself to quickly evaluate property deals because it is so fast. It also completely removes emotions from the deal. Taking action with this tool will make the rest of the tools and info on the site free, that's how useful it is.

Though I say it myself this tool is an essential tool for all serious investors. However, there are plenty of others that offer this sort of tool for free online and I have seen many spreadsheets, I've just found (probably with a fair bit of bias) that mine is easier, less emotional and more importantly, helps you to spot profit much more quickly.

It is not an 'everything' calculation, just one that will get you in the ball park of evaluating a deal in around ninety seconds. And it was good enough for me to buy the first few hundred in record time, so I think that says it all.

However, you don't need the site to go and do this, you can do it with basic maths or you can find another spreadsheet that you are comfortable with. So, basic maths lesson now:

- Property purchase price £100,000
- You can rent it for £525
- Lender will give you 85% mortgage and wants a rental cover of 125% at an interest rate of 5.5%
- The mortgage would be 85% of £100,000 = £85,000 and the annual interest would be £4,675.
- The lender wants 125% cover over the mortgage interest so the rent needs to be £4,675 x 125% = £5843.75 divide by 12 (months) = £486.98.
- The rent you are able to charge is £525 so therefore you can buy it, with an 85% mortgage.

If you then want to re-value it for £125,000:

- A new lender will give you 85% Mortgage and wants a loan cover of 110% at an interest rate of 5.19%
- The mortgage would be 85% of £125,000 = £106,250 and the annual interest would be £5,514.

- The Lender wants 110% cover over the mortgage interest so the rent needs to be £5,514 x 110% = £6,065.81 divide by 12 (months) = £505.48.
- The rent you are able to charge is £525 so therefore you can re-finance it, with an 85% mortgage.

Sometimes, you will only be able to get these to thereabouts work and you may end up leaving some money in the property (well for a while anyway ☺).

Side note: - I make a point regularly on the site that the lenders criteria will soften over time and as rates go up they will move the goal posts to make it possible for us to still borrow money. I'm sure people think when they hear it that I may or may not be right. Well I first wrote the figures above in March 2006 and it's now September 2007. The mortgages we were using at the time were the Mortgage Express 5.19% rate. Today after five interest rate rises totalling 1¼% the Mortgage Express rate is 5.14%! But they are making more out of lending you the money today than they were eighteen months ago. Now that is how they will continue to be able to keep softening their criteria and as they slowly understand the market they are in more, their calculation rates will become easier. Back to the point.

Seriously if the maths shows that there are a few thousand left in, then there's no reason you shouldn't buy your first one. The important thing is to get stuck in. If you're using the site tool then it will say 'Don't buy it' even if there's only £1 left in. Don't let that put you off, only you know how much money you are comfortable with tying up on your first one. The most important thing on your first property is just to take action and buy one.

So if the maths come close to working, buy the bl***y thing. Get in there. Put your toe in the water. Do not keep waiting for that elusive deal. Just buy something. Just get on with it. Because you will learn more and you will get better at it! Even if you buy something that is not as good a deal as you could have bought in three weeks' time, forget it. Forget that deal you can't buy in three weeks time. You buy what you've found after following my system to find it. You get on with it and take a leap of faith.

Powerful statement coming.

Within 12 weeks of reading this book, if you haven't bought a property, you are not going to - unless you read the book again.

Your life will have gotten in the way and the inspiration that I have helped you obtain will fade into a distant memory. And you will go back to the plan that isn't delivering on what you wanted from your life now anyway (does this sound crazy, because the chances are this is what you will do in your effort to remain as one of the 99% who fail).

So all you will have gotten from this book is disappointment that yet again you didn't seize the opportunity that was so clearly presented to you. This is one of the key reasons I created the site, to give you access to all the other readers who are taking action so that it will help keep that inspiration in you. You deserve to change your life and your family's lives, you just need a big enough **reason why**.

I have changed hundreds of people's lives and with this book and website, I will change many thousands more. Just think about how much better your life will be if you use this book to create the wealth for you and your family. And I'm sure you would agree that your family deserve you to do this too.

I find that the thought of what I can do for my family is far more inspiring for me than ever thinking about what the wealth I create can do for me. So why not pause for a moment and picture the job done and you having more wealth each year coming in automatically and just what you would like to do for your family…

And as for the work that is required to create this **certain** future, you can do this. You really can do this.

When setting your strategy, you have to set time constraints as well. As I just said, within 12 weeks, if you have not bought a property, you are not going to.

Set yourself a goal. Write down, this is what I must do. Write down a list of bullet points of what you must do. I must raise equity on my house. That will take this amount of time. When I have done that, I must start with this procedure. Four weeks before I get my money out, I must start the next bit of research in the market. Plan it. Plan it. Put it in your diary. Go onto Outlook. Get it in there. So, plan your time. Take time off to do it. Take holiday days off to do it.

If you don't plan for it, if you don't bother to make a plan, then you are planning to fail. So, you have got to have a plan for all this stuff.

My plan was, I am going out to buy a property now. That was it. That was my plan. And that is what you have got to do. What? Do you think I just woke up one day and I was a property expert?

If you won't write a **Must Do List**, then it will not happen for you and this book will just become another point in your life, where you think back to your perception changing, but nothing else – Do you want that, or do you want wealth forever and no regrets?

How much time can you really specifically devote to this? Because if you cannot devote time to this, then basically you might as well go straight down to the estate agent now and tell him, I want a one-bedroom flat that rents well. And when he says here it is, get in the estate agent's car, go around to the property, have a look at it, put an offer in 10% below the asking price and keep raising your offer by £500 until the vendor says yes. And that is how you have bought a property and congratulations, sit back and wait and you will have actually done it.

What is more, you will have done a better job than the vast majority of people who will read this book and go, I can really do this, but then never actually get round to doing it.

Every single one of you who does not own a property investment should do exactly that: just go and buy one and forget the research in order that you take action. Once you have done it once and you have proven to yourself that you can, you will have plenty of time to apply the skills I am showing you in this book later on, in the future.

Bit deep isn't it, but the point of this book is to make you create money. The point is not to have you think I am wonderful and have you buy everything I ever write. That is just a benefit to you and me.

No, the point of this book for me was so that I would get my message out to more people, that I would be recognised as an innovator and a nutter at the same time. That was just some of my initial motivation. Not really. The book means more to me than that. The main point of this book for you is to make you create wealth for yourself, to raise the financial intelligence of more people than I could do by talking to them and because I wanted to!

But don't get me wrong I'm not all just about being altruistic here. I get paid for my knowledge; I want to make it quite clear I'm in this for the money. But it's probably not where you think the money's coming from.

Quick side track to give you my reason why...

I believe in the Universal laws and one of those laws is the law of reciprocation. And I believe the rule that you can't out give the Universe.

So the way I figure it is, if I teach people my techniques on creating wealth then they will go on and create a lot more wealth for themselves than they could have done, so I will have given big time to the Universe, and as I can't out give the Universe then by reciprocation I will at some point be rewarded in some way for the actions I have taken here.

Who is to say whether I'm right or not, as I have no intention on ever trying to collect on that supposed debt.

All I am trying to do is look for more ways to give because I can have anything I want as long as I find a way to help enough other people have what they want.

Now some will ask why give these techniques away when you can just keep them for yourself and have an endless supply? Well to me it is an endless supply and if it were to dry up then I would find a way to make more money elsewhere, as there is no end. Some will say, well you could give a lot more if you gave it away for free - but nobody values anything that they get for free. As far as I'm concerned I will always be fairly compensated for the wealth I help people create. What's more, without financial compensation, I wouldn't bother to create the information in the first place, so that would be a ridiculous waste.

The point is I will always make you a lot more money than you will ever pay me and that is the way it should be.

Back to the point. So, you don't have time to go out on a Saturday morning and do that? Just go and buy one, irrespective of getting your money back out? After all, your previous argument for not doing this was not understanding the property market, or not knowing if you are buying well. Well both those excuses, sorry, arguments are gone now. So if you say, no, I haven't, then you're lying to me. And you are lying to yourself. Everyone has time to do one thing. If that is all you want to do, just do that and you will have done it. You will own an investment property.

How much time can you realistically devote to this? Don't say about a week if that is unrealistic, because what is the point? If you are going to buy one property a year, which is easy, then you will need to do 16 hours of research, 16 hours of legwork, 3 hours negotiating, 3 hours financing and you will buy one. To refurbish and refinance it: 8 hours organising the refurbishment and then 5 hours to refinance it. A total of 51 hours. A total of five full working days if you want to go out and find a reasonable deal.

If you want to go out and buy a property on Saturday morning, you need just three hours. That is all you'll need. That is all you'll need, if you want to do it simply!

If you want to do it a bit more professionally, you'll need 51 hours. If you want to become a real expert using the Zulu principle, you will probably need to double that time to get a real, real deal. So, maybe 100 hours, 10 days of your time.

So, if you set aside three days a month, in three months you would have it, you would have your deal done, sorted. So, 12 weeks from now, you have bought a deal, a real deal, 20-25% below market value (BMV), which is not bad, is it? 51-100 hours to make £15 to 30K tax-free. Oh, and £10K a year for the rest of your life.

You should re-read that last paragraph as it may just change your life. But what am I saying? We hate going over something more than once because it's a waste of our time, don't we?

Repetition is a master skill and if you practice it by re-reading the most powerful books you have read, it will help you create wealth. But it's your choice.

Think about it: 51 to 100 hours to make £15 to £30k. Not bad. And £10k a year for the rest of your life. Look at that leverage. Look at that time. You have put a little bit of time in to make £10k a year for the rest of your life. For some of you, £10k a year was what you were earning a few years ago. And this is £10k tax-free, as well. (We will cover that properly later). So, that is the equivalent of £15 - £16k a year before tax.

Are you getting how powerful this is? You do just that 51 -100 hours and that is it; that is set for the rest of your life. Every year, on average, it is going to pay you out that money. Not as standard. No. Some years, you do not get it. Some years, you get £30k. And some years, you get b*gger all! But most years, you will get some money. So, you do the effort once. You put that 51-100 hours in. You make the effort. You do it just once.

If you put in those three hours on a Saturday morning with the estate agents, you will get the same result. Yes, you will get the same result! You will not get the £15 to £30k tax-free at the start, but you will get that £10k at the end of the following year and then the next year and the next year and the next. You simply sit and wait and are patient and you will be rewarded for your patience.

So, for three hours you can have that. Can you handle going to an estate agent and buying a flat? Can you handle that? Because if you can't, you are in the wrong business!

I love this, because that to me is so powerful. I mean, now, to me, it's 12 minutes; 12 minutes is what I take to buy a property. I can only buy so many because I have only got so much money. But it takes me just 12 minutes to agree a property. So, my own leverage is unbelievable in that I buy a property for myself that makes £10k a year for the rest of my life and I spend just 12 minutes on it once. Wow!

If you want to do two a year, however, which I advise you to do, then for a further five hours you can double your return because you will have to add another zero hours research, zero hours legwork. You will have to add one hour negotiating and one hour financing. You will have to have two hours organising the refurbishment and snagging, and one hour refinancing it.

So, for an extra five hours, you have bought two properties. Now, that is leverage. You have now leveraged your time even better, haven't you? Instead of 51-100 hours, you have spent 56 -105 and you have two properties! So now you are making £30 to £60k in the first year plus £20k a year, on average, for the rest of your life. Wow!

Is that not good? Well I thought it was, which is why I bought so many.

So, you spend 56-105 hours once and you have £20k a year for the rest of your life. How is this a bad thing?

Can you see why I got interested in property? What will get you interested? Is this the sort of thing that might interest you, might make you think, oh, yeah, that is a good idea. Maybe I should pay more attention to this thing I keep hearing about on the news, property.

Or is this bloke who is speaking, who is writing this, just a complete nutter? Yeah, what is he talking about?

I mean, after all, what does he know? He's only got several hundred properties. He's only buying for 100 different people in the next year alone, from an amazing variety of backgrounds. He is only going to buy for another 250 different people in the next two years. What does this guy know? What does he know? No, it can't be that simple! This is simply wrong! Isn't it?

Or, you can go the other way, of course. You can go on Saturday morning and you can put in your three hours. And instead of buying one property, you can see two in that time and buy two properties. And you can leverage your time by not going down to the estate agents, but picking up the phone and spending 20 minutes until you find an estate agent with two properties for sale and go and buy both from him.

So, in three hours you can leverage your return to £20k a year for the rest of your life. I don't know about you, but I think that is powerful. Now, the only stumbling block in all this, the biggest problem you have got with it, is believing it!

It is what you believe and all the rubbish everyone else tells you that gets in the way. Even the property experts themselves struggle with this point!

Now, that is your strategy. Whether you want to become a buy-two-a-year in three hours or buy-two-a-year in 56 - 105 hours, that is all you need to do. That is all you need to do! And you will make money for the rest of your life, £20k a year for the rest of your life. Or over £30k if it was earned income. So all you have to do to create a wealth strategy that creates you a greater incoming source of wealth annually *forever* which is greater than the average wage in this country, is invest a maximum of £60-£80k or 106 hours of your time!!!

It sounds too easy, but that's it! As I said, the problem is believing it! And then the next problem is doing it within twelve weeks.

Well, there you go. I have just given it to you, probably the most powerful financial message you will ever hear. For it to work, you have to answer two questions: First, have you really believed it, and second, have you really heard it? I can only show the way; it is up to you to walk the path. Some of you don't need to read any more, and in fact the more you read, the more it will stop you, so you might want to stop reading. Your strategy is set.

But if you are a glutton for punishment, or haven't quite convinced yourself that this really works, read on.

24

You Don't Need To Be An Expert

Becoming an expert is only necessary if you want to get rich fast. Effortless property investing is my preferred way now, but then I have been through the pain and I now know the better way, don't I?

Okay. So, after the last chapter, I bet you want a few more details. My favourite kind of property investing is the effortless kind. If you are lazy, why bother becoming an expert, especially when you are competing with experts like me? Why do you want to do that?

You do not need to become an absolute expert anyway. You just need to have a little bit of knowledge. People say a little bit of knowledge is dangerous but a little bit of the right knowledge can be a wonderful thing. A little bit of the right knowledge can be very, very powerful.

Anyone can do this. Most of the muppets you watch on the TV doing up .their investment property can manage it, even though most of them tell you to sell, which we all now know should be just a beginner's mistake.

But even my friends, the so-called experts, even they still advise me and others to sell, which means what... are they really as expert as they think they are? Or are they amongst the vast majority of Property Investors who have made it without really understanding how they did it or why?

Not that they need to, of course, because any damn fool can make money by mistake in property, even a lot of money. That is why I caution you to think about it the next time you are watching this one or that sharing their secrets: just because they have made a lot, does not make them an expert.

I read Fiona Fullerton's book. On the back page was a very insightful comment that went, 'Ok? Just go and make loads of money from your property and tell everyone how easy it is' which I thought was an excellent comment and made me laugh. This is the Property Investors' motto: after not being able to get the message through to people about why and how it works for them, they resort to that – as did I, before I figured it out! Hopefully I have not offended Fiona here, as that was not my intention at all.

The point is, you do not need to understand property to make loads of money from it. Property is not about the light fittings or the wall colour or the tenants. Property is about growth, 1 second at a time, 60 seconds a minute, 60 minutes an hour, 24 hours a day, 7 days a week, 12 months a year, **every year for the rest of your LIFE! WOW!**

But that is just when it really starts. When it really gets going is when it works for your children and changes their lives. I mean, look at the Duke of Westminster. Do you think there will be some point in his life or in his children's lives, or in their children's lives that they will not 'automatically' recover the title of richest person in Britain? Well, if they start selling they may fail, but we all know that would be just silly.

Went off again didn't I? But even the worst of those people on the telly, virtually all of them, manage to make money unless they are daft beyond belief. Now do not get me wrong, some are good. But some of them sure step up where stupidity is concerned – it makes me wonder sometimes, if the TV shows are having trouble finding people to volunteer so they just have to take everyone who does. And there they are – those who should not be allowed – calling themselves experts and giving advice that a lot of the time is simply appalling.

Am I being too harsh? I don't think so. My point is, when you go to an expert for advice, the first rule is, **Make sure they're an expert!** I have spent a small fortune learning this simple piece of due diligence! Mostly, the reason we fail is that we do not do enough research. I drove my wife nuts with all the research and analysing what I was intending to do, before I went into property. She was heavily pregnant with our daughter and all I could think about was growth and making a fortune.

But she knew when I said something was going to go up in value that I was right, because she had watched me do all the research. I think she forgives me now, but it has taken a Mercedes for her birthday, a Ferrari for Christmas, several very nice holidays, loads of clothes and some rather special jewellery. No… only kidding!

Back to the original point. You do need to have done at least a small amount of research if you are going to flip a property and get it right. If you are going to flip a property, that is risk, because you are relying on the fact that you can sell it at the other end. You do need to take risks in property, but when you get good at it, they become so small, that the word 'risk' is not really up for the job any more.

When you get to the point where you are asking an expert for their advice and they are busy trashing the advice I have given in this book, it is time to ask yourself a few questions:

- Is this person speaking from a position of expertise, or is this person giving an opinion of Andy's advice without fully understanding Andy's experience and proven point of view?
- Has he done his homework?
- Has he researched the market?
- Has this person got my interests at heart or is she/he working on a personal agenda to sell books/seminars/tapes and make their real money from me?
- Is this person walking the talk?
- Is this person's strategy in line with the one I have chosen for myself?
- Is this person just truly well meaning and believes every single word he is saying and is he simply wrong?

Be careful of the advice you are willing to accept because it will affect your financial future. Plenty of people told me I was wrong at the start. Now I get told by my family, friends, partners and clients every single day, that I am right and how they are so glad they listened to my radical advice over the words of the so-called experts.

Be very sure that advice you accept is coming from a true expert before you accept their so-called words of wisdom. More opportunity has been wasted and lost by taking and giving poor advice than has ever been lost from making mistakes. And this has been caused by those who lack the wisdom but do not stop dispensing their ideas.

I cannot overstate the importance of the previous few sentences.

What we need to do is work on these two questions: 'can we afford to buy it?' and 'can we cash-flow it should something go wrong?' That is it. That is all you need to worry about! It is irrelevant whether you can sell it or not, as long as you are not buying in a ridiculously stupid area or something like that. But this strategy will make sure you avoid that mistake... as long as you follow it of course!

So, what you have got to ask yourself is, 'can I manage to be as much of a muppet as the ones I see on the TV? If the answer is, 'well, I'm at least that clever', then welcome to property!

If you do not reckon that you can come up to that level, even meet that grade, then maybe you'll prefer your real job. The rest of us will all stay here making an absolute mint from property investing (even if most of us don't understand it). We will carry on having money for nothing and getting property for free.

Now, for those still with us, there are some things you need to learn. You have to know you are not paying too much. Sorry. Let's start at the beginning.

There's the really easy way and the easy way. The really easy way, as I said in the last chapter, is: **Go down to your local estate agents, check if you can rent the property. If you can rent it for a reasonable amount of money, then as long as it meets the maths,** (which I covered earlier, but I have put them in again after this) **then you can buy the property.** That is it - 39 words! That is the really, really, really easy way. You do not need much more help from me to do it that way, other than to tell you to get started!

The Maths

Property purchase price £100,000
You can rent it for £525
Lender will give you 85% Mortgage and wants a rental cover of 125% at an interest rate of 5.5% (I update the deals we are using currently on my website)
The mortgage would be 85% of £100,000 = £85,000 and the annual interest would be £4,675.
The lender wants 125% cover over the mortgage interest so the rent needs to be £4,675 x 125% = £5843.75 divide by 12 (months) = £486.98.
The rent you are able to charge is £525 so therefore you can buy it, with an 85% mortgage.

Right now, we are going to do it the easy way. The rest of this chapter is going to be devoted to the easy way. And the easy way is the 51-100 hour a year method which you can turn into 56-105 hours if you want to buy two properties. Or you can turn into about 61-110 hours if you want to buy three properties. Get where I am coming from? Okay.

You have to know you are not paying too much. How you do that is to Zulu it. This is what you need to become an expert quickly in a very small area. I'll cover how to do that shortly.

You have to be able to fund it and know how much you can rent it for. How you do that is by following the maths described on the last page and then the same calculation with a second lender as described below. All right? However, you can use the software I used. This software gives you various other useful calculations as well as being very quick to use. And you can find it on the membership site.

You have to know whether you can get your money back. If you can get your money back and the math works, wonderful, buy the property. Do not worry too much at the moment about how to find a property worth that much more than you are going to pay, we will get onto that later. I'm just trying to get the purchase and refinance concept through at the moment.

Does the maths tell you that you can get your money back if you then want to re-value it for £125,000?
A new lender will give you 85% Mortgage and wants a loan cover of 110% at an interest rate of 5.19%
The mortgage would be 85% of £125,000 = £106,250 and the annual interest would be £5,514.
The lender wants 110% cover over the mortgage interest so the rent needs to be £5,514 x 110% = £6,065.81 divide by 12 (months) = £505.48.
The rent you are able to charge is £525 so therefore you can buy it, with an 85% mortgage.

Don't buy any of the following:
- You do not want a flat above a shop, especially if the shop is a takeaway
- You do not want a flat next to a shop
- You do not want a flat next to a pub

- You do not want a property with anything commercial around it at all, really AT ALL!
- You do not want to buy a flat that has historic bad management problems.
- You do not want to buy a property in a block that has structural defects that are known about.
- You do not want to buy anything out of the ordinary.

You want to buy a standard flat. It can be a converted. It can be a purpose built flat in a block of a few other flats, up to a maximum of, say, 20.

That is what you are looking for. You are not looking for a particular property, oh look, I have found this fantastic deal or anything weird. Don't think, it is really good, I can make this work - even though it is slightly outside the formula he is saying. Forget it! Move on! There is a deal that fits, somewhere in your weekly paper. If it is a balcony-access flat, it does not fit! You don't want that! Keep it simple and standard!

There are certain criteria lenders do not like. They do not like it for a reason, so just buy what the lenders like. They know what they are talking about, after all they are prepared to lend 85% of its value, and they have been doing it a lot longer than you!

I am not going to add in too much here as it can get complicated, but here are a few things to avoid.

- Above or beside commercial
- Anything over 5 floors
- Balcony access

- Anything that may have structural problems

Try not to waste time or money buying in large ex-local authority estates. These can work, but you have to know what you are doing and there is enough property elsewhere, so why bother? You can get your best profits from those sort of areas, but there is enough property elsewhere. I am not saying they are bad, but they can be grief, and the easy way is to avoid doing grief!

They are just outside your strategy, the easy strategy and that is why it's called easy – because we do not do grief. Buying in a local authority is outside the easy strategy. Keep telling yourself: You are buying the easy way and only the easy way.

People say, 'don't buy something you wouldn't live in'. Those people will leave lots of money around for people like me. I live in a 4,500 square foot house, with planning consent to convert to 11,500. My children race space hoppers around the ground floor of the house. And it's on a circuit where we only see them every 20 minutes!! But seriously now, I would never live in a 1-bed flat, because my life has moved on from that.

Location, location, location? Whatever, whatever, whatever. Too general. Be specific. Those clichés are just more rhetoric to slow you down. All you need to know is, can you rent it quickly and for good money?

How do you rent it? You go and speak to agents. You don't have to do too much. Just pick up the phone to them. Why don't you just say, can I rent the property? I am thinking of buying a flat in this block. How much will it rent for? I am thinking of buying a flat here, how much will that rent for?

Ring up three agents and they will give you three different prices. Don't pin all your research on what one agent tells you. Ask them, how long do you think it will take to get a tenant? Then look in the paper and see if you can find any properties for rent in that area from the agents you have just spoken to and see if what they have just told you matches what they are saying in the paper that week.

Well, that is clever, isn't it? That is rocket science. That you do not automatically believe what you are told by people looking to make a profit – that you check out what they have said and compare it to others in their field – revolutionary!

There are no emotions when you buy a property. You simply won't be needing them. So, before you start doing anything, you will be wanting to switch those emotions off because they will only get in your way. I am not interested if it has a nice red brick exterior, as a very good friend of mine said to me the other day when I bought her an investment property. (And she is a property investor.) She said, 'Oh, it's such a lovely property you have bought for me.'

I don't care. I don't care if it is a nice property or not. I care if the maths work and if it is going to rent, if people are going to pay me to rent it and if the area is nice. That is all I care about.

It is a property. I am doing this to acquire the debt. You do not need emotions when you are doing this. They hold you back. I am slicking you down here to get through and get property bought as quickly as possible. And the person who told me that, you know who you are! (M.D.)

Now, let's work on how you find the first property and Zulu it. The first rule, you have to know the area you're investing in. Deals are hidden in plain sight.

A few years ago, I would occasionally go, 'I haven't bought property for a couple of days. I want to buy a property.' Or a week even! Sometimes I would start to get withdrawal symptoms at about a week. So, I hadn't bought a property for a few days and I would think, I have to go and get one today. I would be on the phone to an estate agent about some other deal – this was when I used to have to phone the estate agents. Now I don't have to do that sort of thing. And I would be chatting to him about this other deal and he would say, 'Oh, I have heard of this really cheap property going in Tower Road in Lancing.'

Now, in Tower Road we already own several properties. It is an ex-local authority area and about 40 per cent of the street is still local authority. I know that because I had to find that out for a particular mortgage lender. Remember my advice about buying the easy ones!

Anyway, the estate agent said there was a property for sale. It was a three-bedroom terrace and it was up for sale for about £115k. I have got one down that road valued at £155k, so I thought, well, that is not a bad deal. Not bad at all. Yeah. Okay. I will have a look at that.

So, I said, which agent is it? And he told me. So, I phoned her up and said, 'Hi, I understand you have a property for sale for £115k in Tower Road, Lancing.' And the lady went, 'Yes, we are doing block viewings on that at 4:00pm.'

Block viewings. Do you know what block viewings means? It means everybody knows about it. Everybody knows that property and everybody's going to be there because the property is going up for auction. That is a place where people go to play by somebody else's rules. I have found property investment works best when I play by my own rules.

And I went, 'Oh, no. Thanks very much anyway.' That property ended up being sold at auction for £148k. The person who bought it was a first-time buy-for-let investor who then spent £12k on it and the property was then valued for £150k. Apparently it sold at a loss after about a year. This is an example of someone you might meet at a party who will now be perceived as a bit of an expert by the people they talk to and will go on to warn everybody off becoming a property investor because it simply does not work. After all they've tried it once, got it completely wrong and now they know everything and they are an expert.

Now their idiocy is going to hold their friends and acquaintances back from possible financial freedom, as well as their own, for that matter! Well, that was clever, wasn't it? Another perceived expert. If you had met them in the pub, you might have had an inkling that what they were saying was not worthwhile, but if another good trusted friend introduced you by saying, 'I know someone here who has just got into property investing', instantly you would have perceived them as a little bit of an expert – do you see how easy it is to accept bad advice?

What I chose to do that same afternoon was this; I was really peeved because I wanted to buy a property that afternoon. I went on the Internet and I went to my favourite local website and I went through it.

I think I might have spent nearly 30 seconds after entering my criteria. I looked through the list and it was like, page one, no, nothing there. Page two. Oh, look. One-bedroom bungalow type property, leasehold, in East Worthing for sale for £85k.

I thought, well, that is handy. I own the one next to it. And that was valued about three months ago for £115k. So I thought, 'that will do'. I picked up the phone to the agent I had bought other properties from. I said, 'Yeah, you have another one of these properties down this place.' And he said, 'Yes.' I said, 'How long has it been on the market?' He sad, 'Oh, about three months.'

See? I am buying property and I had still missed this little gem! So, I said, 'How much interest?' He said, 'Not much interest at all.' So, I said, 'All right. Will the vendor consider an offer?' And he said, 'Yeah, yeah, yeah. The vendor will consider an offer, but they need close to the asking price.' And I said, 'Why do they need close to the asking price?' He said, 'They have bought another house and this is out on a bridging loan.'

This is where the chain probably fell through on their property when they were trying to buy another and so, rather than lose their new home, they asked their bank to bridge the gap between paying off the lender of their existing home and waiting for the sale proceeds to clear their bank.

So anyway, I went around there. I jumped in the car, ten minutes later I spoke to the agent and I went, yeah, okay, I am willing to pay £78k straightaway. Did not need to negotiate too much because I knew I had £115k revaluation on it straightaway.

I came back to the office. By the time I got back to the office, he called and said, 'They will not take £78k, but if you pay £80k, they will grant you access for four weeks between exchange and completion.' I had asked for access between exchange and completion as I like to get in and refurbish while someone else is paying the mortgage. Well, I would have been willing to pay up to £82k in the first place, so I said, 'Yep. Okay.' Deal done. I bought it at £80k. I made £35k pounds, less my refurb cost and arrangement fees, so I made about £30k that afternoon.

I personally went to that auction the same afternoon and watched that first time buyer lose a load of money and waste a load of time. Over the next year I saw that person dismantle a life that was so full of wealth potential. He gained some experience; it is too bad it was the wrong type!

The thing is, that auction property, all right, I admit it, I do not like auctions. Yeah, you can get good deals there. But the problem is, all the sheep go to the auctions. Sorry. I mean, crowds go to the auctions. Everybody knows about them. Everybody knows about the property. You do not know how many people have looked at it.

What I like is seeing a property that has either not come to the market, or has been on the market for months and everybody else has overlooked it. Right? **The very best deals are the ones hidden in plain sight!**

Auctions are where the flocks go. You do not want to play by their rules. You want to play in a game where you get to make up the rules. When I buy a property, it is by my rules. It is like when you're a kid, we're playing my way, **BECAUSE IT'S MY BALL!**

25

Can I Do This Anywhere?

You need to choose a reasonable sized town, say 25-100,000 people or more. Everywhere is good for property, but you don't look for a property deal in a one-horse town. You can find them, but you don't need to and they are not in this strategy.

If you live in a village, then you need to go to a town to buy your property. Buy your property in a town because you need a railway line near it. Do not buy a property where there is not a railway line because you have got to have easy access to it. You know, it really does make a difference.

The best deal for you is either on, or virtually on, your doorstep. You don't want to go too far afield. You get lots of people who say, oh, you'd better go to the north of England because that is where the property's rising the quickest. No. The best deal for you is on your doorstep. You do not want grief, you are looking to do this the easy way – get it? If you live in the north of England, then BUY THERE! Amateurs go out of their way to attract grief. You want to avoid grief and attract profit.

If you want to increase the time you have to spend on this, just imagine how much time you would have to spend if you employed this north of England strategy that so many amateurs advise others to do, because they cannot do it in their own location. You live in a town 300 miles away from where you want to own property. Does this sound like madness to you? Because it does to me.

Well, if you did buy 300 miles away from where you live then that timescale I have just given you – the 51-100, 56-105, 61-110 hour time scale – you can increase that by what, a factor of six, to get the same sort of deals. What were these people thinking about; why listen to some damn fool telling them to travel 3-4-500 miles to buy property, when there is plenty where you live?

You may have noticed that there is plenty of property in towns near you, because you may have noticed that there are all these people walking about, and you can bet they do not all own their own property!

Do these amateurs think that buying property at less money makes up for all the grief? I don't. Why else would you want to buy in a different area? Why do people want to do that? Is that because they believe that the grass is greener? I think they possibly do!

There is plenty of property on your doorstep, whether it be central London, whether it be Glasgow, whether it be wherever. If you are in or near a big town there is plenty of property to choose from.

I mean, I can make property deals on property in the countryside. There is no issue at all on how to do it. I know exactly what to do. I know exactly where to look for them. You can make money on property anywhere and at any time. But, we are not in it for that strategy. You are in the strategy to make money the easiest way possible.

So, the best deal for you is on your doorstep and you have probably driven past it in the last month. So, keep your eyes open from now on because they are going to start appearing to you.

The first place you look is in the local freebie property papers. This is the first time you have got to spend money after the investment of buying this book. You need to buy a big black marker pen and a red one.

Of course, everything is not a one or a two-bed flat. Unless the property is a one or two-bed flat, you do not want to even look at it. Don't waste your time. Don't let yourself get distracted. Just look at the one and two-bedroom flats; nothing else. From the first time you look at this paper, you are banned from looking at anything else. All right? So a black strike goes through every property that is not a 1 or 2 bed flat. Now, take your red marker and put a line through the ones that look too expensive or too far outside your area. There we go. Properties that are not 1 or 2-bed flats you have put a black pen through. Properties that are out of reach you have put a red pen through. Okay. Let's read what is left. No -absorb what's left. Get to know those properties. Look at them. Read them. Understand them.

Now, practice the mortgage formulas. Practice seeing what money you could get back at refinance. Look at what it is selling for, look at what you think you could negotiate without picking the phone up to the estate agent and look at what you could possibly get it to value for, based on the fact there are other properties in that paper valuing for more than it is listed for right there.

Some of those properties with the red lines through will be the ones that are too much money. So, practice seeing what you could get back for it.

Okay. Stop here. Go and get the freebie paper and do this. This is it. **In the words I have just written and the technique I have just shown you lies the secret to your wealth in property.**

You are going to learn more from what is written below, but nothing I have written below is going to convince you to believe that you can do it, anywhere near as much as doing this now. This is the treasure map, people. I have just taken you to where the treasure is. I have marked the spot. It's here: **X**. I have told you to stop and dig here.

If you are too stubborn, too afraid, too foolish to just listen to me and do the one bit you need to do to discover the treasure, then carry on reading. Maybe you are waiting for something else to inspire you; maybe you think you will remember to come back and dig up the secrets that will change the direction of your life another day. I have led you to it; I have put the shovel in your hand, **but only you can dig!**

So you have dug a little, and what did you find? You found money, didn't you? But it can't be that simple, can it? If it's really that simple, why is it still there, why hasn't someone else taken it? Because they have missed it, that is why!

Okay. At this point, some of you are still waiting to be convinced; some of you will have found a little and some of you will have found a lot. So what is next?

Do the same thing the following week. There is no need to rush in yet. As Dolf De Roos said, 'The deal of a lifetime comes along once a week'. Don't throw your papers away. Keep your first week. Then, add your second week, then your third week, your fourth week and so on.

One thing you must do each week is to do the same thing with the Internet that you have done with the newspapers(except don't write on the screen ☺) You have to use the filters instead to filter one & two-bed flats in your chosen area and put a price limit on it. By the third week, you should start noticing properties that look the same. You will see Victorian converted flats in the same area, for example, but there's a £10k, £20k, £30k difference in price. You will just start noticing them! You will not believe me until you try!

You should by the third week, be able to recognise when a new property comes on the market, recognise when a property goes from 'for sale' to 'sale agreed', when a property drops off the market. You should start to recognise these things because you are looking at the listings every week. Your focus is on one and two-bedroom flats in your target area. So, you're focused every single week.

Do not choose two towns. Choose one town. Worthing and Littlehampton, I could have bought in both. First, I focused on Worthing until I got it right. Then I focused on Littlehampton and then on Lancing. They were my first three buying areas. Lancing is really part of Worthing but it is a different buying area and has slightly different characteristics. I focused on each one until I got it right.

The reason for doing the thing with the papers is that it gives you a feel for the whole market. You are looking at properties all mixed up and you would be amazed at how much information your brain is actually taking in. Reading the property papers is a great way for finding the occasional deal as it will give you the whole market on each page. The papers will help prevent you from making a mistake.

Then when you know the market you add the internet into the equation. You need to use both to keep your strategy extremely effective. I use the Rightmove website because I find it the easiest and here are the selection criteria I enter to find deals in every town. Town, +3 miles, flats, and finally lowest price first. This will sort the deals for you in a nice orderly fashion.

In the 4th week, you're ready to pick up the phone to find out about some of those properties that are £10k, £20k, £30k difference. You say to the estate agent, 'Hello. Yeah, I have seen a property in the paper in Crescent Road and it is up for sale for £119k. Could you tell me a little bit more about it, please?'

And then let them talk. And they will tell you, well, it is a one-bedroom flat. It has got this, that and the other. Make notes on what they say, because there will be clues to the deals in their words. Let them waffle a bit, remember that they are teaching you at this time so pay attention, and in future you will learn to ask better questions. People love talking so let them talk. They will say 'It is a lovely this, that and the other'. After they have finished their spiel, you then say to them, 'Yeah, can you tell me what the vendor's (current owner's) position is, please?' Use the term vendor.

That phrase says a lot about you to the estate agent, so learn it word for word. You are friendly, but you want an answer with 'Yeah'; then you are asking for very relevant information with, 'can you tell me what the'; then you establish that you are not an amateur with, 'vendor's position is', then you are courteous, 'please'. This sentence sets you and the agent up instantly. This sentence is the good first impression you are creating with the agent and you only get to make a good first impression once!

And he will say, 'Yeah, sure. They have found a property.' And then it is a case of, what does that mean? I say, 'oh', and I then say, 'Are the vendors a young couple, then?' 'Oh, no, no. She lives on her own, but she is moving in with her boyfriend.'

And it is like I am thinking, well, hang on a minute if she is moving in with her boyfriend, okay, there could be a little bit of, she just wants rid of this flat, so this could be a motivated seller. Obvious really, as it is on the market already then they are motivated, but we want to work up a selling frenzy whenever we can. Or, it is a husband and wife and basically, they have outgrown the flat and they are trying to move up the ladder. What that says to me is that they need every pound they can get out of this property to be able to afford their next home, so they are not going to be as interested in a low offer.

So there are two slightly different stories that tell me a lot about the vendor that I have managed to get without getting off my backside. And more will come to you. You have to put yourself inside the vendor's head and try to look at where you would be motivated if you were in their position. Ask questions about the vendor. What is the vendor's position? Why are they selling? What do they do for a living? How old are they? Ask the relevant questions that will help you get inside their heads.

Oh, they are moving to Kent. So, if they are moving to an area that's cheaper than the area they currently live in, there is another option for you to get money off the price.

Or if they say, they are moving to central London, I am thinking, oh great, they need every pound out of this property, so not much chance of a bargain. Or, I think oh, great, if they can afford to just upscale and move to central London, they probably don't need the money out of this property. Same situation could be read two different ways and it is difficult not to jump to conclusions, but try to keep focused on your research.

If you want to get a little clever, then find a motivated seller. Okay? Why are they selling? Well, it was grandma's flat and basically, grandma's just moved into a home and she does not need the flat any more and we have got to sell the flat because by law, she has got to sell the flat to pay for her housing care.

In this case, it is virtually irrelevant to these people how much the flat gets sold for because they have failed to protect Grandma's money. And the only money Grandma's going to be allowed to keep out of the sale is about £15k. So, whether that property sells for £100k or £110k doesn't really matter. That means you could have a motivated seller there. They just want rid of it because that is what they have been told to do. They don't really care. They don't need it to sell quickly, as they are probably not under any financial pressure to do so, but they are probably fed up with the whole situation and just want rid of it.

Then, you could have a situation where, as I have said, a boyfriend and a girlfriend are moving into their own home together, or they are selling up and going to on holiday for a year. Oh, that happens all the time. You know, they decide to take a year out or something like that.

They bought their house five years ago. There is plenty of equity in it. They are going to live off that for a year. They just want their house gone. You have people who are moving to South Africa, people who are moving to Australia, people who are moving to different areas around the country, people who are relocating for their job.

Any of those types of people are motivated to sell and finding out if they are motivated is just a matter of asking questions. The reasons for people to be motivated to want rid of something are endless, so find out the vendor's reason and if their reason is powerful enough, they will take a low offer.

So, when you have asked the estate agent and have found out that this person could be a motivated seller, then you say, what sort of offer would they consider? Do not say, will they consider an offer at this stage. 'What sort of offer would they consider?' means you are not looking for a 'yes' or 'no' answer. You don't want to give the estate agent the opportunity to say no to you. You only ask questions they can answer that give you information, i.e. the offer the vendor will accept. If the agent says he does not know, you need to sort of make a huffing sound that conveys your disappointment in their ability to actually know the answer to your intelligent question. This, in a very nice way, puts them on the back foot. They will come back with some other point at this stage, in an effort to change the subject and you absolutely must ignore answering their new point and instantly take them back to your question by saying, 'Well I really need to know what sort of offer they would consider before I can carry on at this stage.' Believe me, they will ask to call you back and they will go and speak to the vendor.

So, what you have actually said is, well obviously, they will take an offer. You have already said that in your sentence. But, what you are also saying to them is, what sort of offer will they consider? So, you are making him give you a price.

And you are going to drag that out of him several times. Don't offer any information about yourself; don't drop in, well, I am a buy-to-let investor or anything like that. Avoid commenting because it makes you sound amateurish. Skirt around the issue if they ask you a direct question. Don't offer anything you don't need to.

You know, I was watching a film recently, a John Travolta film, 'Be Cool.' And they say to him just before he's going to go and do a negotiation, 'What are you going to say?' and he says, 'No more than I have to, if that'. That is the point. You say as little as you have to about yourself but you get them to say as much as possible.

This is not the time to stroke your own ego. Keep it out of they way as it could cost you thousands at this stage of the negotiations. When you are negotiating like this, get them to give you all the ammunition so that you can use it against them in a minute. Remember as they are talking to you, they are giving you the weapons that you will use against them later. It is guerrilla negotiating and it works very well.

Remember, you don't need to do this if you want to do the really easy way of buying property. This is only for the 51-100 hours a year easy way.

When you find a motivated seller, you will know because the agent will say, 'Oh, they will consider an offer.' Let us say it is up for £119k. 'They will consider an offer of about £110k.' Brilliant. Brilliant.

You have already found a property that is £15k to £20k below what other properties are like in the area and this guy's turned around to you and said they will consider an offer about £10k less than that. That's usually because you have managed to pick up the phone to a young estate agent who has only been there five minutes. And basically, he has let the cat out of the bag at an early stage. Agents who have been round the block don't let you strike oil that easy!

So if they are willing to go to £110k, you know they will go to £105k-ish. So now, it is just a case of how well you negotiate. So you now have the figure £105k in your head. Right now you've got to put a little effort in and get your ar*e off the sofa. See? You get to keep fit, too, as a property investor.

So now, I am walking out the door thinking, well, I know I will get it for £110k. My figures work at £110K. Now, how much will I be able to lower it from that? Do you see where I am coming from? I now know, before I have got off my lazy backside and walked out the door, that I have already got a deal at £110k. Very useful. Saves a hell of a lot of time when you are looking for property.

When you find them, when you find two or three, go and see them. Let the agent show you around. Let them show you some more that they think might suit you as well. Let the agent think and believe that he knows a lot more about property than you do. Chances are, at the moment, he does. They must always think they have the upper hand, always play to their ego, but don't suck up.

The thing is , estate agents never cease to amaze me. It is very rare that you meet an extremely wealthy estate agent. They are so close to real wealth that it is too close for most of them to see it. They believe that to create real wealth you need to buy and sell properties because that is how they make their money: buying and selling properties.

Their problem is, they cannot understand what we do. They really don't understand it at all. Believe me, I have tried to explain it to them. I have tried to help them. And I mean, not all estate agents are nice, but I actually tend to like them. They are very good at selling things. They are interesting to talk to. And the more you get to like them, basically, the more they like you and the more deals they push your way. So I really do like estate agents.

I also try and help them, but no matter how much I try and help them, they just really don't get it. I have never actually managed to really help an estate agent because what I do, well it goes against the grain. So you have got to let them think they're the experts.

Let them show you around other properties, even if it is wasting your time a bit. Because while they are showing you around them, even if you think it is   not something suitable, you never know, it might be. But if it is not suitable, do not be afraid to go, 'No, this isn't really suitable for me.'

The time you spend viewing with the agent is really important and not just because you are looking at properties. This is the time when the agent begins to like you and starts to see you as a customer and stops looking at you as if you are a commission cheque.

So you want to go and see those properties. Well, brilliant because it is the perfect time anyway, because now is the time you want to be getting out and getting used to walking around properties and costing the refurbishments. Go around, walk around them, but don't put any offers in. At this stage, even if you have found the deal of the week, don't put an offer in. If you have found a deal, great. Maybe it is time to put an offer in. We will come to that in a minute.

But, let's say you don't find a deal. Just walk around properties. Keep walking around them. Get to walk around 20-30 properties in a very short period of time. Say two weeks. You can view two properties in an hour comfortably. Your brain is capable of taking in over 500,000 things a second, so don't waste time in a property. Learn to look and take in things quickly, make notes on the refurb as you walk round.

So, it will take you five hours on a Saturday morning. You will be finished by 2:30, having started at 9:30 and you'll have viewed 10 properties. There you go. It will take you three weekends. That is it. Done. Maximum. That is if you really want to go and do that much. In my opinion, you will probably only need to see 8-10 properties and you will get a feel for how to view them and how to cost them on the refurb.

I am going to show you how to cost a refurb really quickly; a really easy way of doing it. It has to be easy because I am very lazy, and this is an area that should be kept very simple; too many property investors get hung up over budgets, I don't know why. You will succeed because you persevere, not because you are perfect.

Standard refurb budget on 1-bedroom flats:

£500	is allocated to each job for electrical works (If they are not required then the money should not be used)
£450	is allocated for flooring
£700	is allocated for a kitchen inclusive of tiling
£700	is allocated for painting inclusive of materials
£500	is allocated for the bathroom inclusive of tiling
£150	for gas check & boiler maintenance
£75	for cleaning
£3,075	**Total**
£462	15% contingency
£3,537	**Total**
£619	Vat
£4,156	**Grand Total**

Now that was not overly complicated for you was it? And remember you aim to bring in your refurbishments under budget, because a budget is a budget -NOT a target.

Standard refurb budget on 2-bedroom flats:

£500	is allocated to each job for electrical works (If they are not required then the money should not be used)
£650	is allocated for flooring
£800	is allocated for a kitchen inclusive of tiling
£850	is allocated for painting inclusive of materials
£550	is allocated for the bathroom inclusive of tiling
£150	for gas check & boiler maintenance
£100	for cleaning
£3,600	**Total**
£540	15% contingency
£4,140	**Total**
£725	Vat
£4,865	**Grand Total**

All right, we are at week four, same again. Except that by now, you should have found several properties with the £10k-£20k difference in price. On the phone, as before, ask questions before getting off your backside. You should now be able to tell when a new property comes on the market, when one sells, exactly as I said. You notice a new prop, you notice when one sells, guess what? You have just become an expert in your area on those property types by using the famous Zulu principle.

Quick interlude here. *Zulu Principle* by Jim Slater was a book about share trading. But the message is the important bit as it fits virtually anything you are interested in. The Zulu Principle was described in the 1960s as being the expertise acquired rapidly in a single obscure subject, like Zulus, by conducting an in-depth study of library books and magazine articles. Obviously, we have the internet now as well. Your quick and focused research can quickly turn you into an expert.

Well, guess what? You are an expert on one and two-bedroom flats in your chosen area right now. You now know 80% of what somebody like me knows. Just by doing that, you are 80% towards being an expert.

Now there is nothing there you can't do, is there? This is only slightly more difficult than walking down the street and chewing gum isn't it? You can do this, and it is not hard if you try.

And basically, you just need to keep doing this. You need to keep viewing the properties until you have found that motivated seller. Or, you can just buy one of the ones you have found that is a reasonable enough price and you are not really worried about tying up a bit of your lender's money. So, don't wait too long to find this motivated seller. If you think you are close enough, as long as you can recover 75% of your total outlay on your first one, then jump in.

If you are one of the guys who wants to guarantee himself that he's getting the best deal there is out there and do the 100 hours thing to get it to work, then you need to wait until you have found that motivated seller and you need to wait until you have found it 30 – 35% undervalued. Don't wait too long though. It is better to buy and learn a bit, than not buy at all! Always remember it is better to buy than to wait too long on your first one or two: get your feet wet. Getting 75% of your cash outlay back on the first two is plenty good enough as you can always find more funds – is that clear?

If you are one of the other guys who does not mind leaving £10-£15k tied up in the property and you are still going to make £20-£30k, then you should be ready to start bartering and making an offer now.

Just remember, you know your area and you know the estate agents and you know the vendor's situation. Remember that when you do the negotiating. You know all of that, so use it to your advantage. When the agent tells you this is a good deal, cut a property out of the paper from another agent in the same area at the same price and say, well, yeah, this is a good deal. But so is this one. Taking the edge off them. You have caught them off guard. You have made him stumble a bit, because he was not ready for you to come back with that because he is viewing you as just a standard run of the mill person who comes in, who says they want to buy a property, yada, yada, yada.

You now know the estate agents. He now knows that you know the estate agents. He now realises you know your area as well, because you just said it, and this is why you don't talk too much. You get to choose when you are going to let the cat out of the bag, so that it gives you the greatest benefit. And you know the vendor's situation.

So when he says, 'Well, what about if you offer this?' then it is a case of, 'Well, I may be prepared to offer that if they would be prepared to grant me access between exchange and completion.' So, you haven't said you would offer that. So now, you have put the ball back in his court. You have only said 'IF'. And he has got on the phone to the vendor and he is saying, well look, I think I can get an offer out of him at this price if you are willing to grant them access between exchange and completion.

Oh I forgot to say, the best place to be when you make your first offer is in front of the estate agent in his office. This gives you the power because he believes he has a motivated buyer – you, the fish – right in front of him, which means he has a deal in front of him right now, so all he has to do is get the vendor to agree and you are going to buy. After you deliver a low blow and he gets on the phone to the vendor, you start to fidget a bit as if you are changing your mind and thinking about leaving. Remember, whoever wants this deal the most is in the weaker position, so now you are having second thoughts. But you must not say it, he needs to see it in your body language – this is a practised skill, the more you do it the better you will get.

And ask for access between exchange and completion. It saves you a month's mortgage payment, because you will extend it for four weeks and get your refurb done in that time. Saving you a month's mortgage payment is not about the money. You will probably have to concede this point later, when you first start buying property, but at the moment we are establishing negotiating boundaries. Access saves only £500ish, so it is not about the money, is it; it is about playing by your own rules. Why not play by your own rules and make it part of the offer (not that we've offered yet, of course). See? It is an easy trick.

Coming back to us for a second; we d stopped paying the 5% on exchange. We only give £1k on exchange. And because that is all we do we get away with doing it. However, we do get a very belligerent solicitor occasionally, who absolutely insists on 5%..

When I am buying on behalf of a client, I will back down and give the 5%. But when it is for me, I won't do that unless the deal is so hot that it is not worth my while to fight about it. You know, 92–93% of the time, we get away with £1k on exchange so we have very little money in the outlay. And again, we have established a boundary that we can concede later if we want to, to get a lower price. If we had not come up with clauses like this at the start then we would have been 'unreasonable' to ask for them later. But by getting them in at the start, it means they are possible deal breakers and the vendor doesn't know our situation so he doesn't know for certain how critical they are.

In negotiating, the person who wants the deal to happen most has the least bargaining power. Trust me. If you have nothing to sell and you are only buying this from the point of investing, the only way that the vendor has any stronger power than you is if you give it to them. The buyer controls a property deal; the vendor's only control is the power to say no.

If you say to them, look, I want to buy this property and you give any inkling that you care about that property in any way, shape, or form, the vendor has now got control. If they gain control, it is because you have given it to them. You can intentionally give it to them and intentionally take it back, but that is a little more advanced and not needed here. Maybe I will cover that in an advanced section another time.

If you relinquish control, the estate agent will pick up on it in an instant and the score is now Advantage Vendor! You are very close to losing this deal, even if you agree to a price. You must always retain control of the purchase. Once they have it then you are in the weaker position and you've given that away. If you let the vendor have control then your chance of completing the purchase on your terms has just dropped by about 30%.

Whenever I have given control away, I think I have kicked myself because it's like, ah, I can't believe I made that amateurish mistake. And it is easy to do. So, you never give away the bargaining power. The vendor wants this deal to happen most. Do you know why I know the vendor wants this deal to happen most? Because he has put his property up for sale, so he probably has a reason to sell it.

Your reason for buying is to own an investment property. His reason to sell is going to be a lot stronger than your reason to buy. Now, your reason to buy will get stronger as the deal gets better. But Dolf de Roos clearly says, the deal of a lifetime comes along *once a week*. Don't lose control of a deal by chasing it – not ever. Do this and you will be the person at the party telling people how property investing doesn't work!

You don't need to chase. You must be prepared to walk away and lose a little money occasionally. You must think of it as just an expense, a small price to pay to get other, better, more fantastic deals. Some of the deals I've done that people say are unbelievable are not really unbelievable at all. All I do is keep asking questions and making little concessions to balance against their large concessions. I know there will be another prop along next week, because there are lots and lots of properties out there.

So, let us see now. How do we know that it's a deal? Well, it is quite simple. If it looks like a deal, smells like a deal, tastes like a deal, that is good enough. Make a bl***y offer before someone like me nicks it off you. All right?

Why not find more than one deal/ Place offers on both. Offer 10–15% less than the asking price, then wait. Then if you don't get a bite, offer on something else, but leave the offers out there for a while.

If they accept your first offer, guess what? Well done, yeah? No, not well done at all! It means you have paid too much. If you get your first offer accepted, it is because you offered too much!

I had a property recently, well it was actually about a year or 18 months ago now. We had found this prop. It was worth about £140k - £145k all day long. We knew the vendor was in a position where they needed to sell. And so we thought, all right, okay, what should we offer on it? Well, we'd had quite a good run of recent acquisitions so we thought, let's take a chance on this one. Let's put a ridiculous offer in. We will offer £100k.

So we did and they said yes. Most people would have been very happy. They would have just made £45k. We were not. We were really peeved because we could have bought the damn thing at £95k. We gave away £5k! Now I know what you are thinking. You are thinking we should be grateful, and don't get me wrong, we are. But what we do is not just about making money. It is about doing something we love and getting better at it all the time.

The mistake I let us make was getting too comfortable with our success. As we had had a good run, I let that affect my decision on the purchase price. I did not do my due diligence. I did not dig deep enough into the vendor's situation. As it happened, they were a hair's breadth from being repossessed and £95k would have sorted them out as much as £100k. To my mind, giving extra money to people who are not in control of their finances is simply a waste of money, because it will slip through their fingers in a matter of weeks.

I read once, from someone, sorry I can't remember their name, 'I only have one rule on money: never, ever, ever lose money.' Well, we lost money there. We gave away £5k. We made £45k, but we could have made £50k.

Yes, it is only a 'farmer's profit' because we didn't actually make it, but that is not the point. The point is that we offered too much because we did not correctly evaluate the opportunity. The first rule is that you must always get your first price refused. You can always go up on a price. It is very difficult to go down. You lose credibility unless you have a justified reason for going down.

The second rule is that you never increase the offer without getting something in return. As an example, more information is worth money. If the agent says, well, the vendor can't accept that offer because of this reason, would you consider a higher offer? That extra information may be worth you offering more money. Encourage them to give you a counter-offer. What you are looking for is a counter-offer.

It is information that is going to make you money. If I had done a bit more research on that £100K flat I bought, I would have found out more regarding the vendor's position. But because I was being a bit blasé about it, because I had not done my due diligence on the vendor properly, I missed the fact that they needed to sell really badly.

So it is information here that is going to make you dough, because you make money when you buy a property, not when you sell! Don't ever forget that truism!

You have to have a win - win deal. That is another one of Mike's gems. I am sure he got it from somewhere, but he is the one who told it to me.

If you squeeze your vendor too hard and you do too good a deal, the chances are that between you agreeing it and getting to exchange, the deal is going to fall out of bed and what have you got from that? You have a bill with the valuation company, you have a bill with your solicitor and you haven't got a property. So, well done. You have had an infinite loss, all right? Because you are never going to recover that money! So, you must have a win - win deal. It's not optional. Do not squeeze the vendor too tightly.

I pick up deals all the time because I have been willing to concede an extra £500 or £1k, or exchange faster, or complete sooner, or let the vendor stay after purchase. Literally hundreds of minor concessions, when applied well, make deals happen and keep deals in bed. Make a point of conceding something to the vendor that is of little or no importance to you, but that they think is important to you and then bring that up when you need them to back down.

I love buying property. I just so enjoy the negotiations. And if you love something, if you are passionate about it, you are going to be good at it, which is why I am really good at negotiating.

So, if you get a bite when you have put your offers out, negotiate well and that will add value to your deal. I don't go into a deal until I know what their price is likely to be. I always know what my top price is before I go into the deal, and then I start to negotiate up to where I think the vendor's price is.

To use a concrete example, let's say that I know I can make money on £110k. I will start negotiating at £102k to £103k. I'll let them push me up to £107k - £108k and maybe even £110k max. But I will probably walk away at £108k, knowing that 75% of the time they will call me back and negotiate me up to £110k. Don't be afraid to walk away.

When you make your offer, each time you make your offer, restate your benefits. Don't be boring about it. Say it in a different way if you have to. Say it with a laugh in your voice. Say whatever you have to, but restate your benefits to the agent when you make the offer.

Remind him why you are such a good purchaser, why he should let you buy. And why he should go back to the vendor and work on the vendor to get them to accept your offer. Restate your benefits. That will save you thousands at this stage. This is the bit where you are making your money. This is really where property money is made. Have your benefits written down.

You move a bit, they move a lot, but be nice about it. You offer £102k. They say, well, we wanted £115k. Will you increase your offer? No. Will you tell me how much money you would like to pay? £102k. Well, we will take £112k. And then you go back and say, well, £112k's still way out of my ballpark, I am afraid. I **would** be willing to go to £104k.

They will go, oh, crumbs (or similar word), you know. And then you **MUST** restate your benefits. Give them the reasons why they should take your offer, give them slowly, and confidently, but make sure you give them all without pi**ing the agent off.

Well, I have nothing to sell. I am ready to go right now. I can put this in the hands of my solicitor this afternoon. We can have an exchange on it in **just** eight weeks. We can have a completion within ten weeks or nine weeks, whatever. Restate your benefits.

The vendor will be thinking, what do we do? They will say to their boyfriend or girlfriend (whatever), 'well, what we need, what we really need is to get £108k out of this. But you said we must get £110k. Yes, but this person is ready to go and that means we could have actually sold this and we can get on with our lives. I think we can afford to let it go for that. Yeah, you are right, Ok. So, what about if we go back and say to him that we will accept £110k?'

So the agent comes back to you and says, they will take £110k! You go, now, look, I am willing to move a bit you know, but I am sorry, I cannot meet that! All right, you have got me. I give in. I will go to £105k! But, I really think that is about the final I can go to. You have got to tell him that, more or less – that is it! Right? That is it.

Did you see there? I just put in the **more or less** bit. So, I slipped that in on purpose to the estate agent. That is more or less it. then you say, 'Well no, no, that is it. £105k is my final offer.'

So, the estate agent goes back to him and he says, look, I think I can get £107k out of him, but I think that is going to be it. So reluctantly, the vendor agrees to lower the price to £107.5k. You very quickly sigh, and then pause for about 10 seconds (If you have trouble pausing, then I use the line from Reggie Perrin. CJ said it, '1,2,3,4 make them wait outside the door, 5,6,7,8 always pays to make them wait, 9,10,11,12 come!'), then I say I will pay £105.5k and complete in 10 weeks, but that is my final offer (do not pause after you deliver the price, get the whole benefit out).

The estate agent goes to the vendor, look this guy will buy right now for £105.5k, and he will complete in 10 weeks. I can get £106k out of him if you will accept it. This is a good offer and I think you should accept it. Vendor comes back and says, we'll accept £106k.

So the agent comes back and says £106k and it's a deal. You sigh again and reluctantly, you say ok! **You let them win the last round! You always let them win the last round. If you win it, watch the deal like a hawk. Chances are they are thinking they failed. They will not like that emotional feeling so the deal is built on sand! Letting them win builds the deal on solid ground and the foundations are reasonable. Just remember that until exchange, you are in an earthquake zone!**

Now, I could have gone in here and got this property for £105.75k. Or I could have negotiated hard and got it for £105.5k. Or if I want to be really, really pedantic, I could probably have got it for £104k. But, when you negotiate on a win-win deal, I let them win the last round. And I go, fair enough. **I don't want to be unreasonable now (this line saves deals later).** They are seeing me as a reasonable person.

Hear those words, **'fair enough'?** I am the one who is being reasonable with them and I have knocked their price down by £9k. But I am the one who is being reasonable. Isn't that fantastic? Even though they are being reasonable too, I have taken the high ground. And the agent goes back and he says, I have managed to get it through at £106k.

Now, before I had appeared as a buyer, the estate agent would have been an idiot if he had sold it for anything less than £110k. But now, the estate agent looks good to the vendor. So, through clever negotiating, I have made it look like the estate agent did his job really well, the vendors got what they wanted and I came across as a bit of a loser on the deal, but a nice guy who let them get rid of their property for a good price.

Do you see how I have used words to phrase what happened means that we have a win - win situation? They won the last round. There is no bitter taste in their mouth. The last thing they think about me is a nice thing. I have not left them with a bitter taste.

That £500 I have paid extra will mean this property will go all the way to exchange. Remember: only once it is exchanged is the deal built on rock and you are out of the earthquake zone.

And you know, I could have thrown in there, well, I want to do £1k deposit, or I could save that for later. That is always a good one to drop in later, if you know the agent well. Then, you can do the access between exchange and completion and all those sort of deal variations. It allows you a little bit more negotiation if you drop it in a bit later. After you agree on the price, you must be true to your word and you never ever chip the price; the fact that you do not chip the price gives you credibility that is gold dust! (Unless the valuer throws something up which, of course, provides you with the opportunity to re-negotiate downwards. Just knowing what to do here, will be worth literally thousands to you over your new lifetime as a property investor, but it is too detailed for this book.)

As I said, try and let them win the last round when you can. A minor concession somewhere near the end, preferably at the end. Right at the end, I like a minor concession. But at least the last stage before the end, you make sure they have won something.

Okay, you've done it. You've got your deal. Now you have got to come up with the goods. You have to complete on this property in a timely timescale. You have got to do it. You have got to basically know what is going on and make it happen.

Because if you have bought from this agent once and you have made it pleasant for him, guess what? He is going to want you to buy from him again. And you are going to want to buy from him again. And because he knows that you are a good purchaser, he will go out and find a deal for you.

This means that most of your hard work will be done for the next time. Or what you can do is, you can mess them around, take ages to do each stage of it and the estate agent will not ever want to hear your name again, let alone offer you a deal. So, you have got to come up with the goods. It is really, really important!

Remember, it is all still a game until you get to exchange. So, if your surveyor goes out and says, there is this problem on it, then go back and re-negotiate. Get some money off. If the surveyor goes out and basically you find something untoward, like you have been told you it's £750 a year maintenance and it turns out to be £1.4k a year maintenance (£650 more than you were previously told), you should be able to negotiate £600 x 5 = £3k off the price.

Now comes the really good bit. Ask for it back at completion so you get £3k back at completion. Instead of having it taken off the price, you now get an 85 per cent mortgage on the full amount and get £3k back. Now that, at times, is going to be 25% of your deposit. That is a bit clever, isn't it? It is a trick. I do not use it very often now, but we do use it occasionally. If their solicitor is uncomfortable with that, then adjust the deal so that they will pay £3k in advance maintenance payments.

I used it a lot at the start when I had no money to do deals with. Now, it is just like, well, it is just another bit of negotiation and we don't need to do it as much. We hardly ever do it but you may find it useful.

Or maybe it is a case of implying it. Imply that is what you want and then concede to make the win-win deal look even better for them. So, use it. Whatever comes out at valuation, use it to your benefit. The valuation is a time for profit.

Remember: you are in charge. You are the buyer. Once the price has been agreed, the only option the vendor has is to pull the property from you. If it gets to the stage where the vendor is threatening to pull the property from you, say, yeah, pull the property from me then. Restate your benefits, but say, pull the property from me. And then remind the vendor of the problems he had before you came along. You are in charge. You are the buyer. Once the price has been agreed, you call the shots. It is your deal.

26

I Suppose I Ought To Cover Mortgages?

As you may have guessed by now, this book wasn't designed as a property investment manual. It was designed to inspire you to get into Property Investing.

I choose the word inspire very carefully, as this book isn't here to motivate you. If that's all it did , then you would continually need further motivation. But with inspiration, you won't need any further motivation from me.

Why is it that when choosing a mortgage we usually either go to someone we know who was probably recommended by a non-expert? Or from a search we have done online? The importance here of what professional to use cannot be overstated.

I'm not going to advise you on mortgages. Even though I have personally been responsible for more than most IFAs ever have been, I am not licensed to give advice, so I want to make it crystal clear that I am not an expert on mortgages and I am not giving you advice! Ar*e covered!

The first rule is that you must use a Mortgage Packager and not go direct to the lender. Forget that it is a cheaper deal, as that is just an expense of doing business, and I'm not going to go into details here about the mortgages as the book's long enough. I've written over

20,000 words (over 1/6th of this book) on mortgages on the site already and I'm not done. Why? Because they are constantly changing. And mostly it is stuff that you only 'may' need for reference. You can do this without ever being a site member, the site is there for people who think that the investment of their money will make them more than they are investing.

You can use an IFA, but only if he/she guarantees you that they will go through a mortgage packager. They will know how to find one, or you can get the info on the site. I'm not going to stick the details of who I recommend here, otherwise they will be bombarded with enquiries that mainly don't go anywhere and their standard will drop. So if you want to find out who I recommend and why, then you'll have to search the site for it.

I'm not making this bit easy on purpose because there are plenty of IFA's and packagers out there. Some of them are good, and some not so. Who knows you may find one better than I've found.

So why do you need a packager?

A packager puts the whole case together before they go to a lender and as such, if the valuation comes in wrong, then they can instruct another one before they send the info to the lender. When you get a down-valuation and your lender knows, hopefully you'll realise the value of using a mortgage packager, so you won't make the same mistake again.

A valuation or val can come in wrong for any one of a thousand or more reasons. But if you go to the only lender in the country who can do your particular deal with a val that isn't right first time, then you'll have to jump through some hoops to get it to work! That's even if they'll let you jump through them!

With my style of investing, you need two mortgage lenders and you use the first like a bridging loan company.

You want them to offer you a discount rate with NO REDEMPTION PENALTIES and a cheap arrangement fee. This mortgage does not need a packager, but it is very unwise to use more than one mortgage arranger at a time.

Then when your refurb is finished and usually within six months, you go for a second mortgage. Whether you have to take a tied redemption penalty deal will depend on where you are in the country. The majority of people will have to do that. And you tie the property up for 2, 3 or 5 years. You have to estimate which one is best. At the time of this edit (September 2007) I am looking for three year deals but I'll take two years.

Most mortgage lenders have a restriction that does not let you refinance within the first six months of ownership.

Why? Because they do not understand what they are lending against. I know that may sound crazy but it is true. They don't understand it. Therefore their only way of being progressive is to look at what has happened and then change their policy. This is why the majority of lenders will always be 3-5 years behind the game.

The most progressive lender currently is Mortgage Express and they will lend immediately on ownership, i.e.

you can refinance one second after you have purchased the property. All they need is a valuation to stand up - a nd of course the purchase funds!

So this means you NEVER want to use Mortgage Express for your purchase mortgage. (Obviously this is current info and I regularly update my recommendations on the site.)

This information could be out of date tomorrow because we are moving into a world of more and more creative finance. As I write this, I am currently in the period between exchange and completion on another property that I've bought for my mum. I paid £385k for it. But I got it to value for £475k and when it completes shortly, I won't have put £1 in, and I'll have cash back as well!

As I said earlier, this book doesn't cover no-money-down deals, but this is just to give you an idea of what is possible. And my mum's property is not one of those new build deals that are so popular now either. My mum's property is 10 years old and I bought through a normal agent. The full story of how I did it is on my personal blog on the site.

When it comes to buy-to-let, most lenders will consider you as long as you earn more than £25k/year. Mortgage Express actually requires £0 income, because they are more intelligent than most lenders, and they loan based on the investment alone. As I've said, most other lenders are 3-5 years behind the times, and I think MX (Mortgage Express) went over to it two years ago. But I would always advise approaching any lender with over £25k earnings that you can self certify.

There are ways you can do this without breaking the rules if you don't earn over £25k. I'm not going to cover too many here because I will be hauled across the coals for this sort of info, but there are plenty of membership site forums on property investing where people can offer ideas on how to get over this one. But an obvious one is, say you have less than £25k or no income but own one or several investment properties where the rent total brings you over £25k a year. Then you can self certify your income as over £25k. Most don't ask what you have got left so you can self certify that your income is over £25k. You have to think creative here.

When approaching your IFA, consider your responses carefully so as not to trip yourself up. You can't break the rules, but you can answer questions in the most favourable way possible.

27

The Shortcut Can Often Be The Long Route In Disguise

Anthony Robbins talks about how self help books don't get read, as do many experts in the self help/knowledge industry. Some say that just 1% actually gets read and then only 10% get acted on. That would mean just one person would take action for every thousand books sold! Personally I would say 1% of books sold probably get acted upon, but it's only my opinion.

Is this awful or what? I was determined when I wrote this book that because of the content and the way it was sold that I would out perform that pathetic percentage.

Well the good news is, that I have considerably out performed it. I don't know what percentage of books doesn't get read and I don't know what percentage of people take action and then don't let me know. But I do know what percentage definitely have taken action thanks to the hundreds, soon to be thousands, of emails I receive.

Currently over 8% of people buying the book have sent me emails thanking me and telling me what they have done and every time I meet a group of people, the minority have emailed me but the majority say they have taken action and not emailed me. So I think it's fair to say that at least 20% of the people who have bought the book actually take action, which out performs every self help book that I have ever heard of. Now that's something I'm proud of and the Universe owes me BIG TIME! ☺

The reason for telling you this is to give you something very positive before I give you something that can be taken negatively, depending on your attitude.

One of the spin-offs I created when I wrote this book was the number of people who went into off plan property investment with the one goal of overall portfolio value as their primary goal.

The primary goal, for those who have not read between the lines, is cash flow. And then second to that is Property Investment which leads to overall portfolio value.

Now before I start, I am not dismissing new builds or the companies that sell them. New builds/off plan properties can work really well. They are just not my recommended strategy, well at least not for when someone is starting out. They can be done when someone is starting out but they are quick and easy and you can easily over-do it because they can be free to get hold of.

Here is an article I wrote on the site recently entitled 'Is this shortcut the long route in disguise?'

START***

A common question I am often asked is whether I buy new build property or if I would recommend that someone else did. Firstly, I say no I don't, but that doesn't mean to say I wouldn't.

I think when some people make the choice to go into property investment what happens is that they are overloaded with information, and frankly they don't know which way to go. So what happens at the end of it is an emotional trip whereby they become certain that if they don't do something now, they will not take action and all their efforts will be wasted.

They've studied everywhere and they want this elusive fortune that everybody except them is able to get hold of, so in an emotional state they make the decision to take what looks like the easy route. You know the one, the one where everything is done for you. All you need to do is sign on the old dotted line and cough up either a small or no deposit to get to be the proud owner of your first investment property.

Now I am not saying that buying a new build property is wrong. I am saying buying a new build property is wrong when you don't know the market that you are buying in. Without this due diligence, you are just throwing the dice and hoping it will work out. The funny thing is that it certainly will if you have the cashflow to sustain whatever comes along for the next 10 years or so.

Those who don't know their market and haven't done adequate cash flow provisioning are suffering the worst fate that any property investor can suffer, repossession. I am asked by people regularly how they can get out of the mess they are in, they bought £1,000,000 portfolios or much more and they are now being eaten alive by mortgages with tenants paying a lot less rent than they have going out, or no rent. The worst case I have seen was a £4,000,000 portfolio that only cost £25,000 to get hold of, but only has one tenant in the whole lot of it. These poor people were losing nearly £20,000/mth and were already four months behind with their mortgage payments when they spoke to me.

The lure of easy money is very clear when I look at new build, but in my estimation, only 5-10% of the new build properties deliver all that was promised. The rest under perform. Now, if you can handle that under performance then there really is no big deal, and why not sit and wait to make your money. Just beware of the pitfalls. The biggest rise in auction properties is coming from newbie property investors getting rid of their new build properties.

There's a link to an article below that a member sent me from the Daily Telegraph which really demonstrates just how precarious this market really is and just how seriously this market can damage your wealth. Flats that were previously sold for £249,995 last year were sold at auction for just £140,000.

Just buying any old property and expecting to make 10%/year growth doesn't work! You have to know you've made money and released your equity or you have to buy in an area where there will be more than adequate demand.

Think about it. If it's a new build and there are 10 in the block in a town where they are not building any more new builds for at least 18 months, and they are not building within 500 yards of this one, then it is probably a good bet (but still a bet if you haven't done your due diligence).

If it's a new build with a 30% discount and cash back on completion in a block of 50 flats in a town centre where they have recently built over 1,000 new build flats, then it is probably a bad bet. It's not rocket science is it?

You can't just abdicate control of your money to some developer whose job it is to sell you his property for the maximum he can make out of it.

The advantage you have when buying a single unit at a time and doing it my way is that you are protected from the herd. With new build you are running with the herd and none of the herd is likely to have much of a sense of direction, as they all probably made the decision to buy in the same way you will have done.

Now I am not saying don't do it - just consider that this little shortcut may well be the long route in disguise.

Best wishes

Andy

Here is the link to the Telegraph article. Read both pages of it:

http://www.telegraph.co.uk/money/main.jhtml?xml=/money/2007/07/23/cmbuytolet23.xml

As I said I am regularly emailed by another person who is about to go under because they underestimated how hard this area really was. The common mistake they make is cashflow.

New builds can work, so this isn't a new build bashing! I just wrote this book to make people wealthy, and if readers are going into the new build market because I have convinced them of the virtues of property, I don't want them going in blindly. I could make new builds/off plan work very successfully, but I haven't yet as I have never had the need.

There are hundreds of property companies selling off plan properties, and some of these can work as I've said. But the majority, (and call it an unfair generalisation if you will, but I see too many people fail here not to give this an adequate warning), really struggle after the sale. They struggle with mortgages, they struggle with renting in the first place, then re-letting, and achieving the rents needed to even get close to mortgage interest.

These cash back on completion deals are there for a reason. The reason is that they have to make the deal so appealing that you'll take it, so you won't mind as much about the cash burn you've got for the following years, basically because the price was too high for the rental market.

There are many other pitfalls in this market, and I really don't want to cover all of them as it is unfair of me because I'm not giving more balance to the view point. I'll be happy to bring a balance on the site when I'm asked. But this book is really to cover just one style and this is stepping outside of that style.

One safety net if you do go into it is to get your own valuation carried out, from a valuer on your lenders' panel and NOT the valuer that the builder used. You'll see why on receipt of the val that it was worth blowing the £200-£500 to find out before you said yes. Always remember, their job is to sell you a property today, and as Dolf De Roos said, 'the deal of a lifetime comes along every week!' So walk away and make your decisions slowly, very slowly. I have members on the site who've rushed in and tied up all of their capital because they didn't do their homework first.

Quite often the money down but all of it plus cash back on completion deals seem like the Holy Grail, but the shortcut can often be the long route in disguise. My way of doing it seems like more work, but you have put your work in at the start and after your first re-mortgage you are virtually free of risk. With off plan and what are known as gifted deposits, it is really easy at the start. It only becomes difficult when you are trying to re-mortgage, let or re-let the property, value the property for a refinance, or worse. Valuing the property on purchase can often be tricky despite what you are told, so read the fine print and get your own val done first! Don't be cheap here; otherwise it could cost you a fortune. Look at this expense for what it is, an insurance policy against you losing your wealth.

As I mentioned briefly in the article, one email I received was from someone who had managed to acquire a new build portfolio worth over £4,000,000 with just £25,000. He and his partner went into it with reserves of £180k. Twelve months in and only one of them let, all of their money was gone and they were in arrears going backwards at about £18,000 a month. I doubt they will have survived, but I have not heard back and they were already at breaking point. Try and avoid this if you can!

The highest growth in auction properties at this time is coming from first time buy-to-let investors and their properties are the new builds. The companies you buy from are not responsible here. You are!

A friend of mine was actually threatened with prison if she did not complete, following a property she bought two years earlier for £185k with a gifted deposit of £40k. Yes, makes you think really, doesn't it. Is this really a shortcut? In other words, the company said she was buying at a discount, so a no- money-down deal. Nice! Yet when it came time to finance it, the best valuation she could achieve was £165k and the best loan she could obtain was £140k. She was one of the fortunate ones who could come up with the money to complete, unlike some of the others!

Then there are the people who complete together with the other 30, 40 or 50 flats and they are trying to rent theirs out at the same time as every other landlord. This causes property deflation, but that's the least of their worries! They now can't rent it, or if they can, then they are doing it for far less than they thought they were going to have coming in. I have seen people go under here as well.

New build and off plan can work when done well, and I can make it work. But it is not as easy as it first seems and it is probably the long route in disguise. At the start it is easy, and then once you are trapped, it gets hard. My way is hard at the start and then once you are trapped it gets easy.

The off plan route has a hidden-in-plain sight dark side as well. What happens to you when you look at those new properties in the stylish new blocks, with brochures filled with pictures that have been dressed to sell?

You start to think, 'Well who wouldn't want to live there? They are going to be so easy to rent. I am going to be able to show this brochure to my friends.'

You've already been looking at those previously-owned, converted or 1970s properties and subconsciously thinking, 'Well, they're not very nice' or, 'Well I wouldn't like to live there.'

You know what's happened, don't you? You've let your emotions in and I've already told you there is no room in property investing for your emotions. New build/off plan is a desire product. It is something you want. Hell I want them! They look great! I would love to be buying loads of beautiful properties around the country, and I would love to be able to say that I own four flats in Gun Wharf etc and that they are each worth £300,000. That's nearly double the average property in my portfolio, so it would be a lot less work for me to buy them at the start.

So why don't I?

Because I don't make property buying decisions on what I want, or what looks easy. I make my **Investment decisions** on what makes money now, what makes money in the near future and what makes money in the next five to seven years. I make my decisions on whether they make money, nothing else!

I'm nearly finished here with this warning and to all of you who are already going, okay Andy, I get it, please don't go on, then skip to the next chapter - as long as you know that **I haven't said don't buy new build. Just do your due diligence and think slowly.**

A couple of last points and then we'll leave this off-track area alone.

Why do you think I like to buy the low-end properties? Because the mortgage lenders set the terms and it is easier for me to get full 85% loans on properties worth under £180k than it is for me to get 85% loans on properties worth £360k. So I buy at £85k, knowing that for the next seven years, I'll be able to release money even if the lender's policies don't become easier (which they will, but that's not covered here in the book).

Now when you buy an off plan flat for £240k that is apparently worth £315k (looks appealing doesn't it - especially after reading what's in this book?) let's say you get a mortgage for £250k and get all of your costs back and some cash.

You're not worried that you need to pay monthly charges of a mortgage at £1,250, a managing agent of £140, cover voids of £100 and pay the maintenance and ground rent of £150.

So really, you need to rent that for £1,640 just to cover expenses. The mortgage lender has lent it to you on the basis that you'll rent it for £1,400. You think, 'well that £240 is manageable, after all I'm getting £4k back at completion!' But what happens when yours and the other 33 properties that were all sold to landlords go up for rent on the same day? None of you know that the local market lets are really only £1,100/ month at best (despite what the valuer has said) and now there's an over flowing market of properties all identical at this price point. What does that do to the market?

Well, it's excessive downward price pressure. The rents are now going to be at or less than the rent levels of previously-owned properties. So now, if you can actually get yours rented, what you end up with is £750 a month and that's before the managing agent's fees so you have an outgoing of £1,640 and an income of £675. If losing nearly £1,000 a month on this one property is not a problem to you and you can afford this sort of cashburn, then you can still make it work. But what if you bought two or three? How long could you stomach £12k, £24k or £36k a year? And that is on the basis that you actually get it rented. There are no stats that I could find on how long it takes to rent properties in their first year, but I'd imagine that it's an average of 4-6 months. So your cash back at completion didn't last too long there!

Now I've painted a bad picture here and it does not happen to this degree in the majority of cases, but it does happen far, far too often to be a considered a freak occurrence. And there some of the elements mentioned there in every new build experience. Just attend a few auctions if you doubt what I'm saying here. All of this can be avoided by due diligence.

But that wasn't even my point here. My point was to tell you that let's say you got through that minefield, and let's say you made it work as the average one does and then you were only burning £200 to £500 a month like most do. Then all you need to be able to do is refinance the property when the price goes up to £400k and release capital to cover the cash burn. Obviously to get it to that point could be a lot longer than you think, because the property may not have actually been worth £315k!

Just because it has been valued by three different valuers, does not mean that it is worth that price. Never forget that.

It's a lot more difficult to release 85% at a level of £400k than it is at £180k and that's because the mortgages loaned on rental income are in the minority of cases.

So if you go into that market, understand that it is not the safest route to wealth, and that it does look a lot quicker than the way I am showing you to do it. Funny thing is, it probably is in the first few years, but after three years doing it my way the foundations of your wealth will be properly constructed, whereas do it the other way and you could still be building on sand.

That's enough! In conclusion, buy new build if you want to. They can work, just do your due diligence and leave your emotions at the door of the show home. You have been warned!

28

Having Fun with Builders

Here is the simple, but effective Golden Rule: You only refurbish what you have to. Not a penny more. You have to get a balance between what it will rent for and what it will value for.

Basically, you are trying to get a property to feel right when somebody walks in. It doesn't have to feel that it is the most wonderful property on the face of the planet or the best flat they have ever been to. All that is pretty irrelevant.

The valuer wants to feel this will rent easily. Why? Because the lender wants to know that you are not going to have trouble paying the mortgage. What matters most to the lender is that it will rent easily. What matters second most to the lender is the value of it.

So the first thing is, as the house doctor says, kerb appeal. If it looks c**p from the road, then you bought the wrong one. The valuer has to feel that the property is rentable or your valuation will suck. They have to feel it is a saleable property as well – even though you are not planning on selling – or the valuation will suck.

When the valuer walks through the door of one of our properties he sees barley white or white walls. This gives the re-furbished property a 'new property' feel. Whether you like barley white or not, I do not care and <u>NEITHER MUST YOU</u>! What you think and feel is irrelevant. Believe me, more money has been wasted on property development by people who refurbished to suit their own tastes than probably any other area of property investing.

You need to have the tenant to think in the first fraction of a second, 'Oh, this is quite nice.' That immediate positive feeling will be pretty much the only thing they remember at the end of a day of viewing properties. That is what you **must** aim for and hit every time.

So, your first priority is kerb appeal. They **must** have an immediate positive feeling about that. Your second **must** is to get that second hit of 'quite nice' appeal when they go through the door. Those two **musts** seal the deal. This is primarily why we can rent property quickly.

Neutral works best when it comes to floors too. A beige colour, not dark brown, but a darkish beige carpet hides most of the dirt and it looks pleasant when they walk in. Again, we are doing this for valuation purposes and tenants as well. When they walk in the first time, it is clean and fresh and has carpets that were vacuumed the day before. So the place looks brand new, both for the tenant and for the valuer. If you are re-letting it, check for smells and if you think you need to get the carpet cleaned, do it – people who rent can smell things too.

If there is anything amiss – anything that is unfinished – we always comment on it. We say, oh, they are just finishing the top at the moment. This tells the person viewing the place that if there is something amiss, you know about it and it is being dealt with. You don't want to wait for someone else to point it out. Your failure to notice something or hanging back and waiting for them to say something to you about it means that you may not be a good landlord. In some cases that may be all that is needed to pass your rental property by. So do what needs doing and own up to anything that is amiss, but don't spend a penny more on the refurbishment than you have to.

Neutral is the key word here. Do not personalise it, ever. You should always be thinking de-personalise and neutralise. If you want to personalise it, buy another home and personalise that. Never ever personalise rental properties. You are selling this property to your prospective tenants and to valuers.

I don't care what you think about this, 250+ properties and going strong means that I am right! I could tell you stories of people who I have helped who still do not get this. They have come to me and said, 'We are going to paint the house a really pale mauve and make features of the chimney breasts.' They wasted time and money personalising the house and then had trouble getting it to value right and finding a tenant who wanted to rent it. When they did eventually find a tenant, the tenant only agreed to take it if they could at least re-paint the lounge to a neutral colour. This is just one example of a countless number.

This is a flat that rents out to people. It is their home, NOT YOURS! You are not in this because you want to go around and look at that flat. If you were in this because you wanted to sit at your dinner table and say, 'Oh, yes, I did the lovely peach coloured walls in our investment property' then fine. But that is just a waste of money and a waste of time. And to you people who are thinking, 'Well, he has got great ideas, but he is not quite right here'

- yes I am! I know what sells and what doesn't and that is why I am unemotional about property. Other than the pleasure I feel towards my property when I get paid by it, it is an object to me; an object that provides for mine and my family's future.

Redecorating to suit your taste, a) Probably costs more and that means it is a waste of money, and b) Puts more people off renting it, which means it is a waste of time and a waste of money. You did not get into property because you want to be an interior designer; you got into property to make money. In order to make money, one of the Golden Rules is not to waste money!

All right? I hope everyone's got it and I hope me banging on about it will at least stop some of you from wasting your profits. I know that by the time you have bought the property and it is time to start the painting, the words written here will be long forgotten, but I have to try!

I change the colour of the paint I use in refurbishing to match the colour of the paint that is being used in all new build houses. The majority of them are having that sort of colour at the moment so I do the same because I know the valuer subconsciously associates new and value. Does this work? Who knows? If I have to paint, I might as well use a colour that may have an edge and wins a better valuation or two along the way.

When valuers go around, if the impression in their mind is that it reminds them of a new property, chances are you will get a better valuation. Even if it is a refurbished property, which all of the ones you should buy are, painting it like the new builds leaves a subtle impression in their mind that it is a new property. Subtlety when it comes to valuations is very, very much the key. (We will come back to valuations shortly.)

So, don't personalise it. It is not a reflection on you; people won't think you have no taste! And who cares if they do? You will be sleeping at night on a big pile of money! It is important to keep the reason you are doing this in your mind all the time, so that you can continually ask the most important question in refurbishment. This question will serve you well and save you money each and every time you are about to spend some. Here it is, here it comes, learn it, keep it in your mind, it is very powerful:

Will it add value?

Our business mentor, Mike, said to us once, 'Boys, when you spend £500 you want to know you have got at least £500 of value!' Words that have served me well. Initially, you think, 'yeah seems pretty simple', but this is one of the core things that has helped me to become rich. If you apply this simple question to everything you do and every time you spend money, you will easily find the reason why you are not rich yet.

So, back to the question. You are standing in a DIY superstore and you're buying some light fittings. You are about to pick them up. Before you pick them up, ask yourself, **'If I buy these, will they add value to the property?'** If the answer is no, look for something else. If the answer is yes, ask yourself, **'Could I find something cheaper that would add more or the same value?'** If the answer is no, buy the fittings. If the answer is yes, carry on looking.

That's it. Every single time you go to spend money on your property, ask yourself those two questions and it will save you a fortune over the years. Even though the chances are good that by the time you get to your property, you will forget this and you will send someone else to do the buying, I ask you to remember one thing: **no-one looks after your money as well as you do**, or at least should do!

Also remember that there can be no emotions in buying property; you cannot be emotional about this at all. All right? I mean, you see it on the telly what they do. It is just dire how it is considered the norm to vastly exceed their budgets. That's their profit they are spending. Are they mad?

I know that a lot of this is just done for the TV audience, but I think if you are considered an expert and you speak from a position of expertise, then you should only give advice that is right, whether it is TV or not. If someone's going to mess it up, you have got to try and stop them, or at least show them what is going to happen. Put your neck out, please!

These people have been chosen by the TV production staff to be the voice of experience and educate people in property investment in this country. You would think the least they could do is put some passion behind it. Thankfully, I had never watched any of these shows before going out and doing it myself. If I had done, who knows where I would have ended up? I can tell you that if I went on TV, it would be like, what are you doing that for? No, you don't want to do that. Stop that. Do this.

You know, I had somebody very close to me in business decide he was going to do his own property last year. He spent ages deciding on all the different bits, whether the inset around the fireplace should be one colour or another. I told him just to paint it all barley white. And he said, 'No, no, no. I don't want to.'

In the end, I think he got out of the property without losing any money, because he was using a flipping property strategy. But he spent months with about £50k tied up and made nothing, because he did not use the expertise that was around him. He did not do what he was told to do. He bought the wrong type of property in the first place and employed the wrong strategy with it.

Property is all about numbers and all about your budget. You have got to set your budget right from the start. You set your budget when you first view a property.

I have shown you how to work out a budget, and on my website there is a simple sheet we use to record the work that needs to be done.

Don't be afraid if you go over on your budget because there was something about the property you did not know about or realise at the start. You will catch more things the more you buy. It is called falling forward and mistakes are just an opportunity for greater profit later, as long as you capitalise on them happening by learning from them.

Let's say the boiler dies on you. Let's say there were some electrics that caught you out. That is a mistake. Learn from it and move on, but don't let the future worry of losing £2k on poor electrics or something else you might be unsure about, make you miss out on a £30k profit on a deal. Do you understand what I am trying to say? Yes, you lost a bit, but in the big picture you made a lot and you would not get caught like that on every property – maybe one in eight. So don't waste an opportunity to make money on a deal. Do the deal first, then find out whether or not the electrics will need to be done. Going about it the other way is just wasting time and may cost you the deal.

You don't beat yourself up about this sort of surprise. I am not a plumber. I'm not an electrician. I am not a gas engineer. Sometimes I buy a property and I have a problem with it. Deal with it and take your profit – no emotions. As I am buying 100 properties a year, I just think of it as rolling with the punches. It is simplistic, I know, but it really works well for us. We always ensure a huge profit from all deals so that when the one in eight comes along with a problem like this, it is just a dip in the profit returned.

We bought a property recently, a lovely big Victorian house that we converted to five flats. It was an HMO (House of Multiple Occupation). We did not notice and the valuer did not tell us that there was a roof problem. It has cost us £2k to get it sorted out. That was not in our budget. Some of you will be thinking, sue the valuer. You are probably right, but what good would that do? Yes, we 'might' get our money, but at what cost? I am not talking about monetary cost. I am talking about our reputation. The valuer would never want to value anything for us again and he would probably warn other valuers he knows to look out for us as well.

In property investing you roll with the punches! On this deal alone my profit is going to be between £250k and £300k, even after blowing this £2k and a further £5k on unseen electrical work. What is more, this deal was fully funded by a joint venture partner, so this whole deal has cost me nothing at all but a share of the profits.

Do you see what I mean? Sometimes there are going to be hidden expenses that mean your budget will go over. Deal with it and learn to accept this as just one of the insignificant little snags of being in property investment.

When buying a flat, you haven't got the problem with roofs, you haven't got the problem with the structural because that is the freeholder's responsibility. The chance of getting big, big mistakes is really limited to the electrics and the boiler. So your level of mistakes is not going to be too high on the properties I am advising you to go for.

So do not beat yourself up if you make a mistake and you go over your budget on something like that, because you are not an expert. You are going to make this sort of mistake occasionally. I still make those sorts of mistakes, as I said above. Do you think they bother me? I don't even consider them mistakes any more. I consider them part of the numbers game. I buy 10 properties. One of them has a boiler problem. I add £150 to every refurb budget to cover the one I get wrong. It is called a contingency factor.

However, if you spend money on a nice tap set and a fancy dimmer switch, you *should* beat yourself up about wasting money, because those things are a waste of bl***y money. You don't need them. You want basic. The light goes on, the light goes off. Tenants don't usually view property at night anyway! They won't notice a dimmer switch and if they do, it won't be the deciding factor in whether they rent or not.

If the tenant wants to come in and put a dimmer switch on instead, let him speak to your managing agent and ask if he can put a dimmer switch on. You don't want to put a dimmer switch on. That does not help to rent the property. Keep it bl***y simple, people. You don't have to do this. People go, it's got chrome taps and brass wall sockets. Stuff that! You are not interested! You are not living in it! It is not your home!

Leave your emotions at the door. No, better still, leave your emotions on the sofa before you get in the car to go to your rental property, before you get to the door!

EMOTIONS DO NOT HELP YOU MAKE MONEY IN PROPERTY. THEY COST YOU MONEY!!!

Just say no to emotions when you think about refurbishment. Any emotions at all are a bad thing when it comes to property investment, especially on a refurb, because refurbs can eat your profit very, very quickly - as you will have seen by watching the TV.

Tenants will often put the things that are missing in the flats for you. When I first started renting, the managing agents said this will not rent or that will not rent because it does not have a shower. This is bul****t, as long as the prop's in a good location, it will rent. And there is a benefit to not having a shower: you would be amazed at the number of times tenants approach us and ask to fit these sorts of things themselves. We say yes, of course, as long as it is done well. And what do you think the benefit is for the tenant? They now have what they need and want in the flat; they have invested their own money in it; and they want to see a return on that money, so they will stay there longer!

If you go and waste money on something, beat yourself up about it. Maybe that way you will not go and make the same damn stupid mistake   again!

Get the job out on time. This is really key to profiting in property. If you budgeted four weeks to get the job out, remember that it's four weeks of mortgage payments. Every day has a cost and every day longer that you are on the job has a cost. Work out what your daily cost for the property is and remind yourself at the start and end of each day how much you are spending today. That should keep you focused. Don't forget council tax, insurance, electricity, water, your time and, of course, the mortgage. Add it all up for one year and divide it by 365 and that is what it is costing you for every day the tenant isn't paying you the money, all right?

Your costs

Let's say you have an £85,000 mortgage on a £100,000 property and you borrowed the other £20,000 to carry out the refurb and fund the deposit.

Mortgage interest @ 5.5%	£4,675 / yr
so	£12.81 / day
Buildings Insurance	£150 / yr
so	£0.41 / day
Electricity	£400 / yr
so	£1.10 / day
Gas	£400 / yr
so	£1.10 / day
Water	£400 / yr
so	£1.10 / day
Council Tax	£750 / yr

so	£2.06 / day
Other loan interest	£2,000 / yr
so	£5.48 / day
Total	£24.06 / day
Or	£168.42 / week or
	£729.82 / month

So, that needs to be in your budget as well. When we budget, we budget refurb time. It is on every job. And then, if we manage to negotiate access between exchange and completion, that just improves our situation. We do not budget to have refurb time, to get access between exchange and completion and then not get access and have to add that to the cost. The point is to come in under budget. A budget is not a target – it's a budget and in my opinion you should plan to come in between 5-15% under it as a general rule, as this will demonstrate you are in good financial control.

The eternal question is, do I do it myself and save money? The answer is no, get a builder to do it. You are in property investing for the money; you are an investor, not a builder. Just because you can learn how to do something does not mean you should do it.

Just imagine those six weeks of learning and pain you will go through (depending on your level of skill). Anyone who is blind can hear the pain in the voices of the people on TV as they explain the hell they went through. If you are too deaf and blind to hear and at this point you are still thinking that I am wrong, then let us go a little deeper and make it crystal clear for you that this is a waste of your time as a Property Investor.

Ok, so let us say six weeks at 50-60 hours a week. That's 325 working hours. I am not going to go into hourly rates because this book's long enough. The point here is using other people's time and yours for better profit.

You may save yourself £1k - £3k on your costs if you do the refurbs yourself and don't make mistakes and don't get emotional. But you will do, because you will no longer be able to stand back and view the property as a money producing object once it contains your blood and sweat.

Now let me ask you a question? Do you think you could spend 100 hours researching ways to raise more capital to invest with? Do you think, if you focused on it for just 100 hours, you would become a little bit of an expert in raising money? I know you would, as I have done it – you would be amazed what you can raise if you focus on it.

So let's say you spend 200 hours on it and raise £75-£100k. Impossible, right? Wrong, it is easy when you start focusing on it and if you are interested I may write more about it on my website, as it is not really for this book.

Okay, you have 125 hours left to spend that money on property. With your new knowledge you will find at least three deals, probably five, and you get to choose the best.

I make it sound easy, don't I? That is because it is easy. It is just your fear of not knowing that is holding you back. This is not magic, people! I did not just wake up one day and find a piece of paper in my hand that says I own 100 properties. Neither did Greg. This is simple and you can do it. Just believe and trust in yourself. Do not listen to amateur opinions. Focus on the expert. He is telling you, YOU CAN DO THIS, just do it!

Back to our 'what if' scenario. You have found at least one property deal! You have a wealth of priceless knowledge and a better understanding of your true capabilities. You have a deal in front of you that will have none of your own money in it, because this is all borrowed money. Remember, my favourite way to invest is with none of my own money!

That property deal is worth a minimum of £20 - £25k profit to you. What does that mean? It means that in this 'what if' scenario, you either work for six weeks to save £1-£3k in refurbishing costs or you work for six weeks to learn how to correctly fund your new business, expand your abilities beyond measure AND create £20- £25k profit. It is up to you.

So even you diehards who "really want to do the building work myself", even you lot must see that what I have shown you is not just a little better, but is an infinitely better use of your time. Oh, I know. I know that some, if not most of you, will not take this advice. I know that you will think you know best. I can't help you if you won't see that **you are wrong to do it that way** and that the eternal question, 'do I do it myself and save money?' has been answered: **No! Get a builder to do it. You are in property investing for the money. You are an investor, not a builder.**

The shortened version goes like this: 'Do I do it myself and save money?'

And the answer is:- **'Only if you are thick and do not understand why you are in this business!'**

All right, so hopefully I have convinced a few more of you to come over from the dark side and find a builder. This is really hard. Really hard to find a builder, isn't it? Yeah? No. It is not really hard to find a builder. Do you think that all the builders have gone home? Do you think none of them will want your job? Do you think that there are no good builders out there looking for a good client to provide them with work? Or do you think there are no builders capable of doing it at the price you need it done for so that you can make money

First off, you can find an odd job man if you have to. Look in the papers. Look in the back of your local freebie papers. For example, we have a free paper called the <u>Friday Ad</u> and there are always people advertising in there wanting work.

Your next worry is not knowing if their work is going to be good enough. Well, it is quite simple to solve that problem. Basically, you agree that you will pay them on the day of completion in cash. You will need an invoice for it, of course, but you'll pay them in cash on the day of completion. So the builder has just been **motivated** to get the job done and **given incentive** to get it done right!

Then you tell him that on the day he finishes, you will go around to inspect the job. If you're happy with it, you will go to the bank and come straight back and pay him there and then, **on the spot.** Now he has been **inspired to finish the job to meet your standard.**

You don't give them any more than 10, 20, 30% of the money to buy materials and things like that. You don't give them any of the money up front. You wait until they turn up on site with the materials and you go and check that the materials are there.

When they ask for a deposit up front, say **No.** Tell them that, on the day the materials arrive you will pay the deposit, but you will not pay anything towards the labour cost until the job is complete. **Be straight with the builder and they will respect you for this.**

When they have finished the job and they say,' 'Right, I am going to be finished at 3:00 tomorrow afternoon. Could you come and inspect the job because I want to get paid?' You go, 'No problem at all. I will come around then, or if you want me to come around today, I can give you a snagging list today just to ensure you can finish that as well, so that I can pay you tomorrow.' Clever builders **(90% of them are this clever)** will say, 'I want you to come around right now and give me a snagging list right now.'

So you go around promptly and give him the list. We will come back to what and how to snag shortly, but when you give him the list you **must** ask, 'Will this mean that you will **NOT** be finished tomorrow?' This forces the builder to take responsibility for the timescale and the list. Chances are, they will work late to ensure that they get paid tomorrow and you get your job out on schedule.

The ones who think, 'I am going to get away with this' and think they will talk you into paying them, are going to say, 'No, come around at 12:00pm tomorrow, it will be done,' ,because they are going to say that did not need to be done and this does not need to be done and all those sort of things.

At the point he says, 'No, don't worry we will be done, it will be fine', you must reiterate the point, **'Well I just want to be able to pay you tomorrow and if I find things are not done and I am not happy with some things, then obviously paying you won't be possible. But if you are sure that it is going to be up to spec, I will come then. It is entirely up to you!'**

Chances are, the builder will say **(9.5% of them are this clever)** 'can you come around now'? If they do not and it is not up to spec when you go around, then you just use exactly the same words again and add, 'well, I did warn you that if it was not up to spec, then I would not be able to pay you!' Do not pause there. Go straight on with, **'When can you have your work finished?'**

In this sentence you have clearly put the ownership of the problem on to the builder. He will take the bait! After all, he wants to get paid. If things do get heated just simply reiterate that you just want the job done and that **you want to pay him.**

At this time, even this Neanderthal (0.5% of builders are this thick, so you have got a 1 in 200 chance of finding one of them – it is these idiots and the public's inability to handle them that give this profession a bad name) will realise that it is in his interest to complete the job.

When you go around there, come up with your snagging list. Remember, it has to be acceptable and it must not look tacky. You have to know what looks acceptable. So, what looks acceptable? Does it look neat to you personally? Would you be happy if you had employed a builder to do it on your own home?

If you are a finicky bug**r, then you are not the person to do this snagging list. You have got to get somebody who is *reasonable*. You have got to be *reasonable*. You want it to be *reasonably good*. You are looking for a *reasonably good* standard of finish.

If the tile is falling off the wall or if there are big gaps in the grout, then that is not a *reasonable* standard of finish. That is what known in the trade as a sh*t finish. What you have to do is you have to get them to a *reasonable* standard. So, you go around there and you write out your snagging list to what you think is *reasonable*.

If there's a light switch that is wonky, that is not really being *reasonable*. If you can get hold of the light switch and twist it yourself and make it not wonky it is not worth saying something about. If the light switch is on a 35-degree angle on the wall, then, yeah, there's a problem.

Do you see what I mean? If it is slightly off level, who cares? The tenant won't care. They are looking at the feel of the room. The valuer won't not care as he will look with the same eyes as the tenant. So that's the key: You are looking at this from the point of view of how your tenant will view it. Will they view that lounge as spacious? Will they view that one bedroom flat as spacious? Will they visualise themselves living there? They will not stand there and go, that dimmer switch is wonky, I am not renting this.

So when you are snagging, be *reasonable*. I could do hours on snagging but I am going to let it stop there and look forward to answering your questions on what is *reasonable* on my forum.

You keep that snagging list nice and simple. When you hand it to your builder, you have warned him it's coming. You have told him, right, I have got some snagging here. You say it is only *reasonable* snagging. You could give an example of something else you noticed, but did not think it was really important for a rental property so you are prepared to let it go even though you would have asked for it to be remedied if he had done it to your own home (it is important that you mention this when you first deal with a new builder).

This, if presented well, demonstrates to your builder that you are a *reasonable* person. When 85-90% of builders look at your snagging list, they will agree that it is *reasonable* even if they think it may be slightly excessive. The builder's feelings towards this list matter to you at this point because you want your job finished off well and promptly. The remaining 10-15% of builders will complete the list grudgingly, but even the Neanderthals will see that it is in their best interest to finish the job to the standard you have *reasonably* requested, so that they get paid.

I have not gone into too much depth here, but I do want you to keep in your mind two things that you could be a bit more ar**y about, because these could be useful. If you have got a bit of an ar**y builder he might go, well, that's *unreasonable*. You say, 'well, no, if I'd asked you to do that – and you point out something picky, I would consider that to be *unreasonable*. I do not consider this to be *unreasonable*.

So, when you hand it to him, say, 'Right, here's the snagging list. I have tried to be as fair and *reasonable* as I can, but I do want those changes made. If you make those changes and they are all done and the rest of this stuff that you are still working on is done by 4:00 tomorrow afternoon, I will come here and **I will shake your hand and pay you the money**.'

Do not go with the money in your pocket. Have the money available at 4:00pm tomorrow in a safe place. That way you can actually say to him, 'Right, I will go and get the money'. Do you see what I mean?

So, now he knows it is coming. You warned him. He has managed to do the job to your standards and you have both completed your relationship nicely. That was hard, wasn't it? No, it was not hard at all! Builders are *reasonable* people if you learn how to talk to them properly so that they know where they stand.

Don't promise anything you will not deliver on to a builder. Don't promise him more work or anything like that unless you are intending to give him more work, because he will just think, 'yeah, yeah, yeah, whatever'. And he will think you are more of an ar***ole than he already does.

Some builders do not treat their customers well. The majority of builders do. The majority of builders are decent people trying to do a decent job and get paid a decent day's wage.

You get to choose what it costs to build. You tell them how much you want it done for. It is cheaper than asking them for a price. If you ask a builder, 'How much will you do this room for?' He will say £1k. Most builders when asked for a price only know how to answer in big round single figures of £1k to £9k. If you want to see an excited builder, then offer him a job where he can put two of these single figures together!

Back to the point, if you say, 'I want this room done for £500. Can you do it?' Maybe he will go, "No, but I can do it for £650.' Or maybe he will say yes.

You are probably looking at 35% savings just by changing your phraseology. It is not hard, is it? You think you can handle that? **Because that is all you have got to do to get a cheaper price!**

So, you never ask, 'How much can you do it for?' You say how much you want it done for. You always make sure he knows how much you have in mind. Then he sees if he can make money at that price and you have got a win – win deal.

Oh, and the other key thing is you have to know how much an individual thing is going to cost. If you go to my website, we are continually updating what *reasonable* costs for doing things are. In other words, I will keep you updated on the going rate for items and when we notice if a company has special offers on certain items, if you get into this then, buying from the right place will save you a lot of money. Also, there is a forum where people can let everyone know about the best deals they have found.

But when you talk to the builder you tell him, 'Yeah, well, I budgeted £250 for that.' And he goes, 'That cannot be done for £250. That is a £450 job,' fine, well that is okay. Say fair enough and then go and ask another builder and see what he says.

And then if the other builder goes, 'Yeah, no problem. I will do that for £250', then say, 'How can you say that is £250?' Ask him. Find out. And he says, 'Well, I can buy this boiler for £170 and only £80 work to fit it.'

Then, you must go back to the other one and say, 'Well, why do you say it's £450?' And he says, 'Well, I buy this boiler for £370 and there is only £80 worth of work.' Now, you are seeing that they might not be quoting like for like.

So, you can actually dig deeper on this. You can actually find out why somebody is more expensive. Because that first builder you had, he was certain that he was right on his price. He might have a very good reason for it. It is your job to *extract that reason* from him, why he thinks you should pay more than you budgeted for it. And if his reason is correct, *you should pay it*. Even if you go over budget, you should still pay it because he might have a bl***y good point. You then take this knowledge with you to your next project.

You should be able to get your builder to agree to a fixed price budget. Always be prepared to pay more out of your own choice as it will sweeten the deal with the builder. Do not offer at the start. Get right to the end and say, 'Look, if there is an extra, if there is a genuine extra, I will pay for it. But, I do not expect the p**s to be taken out of me'.

Always pay the price you agreed to pay. Tell your builder, 'The price we have agreed is £3.2k. You will get paid £3.2k. I will not chip you on the price.' You must **never chip** or try to chip somebody on the price on this sort of thing. Once you have agreed a price, you stick to it. You have agreed to £3.2k, so that is what you must pay. This is not an area you work on to save costs, as it will cost you in the long run. You will find that after just a couple of refurbs you will be known for it and the builders will start to cut corners when they work for you and you'll end up on the losing end. Remember that chipping the price is for amateurs. That is for amateurs or people who want to be poor. You will not earn a good reputation by chipping the price once you have agreed it.

If you have set yourself a budget of £4k and he says he will do it for £3.2k, great! Take his offer. Just be sure that he is going to do the work you think he is going to do.

If he goes away and does the job and it turns out that he does the job wrong, yeah, make sure you get a discount on the price. That is not an issue in a case like that. Of course you are going to knock the price then. He did not deliver as promised.

But if he does what he says he is going to do in the time he says he is going to do it, do not chip the price. In fact a £20 - £50 tip will go a long way to make him come back to you when you need him. Tell him about the time scale, make sure he understands your motivation and mention what cost you will incur by him over-running. But don't give him an unrealistic timeframe. Discuss it with him and agree on it between you. If you need it done quickly, ask him if he can lay on extra help. This will probably cost you more on the refurb, but it will help you save money overall as the property will be vacant for less time. Always remember to balance out the extra cost against the time saving before you make a decision.

Then tell him it is going to cost X amount extra per day for an overrun, so you want it done within this time or you are going to want a discount off the price – this is important. You want him to see that you do really incur a cost if the job overruns. To make him understand how much it will cost you, you have to put a figure on it and you have to tell him that you will want a discount if the job overruns. There is no problem saying that. If he disagrees he will tell you so. If he disagrees, get him to give you the timeframe he needs. When he has done that, tell him that still fits within your budget. Then get him to agree that if he overruns on the timeframe he has provided, he will give you a discount.

If you want the job done quicker, what you could say to him is that if he gets out of it in less time, you'll pay him one third, half or all of the time he has saved you as a bonus. It is best if you do not do this the first time you deal with him, though. Wait until you have had at least one successful project with him and you have seen the quality of his work.

So be prepared to pay the extra if he has genuine extras, even if they do make you go over budget. And remember that fixed price is the only way. None of this day rate cr*p. You don't want to be involved in any of that. Anyone who says, I will do this for day rates, tell them, no, not with me you won't. I will not have you do it at all. I will get somebody else to do it.

And if he turns around and says something silly like, I will be surprised if you get somebody to work for a fixed price, he is what is called a moron. There are plenty of people out there who are genuine decent builders. He is one of the people that is not and you can tell by the fact that he is asking for a day rate and doing his best to scare you into giving it to him. Basically, he is telling you, all I want is a job really.

A proper builder will find a way of doing the job for the price you want it done for, as long as the price you want it done for is *reasonable*. They would not take the job on if they thought you were being too *unreasonable* about the price. So they are still making money, because they will find ways of cost saving.

Never pay more than the material cost up front, and do not even pay that until the materials are on site. Trust **HAS** to be earned. Go ahead and say that to them, they will understand. Also tell them you understand that you have to earn their trust as well, and that you will do that by paying them what you promised, when you promised to pay it. This shows you are fair and are looking at it from their point of view.

No more than a deposit from you for materials once they have been delivered to the job. You do not pay labour until the end of the job – Not a penny. If it is a long job, that is a different story and I am not going to cover that here, but I will on my website later.

Most of the refurbs you are going to do are on one and two bedroom flats. The jobs are two to three weeks absolute max timescale. If the builder cannot fund two or three weeks of his guys' time, then he has got financial issues, and you want to move on to another builder.

Agree to a notice period. Agree on a time that you're going to tell him that this job has to start. Tell him you want the job to start on this day and how much time you're going to give him – say at least 4 weeks notice, as an example – before you want him to start.

I always give builders notice at exchange. That way, they know they are going to get at least four weeks notice of a job. If I have gained access between exchange and completion, then I tell them when I start the purchase process that the timescale will be tight on the job, and the notice I will be giving them to start will only be two weeks. As I have told them early on they are ready for it and I already know roughly how many jobs they can handle. If I start to up gear more than they can handle, I go out and find other builders to take the work on.

When they have agreed to that notice period, make sure you give them adequate notice to get in. When you agree to everything, **write it down and both sign it**. People just don't do this! Because of that, what I have done is written out a standard contract. It is a really simple one. It is not a legalese contract. It is just literally written in plain English and I have made a generic one available on my website.

If you can't get out to the job when your builder tells you he is going to complete it, you still have to be prompt with your payment. Let us say you are on holiday or something and can't get back to snag it. Whether the job is snagged or not, arrange to pay 80% of the total bill when the job is complete and tell him you'll pay the rest on your return when you have snagged it. So if you cannot get to it, if you cannot drop everything and do that snagging straight away, pay 80% of the bill immediately. But better still, go down and snag the job that day and pay the bill that day. This avoids the inevitable problems of re-motivating your builder to complete the job. For example, if he is owed £800, he is motivated. If he is owed £3.2k he's more motivated. It is all about the maths.

You have got to think about what matters most to these builders. Does it matter most that they have done a really good job? Does it matter most that their van is really tidy or they had a really good breakfast? Or does it matter most that you think they are nice people? No, what matters most to them is they get bl***y paid promptly.

Dolf de Roos said it best: Pay them quickly. What annoyed me about it was that when he said it, I realised what an obvious thing it was and how foolish I had been to miss it. And I was in the building trade! Pay them quickly. That is it. Simple. When the builder hands you the invoice, hand him a cheque. Just like that. You can look at him and think, right, that builder will probably jump through hoops for me now. That builder is going to think I am wonderful. When I pick up the phone the next time, that builder is going to remember me, and he will think, I do not mind working for him, I get paid promptly. Very likely, he will put other customers off to get your job done first. Because he knows you'll pay on completion.

After you have done three or four or five properties with that builder, that builder is going to think you are the best thing since sliced bread if you always pay at the end. So pay him 80% if you cannot get to it straight away, regardless of the job he has done (always tell him what and why you are doing it that way). If he has done a great job, the 20% will keep him motivated to finish. If he has done an awful job, the 20% you keep back should be enough to pay somebody to come and put it right. A small insult can work wonders at making sure they know you are in charge, but be sure to keep these points small.

When you are first dealing with a builder you should get your backside out there as quick as possible. Be prompt, make him see that you are trustworthy and efficient. Make him see that you are ***reasonable***. When you snag, it has got to be good, not great.

Shop around. Say it is carpets you are looking for. Mid-beige is what we have found to be the best. Go to different carpet places. Speak to different carpet guys. Look in the back of the freebie papers and you will usually find a new one-man-band company who got tired of laying carpet for a bigger company and has struck out on his own. He will be pretty cheap and desperate to please. Give him the work, pay promptly on completion, but do not give him any money up front. They all buy their carpets from Switzerland or Sweden or somewhere like that at the moment. And they can all buy the same or similar carpets cheaply.

Don't promise what you can't deliver, just promise what you can. If you are doing more properties later, that is later, unless you have them already sale agreed. If that is the case, you can talk about opportunities for further work. If he reads into that, that you are going to give him more work, all well and good. Understand that this is not a trump card, the only time you can play this one hard is when you are his biggest customer. Amateurs tend to brag. When they do, the builder loses respect for them.

So, you have done it. On time and on budget. Was that easier than you thought? It is all just a simple matter of being clear about your expectations and dealing with these guys professionally. That is what it takes, what you have done there. That was dealing with builders. If you think you can be that professional and follow that system, then you can deal with all builders.

So what is everybody talking about, then? What is everybody talking about, saying, 'Oh, builders are awful to deal with!' They are awful to deal with when you do not know how to handle them. But now you know how to handle them because I have just given it to you. It is not rocket science. None of this is. Believe me.

You can say, yeah, maybe I am clever when it comes to the negotiations side and things like that. And maybe I am clever to be able to spot the deal. Or am I? Well, not really because, basically, all of this is just a system. There is nothing I have not told you here that is not a system. Even dealing with builders. It is all part of a system.

99% of all problems start with builders because you haven't written down your expectations from the start. Don't say, well, the builder should be doing that. They don't and won't. Small builders as a group do not understand that they should be doing this, so if you want an easy time with builders, do it yourself. Write it down. How many times have I been caught by this simple error? Too many!

29

Managing Your Props

So you want to manage it yourself. Why? Why would you want to do that? This is another eternal question new landlords and prospective landlords ponder: Should I let it myself or use a managing agent?

Well, where do I start with this madness... Let us put it this way. I started by managing them myself, or as I call it now, mismanaging them myself. I thought, great, I am going to save 10% if I manage it myself. And that was when I owned loads and loads of property and was intending to buy loads and loads of property. I can make loads of extra money. Yeah, right! In business, the rule for the middle man is that the middle man has to add value.

Every business is set up for a reason. Now, my business was set up in order to make serious wealth from property. My business was not and is not intended to manage tenants. So I have the option of managing the properties myself or paying someone else to do it for me. Which method do you think I choose?

I have this discussion with hundreds of landlords and to the ones who insist on managing their tenants themselves and therefore keeping their portfolios small, I just smile and say, 'Well whatever works for you.'

Here is my point. It is up to you. Some people enjoy spending their time saving 10% of an income. But those who do have forgotten the primary reason they got into property in the first place. Forget that old saying, Look after the pennies and the pounds will look after themselves. Bullsh*t! In property , you do need to look after the pennies, but the pounds come first, bl***y loads of them.

By focusing on the pennies, you are focusing on **earning** money. But the primary reason for getting into property is to **create** money. I am intending to explore this point in much greater detail and it will be available on my website.

You need a managing agent and a good one, as your money doesn't come from long term wealth creation by saving £600-£1000/year and causing yourself loads of work. That is what you should be paying your managing agent to do for you.

If you could arrange your own mortgage and save the fee, would you want to do that? If you answered yes, and you are not an IFA, then you are still thinking the wrong way. That is not the way a property investor thinks.

If you could handle your own conveyancing and save the cost, would you want to do that too????

The point I am trying to make is that this business is an **'other people's efforts'** business. You create wealth by leveraging your skill and capital against everything else and doing as little work as you can. Even less if possible!

I have a couple of friends who have a small portfolio of about 12 properties. They manage them themselves in order to save money. They have had it pretty easy so far, and only ever had a few non-payers. I asked them to tell me how much time they spend a year on managing their tenants and maintaining their properties. They said it takes no more than 2-3 hours a month to check the rents and chase the late-payers. Then they have to visit each one twice a year – they learned the importance of doing that after a tenant caused damage to a property because they had not kept up a proper schedule of visits. That takes another 4 hours/mth. I don't need to talk about the time bomb waiting to go off at some point called 'Eviction', and believe me they do happen.

So these friends of mine are confident that they are saving money and they are right. But at what cost? They are saving 12 x £575 (In other words, the 12 x 10% they would pay to an agent) = £6,900 / year. Not bad, eh? Wow! What a saving! Of course there is tax on that at 40%. So it is still an excellent saving of £4,140.

All they have to do for just over £4k is to be there when the tenants call, collect the rents, chase the non-payers and check out the properties regularly. They both have full time jobs and have had to give up their free time for their new part-time job and be prepared to live with the time bomb ticking along in the background and waiting to go off.

Let us say it takes them a mere seven hours a month. That is an hourly rate before tax of over £82/hour. Not bad, not bad at all. I can see why people go for this easy money! After tax, that is just under £50/hour. Not many people earn that! I can see why they feel they are doing the right thing.

I, on the other hand, don't do any of that. I work on building my portfolio instead. I spend 15 minutes buying a property and making £20k+ tax free. If I worked on an hourly rate, I would be making about £100k an hour tax free.

Now we all know that is rubbish and not possible. But the bit that is possible is the one property in the occasional 15 minutes. Say about once a week or every 10 days. That is possible for anyone who is willing to set up their own property buying machine and go through the pain and cost of that. My friends could just apply the skills they already have and one quarter of the time they are using to look after their tenants, to find one deal a year and make a mere £10k+ tax free instead. Their benefits would be an extra £5k in the first year for only 25% of the time they are spending already. A little more impressive to create it than earn it. I think even you diehard Landlord property managers would agree to this simple statement. And if you do not, e-mail me and argue with me. I would love to hear you try and beat this and the next point!

The following year, or shall we just say for the rest of your life, you make 10%/year on that property, so let's call it £10k/year forever. I think my hourly rate is better. If you spend too much of your time looking after the pennies then you'll certainly be missing the real profit, won't you?

One last point for the landlords out there whose argument is that you cannot afford to buy any more properties: Could you use the remaining 75% of the time you currently waste in your part time job on fundraising? Just a thought. Whatever works for you.

Seriously, if any of you feel that I have not done enough to put that discussion to bed, e-mail me and when I have more time, I will go into more detail on my website.

My point is that you will make maximum use of your money and your time if you pay someone else to provide a good service to you and then you monitor them. It should not be too much money. Some agents in some areas charge more, some you can get for a bit less.

Remember: If you pay peanuts you get monkeys. This saying really does apply on this sort of thing, because they will not look out for your best interests unless they are getting a fair wage. Think about it: Would you? Basically, if it is chump change you are giving them, how can they afford to give you a good service? Remember: it is worth an extra 1-3% to you to have no problems! So do not be tight, be **reasonable**.

Look at it from their point of view. They need really, 80 to 100 properties a month to make reasonable money as a managing agent. I mean, that's £4k or £5k. It is not a lot of money from their point of view. And from my point of view, when they are doing that much work so that I do not have to, it is well worth my money! I think my time is most valuable spent elsewhere, as I think I have clearly shown!

Managing your own properties is best described by my business partner, Greg. He says it is like going and getting a time bomb, setting it to random, pressing the start button, digging a hole, putting it in the ground, burying it, making sure we do not remember where we have buried it and then carrying on with our life – saying as we do, 'Right, we will just wait for that to go off then.'

Because at some point, that random number is going to come up. Bang. And then you have got a big, time-consuming, costly problem! Your time is taken off what you are doing to go and solve that problem. It could be anything from a leaking tap that has caused a flood to having to evict your tenants because they have been racially abusing the next door neighbours and the police are there. Or having to evict your tenants because they have set fire to the upstairs bedroom. Or having to evict your tenants because the garden wall was knocked down when they drove their car through it – yes, literally drove their car through it – on purpose to see what would happen when they did. The tenants are not here right now, as this is the police on the phone, and the tenants are all in hospital.

These are some of the little gems I had to handle when I was managing our properties myself. The point is, you put that time bomb in the ground, you set it to random, you walk away and you are saving yourself that £600 a year (by giving yourself the job, of course). And you do not know when it is going to go off.

But let us say you own 10 properties. You save £6k a year. You get one of those bug**rs going off. How much time will it cost you, which is un-claimable? That is right: You cannot claim the value of your time back. You can claim the repairs and that sort of thing. You cannot claim your time back so it is money well spent. Spend the bl***y money.

Find the tenants, look after them and handle it when it goes wrong for them? What the hell are people thinking? You want to pay somebody else to do that. This is other people's time and other people's efforts. It is your money. You are paying the money and it is worth every bl***y penny.

Who am I to say you are wrong if you want to do it, though, right? After all, some people like pain and who am I to say they are wrong? I will stick with creating wealth and living in comfort. I like it easy. I like the easy way.

I am just going to tell you how and why I do it my way. That is all I'm going to do. I have now finished banging on about why I know it is the right way!

So how do you find a good managing agent? Believe me, this takes a bit of doing, as they are definitely not all professionals. First off, you interview your agents. You go out and talk to them all. Don't just talk to one. Also try and talk to the manager as well. Talk to the person who is doing it.

Or, if the person is not a manager but still handles all the lettings, right, then that is the person you want to talk to. You don't want to speak to somebody who has been given the job because it is the other person's morning off. You want to go back and speak to the person who runs the operation for that agent. You want to speak to the right person all the time. Don't speak to the monkey. You speak to the organ grinder.

Your time is better spent managing the managing agents. Talk to them. Find out about what they can do for you, what they would do to look after your property. Find out their systems, how you will get paid. Talk. Ask questions. Ask questions. Ask questions.

Once you have asked all the questions of all of the managing agents, you will know who the best ones are to go for. At that point you want to pick two or maybe three and say, whoever rents it first gets the full management.

Then, when the tenant serves notice, the person who has managed it already gets a two week lead on the other agents. By that I mean he/she gets 2 weeks in which to let the property that has just become vacant before it is offered to the other managing agents. That is it. That is all you have to do. The ones who are good will rent the property. And remember, your property is not being exposed to all the unscrupulous agents in the town. It is going to the ones you've done your due diligence on.

If the person you chose doesn't deliver, give them notice. Tell them they are not delivering, right? Warn them about it. Say you want it done such-and-such a way. They will do it the way you want it done and if they don't, change agents straight away.

If a tenant gets into arrears, you should be informed. You want to know. Seven days later, if the tenant is still in arrears you want to know about it so that you can beat the agent up. (No, not literally.) Because your job is to manage the managing agent and his job is to manage the tenant.

So if a tenant does get into arrears and the managing agent does nothing to police the problem, the quicker you jump on it the first time they let a tenant get away with it, the sooner the managing agent realises that they have got to do the job or lose the job. More important for your long-term peace of mind, the agent realises that they cannot accept tenants in your properties who may be a problem.

So, you have got to have two or three agents that you think, yeah, they could do this job and be prepared to switch the property if the one you currently use does not come up with the goods.

How we handle it with our properties is we always have three listing agents on the go at once. And they have all got a sizeable chunk of our property portfolios. If a property comes up for rent, the agent managing that property give us notice that the property is coming up for rent and they have it for two full weeks before the other agents get to hear about it. So they get two weeks to re-let it before the other agents have a go. Bear in mind, our tenants are required to give us four weeks' notice.

If they have been incapable in two weeks of trying, then the other agents get to work on it for the two weeks after that. The idea is that we want to have a tenant going into that property on or around the day the property becomes vacant. We try not to have voids. We budget on a 5% annual void, but our actual annual void is under 2% and that is the way we want to keep it.

In other words, we are looking at a maximum of seven or eight days the property is going to be void as an average/property/year. That is our figure. If you are working on 5%, you are looking at 15-20 days the property is going to be vacant.

If you give it out to the three agents, you will quickly find out who is the key man at the time. The key man is usually the one who has not got a full roster of tenants at the moment. The one who's got the business is carefree about it and more careless about finding new tenants. That's why you've got to be prepared to switch managing agents.

As soon as we start to get a feeling that the managing agent is not coming up with the goods, we go down there. We talk to them again. We say to them, look, you know, if you are not going to come up with the goods, if you are not going to rent these properties out, if you are not going to give us your full attention on this property, I am going to have to move elsewhere. It is you that is forcing me to do this. It is not me wanting to move it, because I don't want to move it. They usually buck up their ideas and sort it out.

Like everyone else in this business, we have gone through our share of very poor managing agents. We have had some managing agents literally steal money from us. Some stole by mistake. But believe me, you will get managing agents who will steal money from you intentionally. You definitely don't want to get involved with any of those sorts of people. If you find that this is happening, you want to get rid of them as fast as you can.

Let's not forget the purpose of the tenant in the property: You are on a capital strategy. You are not on an income strategy. Therefore, the purpose of having a tenant in the property is what? **To cover your expenses**. That is what the purpose is. Nothing more. All you want to do is cover your expenses. Yeah, you want to make a better profit because that keeps the taxman happy. And you do not want to take a loss or at least try not to take a loss. But taking a loss is not a reason not to rent the property as, chances are, you can put the rent up in the near future.

You definitely do not want to intend to take a loss over the long term. You want to basically break even and if possible make a small profit. You know? Anything. A tenner is good. But if interest rates rise then you just may have to supplement the rent in order to cover the mortgage. If you have released excess cash from the property then you can use that rather than using your own capital. Obviously this should be avoided wherever possible but if you want to buy in your own area then some areas of the country will mean that this sort of technique is required.

All you are interested in is having them cover the vast majority, probably all, hopefully a little more, of your costs. You are not in this to make £150 or £200 a month per property. You are in this for the real money and the long term. When you look at it like that, rental profits are chump change.

If you spend your time going for the chump change, you will miss the real money. Remember 'look after the pennies and the pounds will look after themselves'? I agree with that sentiment on the whole, but not in this case. In this case, your job is creating wealth – to look out for the big pounds!

Just get that property rented. Get it rented for as much you can. We always try and push the envelope on the rent. If rents in the town are £500/month, we charge £525. We let the tenant negotiate us down. I had an agent yesterday ring up Julian and say that one of our properties is up for rent for £475. This managing agent said, 'The tenant wants to know, if he paid six months up front, would you let them have it for £450?' I said, yes. I mean, I think it took me a blink of an eye. See what I mean? In our early days, one of our properties rented for £2,000/month and the tenant said if I pay a year up front, would you let me have it for £1,900. I said yes. Even though I lost £1,200, that cashflow bought me two properties in that timeframe! Talk about leverage!

So be prepared to negotiate. You never know when it will work to your advantage.

So to recap, let us go back to the question, why would you want to manage it yourself if you can pay somebody else peanuts to manage it for you? The problem is defining what peanuts means to you. My perception of peanuts is the £600 a year I would pay the managing agent as opposed to the £10,000 a year I make on the property simply by owning it. To me that £600 buys me the ability to have someone else take all the grief and thank me for the chance to do it. Not only that, when something goes wrong, you have somebody you can beat with a stick. Not a stick made of wood: the stick you hold over the managing agent's head is the power you have to take the business away from him and he knows it.

The managing agent will work hard for you if you make sure he knows where he stands. Do not be unreasonable. There is no need to be unfair or unreasonable. The last thing you want is to find yourself having to manage these properties yourself. Try it. Have a go. Have the fun. Go through the pain. Learn. Or you can just take my word for it as somebody who has bought as many properties as I have in a very short period of time. It is up to you.

Loads of people swear by it. They love it. They do not mind having to go around when they occasionally have somebody who does not pay the rent. It is like, if they want to go through the pain, if they really want to do it to themselves, let them. You know? They just do not understand what it is really costing them to manage the properties themselves.

But I could not care less. Let somebody else have the money. Save me the time and trouble and share the wealth, that is what I say.

Even if you choose to use managing agents then still the whole rental area of property investing can be the thing that really puts you off getting into property in the first place. Mostly this is fear of the unknown, because like any other thing in life it is just a skill that can be learned and you can mitigate your pain in almost every way. And in fact if you want to abdicate control of it completely to someone else then you can remove yourself from all but the pain of seeing the money go out the door on an occasional expense.

These sorts of annoyances really are exactly that, just annoyances as they are just part of the business and are therefore unavoidable at times.

Let's look at one area that fills people with dread, which is *'RENTAL VOIDS!'* I have no idea why these scare people so much once I have clearly shown that Property is Free, and all you need to do is cashflow them when they happen. Then when you refinance, you repay your capital reserve from the equity released.

Those who plan ahead, plan a 5% rental void period and deposit a sum of five years of 5% void into their cashflow reserve. If an unexpected expense comes in like a boiler costing £1,200 then this should come from your reserve capital, which can be replenished when you release equity in the future.

Do you see that anything that happens should not be an issue to you as it is all simply cashflow?

30

My favourite bit is when I get paid

The day I realised that this was my favourite bit was a good day. Getting paid without selling anything is just simply the best. You do not need to go and find a buyer, you just get paid. And do you know what? You get paid more as well! A lot more! I am going to explain that in this chapter.

But first, let us take a look at what happens if you sell. You buy a property for £50k. You refurbish it and do whatever you are going to do to it. Basically, your plan is to sell the property in two or three years for £100k.

Now, for the purposes of this calculation, we are going to assume that you have no capital gains tax allowance left. And you are not going to use clever things like using your wife's name and your name and two other people's names to gain the maximum amount of tax allowance. I am just going to keep this simple.

I know that everybody's situation is different. We are just going to assume that you have no capital gains tax allowance and you are going to pay tax at the standard rate and we will assume you are a 40% taxpayer for the purpose of this exercise.

You spent £10k refurbishing it on top of the £50k you paid for it, so it's cost you £60k. This includes all of your mortgage costs and everything. You are now ready to sell it for £100k. You put it on the market. And you wait and wait and then, because it is a nice property, it sells after just two months of waiting for 93–94% of your asking price. Let us say they pay you £94k.

So you have made a gain at that stage of £34k. Well, no, you haven't. You have still got the mortgage payments to make, since it went up for sale as it no longer has a tenant in it. We will ignore those costs for the moment though. You have made £34k. It takes another two to three months before it completes and you have got all the pain that is associated with all of that, obviously.

If your deal is with a first-time buyer, he has a 30% chance of failing to complete when he tries to buy. You do not get that with a buy-to-let landlord, but that is only because first time buyers have not been educated in what it takes to ensure that they can buy property easily.

I will be covering that in the near future, so if you are interested, please watch out for it on my website, or email me and I will let you know when it is available.

So you get to completion and in this scenario the buyer manages to complete. You get your money and you finally have your £34k gain in your hand now. It has taken 6 months from when the tenant moved out to the day you sold. Let us say your £50k mortgage for 6 months at 5.5% = £1.375k. So you are down to £32.625k. Next, you pay the estate agent, and they will probably have charged 1.5%, so there is another £1.41k. You are down to £31.215k. Next, you owe the taxman 40% of your gain. So he gets his £12.486k and you are left with £18.729k. You have made £18,729 on this deal. Not bad. Not bad at all. From one point of view, you have made a good gain and neatly put your asset to sleep so that it will never bother you again.

You could say this was traditional property investing supposedly done well.

Now let us look at it from another point of view. Let us say you get the same property in the same deal; you spent the same amount of money and you've put £10k into it. We will say that the property cost you £60k after refurbishment and now you are going to refinance.

You instigate the valuation at £110k. The valuer goes out there and he will maybe value it at £110k. He might value it at £105k, but is much more likely to value at £100k. Whatever happens, it should be more than the £94k you would have got.

You instruct a mortgage company on a refinance of your investment property. You then prepare for your valuation and this element is crucial to the process. This is where the months of time, (not necessarily your time) have gone into getting the property to this tipping point (that is the title by the way, of a truly great book by Malcolm Gladwell).

First things first; if you have a tenant in it you have got to have a copy of the tenancy agreement. It is no good doing a deal with the tenant to give him a cheap rate as now you need that flat rented for as much as possible. Every £1 of rent means you can refinance to a higher level, if the valuer says the property is worth more. The only time rent does not matter is when the mortgage is irrelevant of the rent, such as an investment mortgage that is based on your own income. Or when the rental cover is so little that it will easily cover whatever the value the valuer puts on the property.

I usually go for a lender on my purchase mortgage that has a 130% loan cover ratio and on my re-mortgage a 125% to 110% loan cover ratio. But some lenders will go down to 100% loan cover.

To recap quickly on what this means, if you have a loan cover ratio of 130% and the mortgage is £100, then the rent will have to be £130 or 30% more than the mortgage. This is to cover you and is a safety net built into the investment by the mortgage lender, it is part of their criteria. When you hear that lenders are 'relaxing' their criteria, it usually means they are lowering the loan cover percentage from 130% to 125%, or softening their criteria in some similar way.

They may also be lowering what is called their calculation rate. This is where the lender is making an effort to help the borrower borrow more, so that they can lend more without looking too bad to people who do not understand mortgages – and we thank them for it! Over the next few years as the lenders understand their business more you can expect to see their criteria softening further.

What it means is, if the lender has an interest rate of, say, 5.5% and a loan cover of 130%, then for every £1 of rent you have, you can borrow £167.83 of mortgage. If the same lender uses what he calls his 'calculation rate', he would say, my calculation rate is 5% and a loan cover of 130%, then for every £1 of rent you have, you can borrow £184.62 of mortgage. Big difference eh! You really need to know and understand the lenders criteria, but as they said in The Matrix, 'It is really boring sh*t!' so I update a list of our favourite lenders regularly on my website. You never know when a lender's product may change very favourably, and when they do you have to be ready to act. I am no IFA and I am not authorised to give advice on lenders, even though Buy to Let lending is not regulated. But I will be saying who I like to use on my site. Lenders only loan tranches of money at a rate, so when the tranche is gone, they pull the product, so being ready to act when they release one is key.

All of this means that you want to make sure you have a premium rental on the property. So, let us say you are renting it and it is going to give you a maximum of 85% loan to value. You know you're going to get 85% ltv because you have your tenancy document. You have your tenant in the property and you have asked your tenant to make sure the place is tidy. You have told him that you are coming around to have it valued, or you are getting it valued before the tenant is in there. Whatever, but make sure the tenant sees that it is in his interest to help you, his landlord, by keeping the place tidy when you want to value it. I prefer not to have my tenant present when the valuer is there, or if they are there I instruct them not to speak to the valuer.

So, now you know that it is a case of how you convince the valuer that it is worth the maximum amount of money that you are asking. Because the valuation is just an opinion. The lender chooses the valuer and their opinion becomes whatever the valuer says. As the borrower, it is your job to present your property in the most favourable way possible. There is absolutely nothing wrong with any of what I am telling you to do here, as the lender is covered by the fact that they will not lend more than their rental criteria. So even if the valuer made a mistake and over-valued it, the lender is protected. Believe me, that is not likely to happen and frankly all you want in this business is what you would be able to put the property on the market for anyway.

You go to the property market in your area and see what comparable properties there are. In other words, if yours is a converted Victorian flat and you find a purpose built flat in the same area, it is not really a comparable property. It would be far better to have a converted Victorian flat as a comparison. So go online or walk the streets if you have to. Go and see an estate agent or get deals out of the local property paper.

You go around and you find properties that are sale agreed that are almost exactly the same sort of property as yours. The price needs to be more or at least the price you are looking to have yours valued for. If you want your property to value for £105k, do not go and find a 'comp' for £90k, (comp is property jargon for comparable).

Once you have found one, you basically use that as a comp, get the full details either sent to you by the estate agent or print it from the net. Then you go and find another one and another one. You find three deals that are reasonable to the value that you are asking for. They are out there. Believe me. You just have to look for them. Go and get five if you need to, just to be sure. I try and always get comp properties from within a 400 metre radius, but this is only a guideline and quite often you can get them from the other side of town and your valuer will accept them.

So now you are confident that your prop is worth this money, if all of these other ones are as well. This is only reasonable, and is an opinion, as is any valuation.

You must always be there when the valuer goes around. This is so you can offer him a copy of the tenancy agreement and details on at least three comparable properties you have found within 400 yards as the crow flies of your prop. You say to the valuer, well this estate agent down the road has this particular flat sale agreed, (sold is much better), at £115k, which is almost an identical one to mine and it is almost within the area, which is why you think this one is worth £110k or £115k.

Also make sure you have the full tenure details with you on your prop, this is lease details, showing start date.

Then the valuer knows it is a 99-year lease. It is a virtual freehold with a 99-year lease with 75 years left on it. Or it's a £750 a year maintenance bill with a £50 a year ground rent. He knows all the details. You have given him that. You have got a tenure document. You are making it easy for him to do his research. You have just made his life a lot easier.

The valuer will go and do his due diligence on the items you have provided him so you can't make it up. It has got to be real. There is no need to make anything up in this business.

When the valuer values your property, he will not look favourably on anything. His job is to work in the best interest of the lender. But what he will do is look at what you have provided him. He does not want any complaints from you saying that his valuation was not good enough. You don't want to complain because that is not a good thing to have to do. I had to do it just once and we have never been able to use that valuation company since.

He did such a poor job this valuer, when he valued a property of mine for £120k, I had to complain. A week later, I had another valuation company go out and value it for £160k. That was too much difference for me. I just had to complain. In his response, he dug himself into his valuation about how he was right and what I had said was wrong. He made such a fuss that I am still unravelling and rebuilding the trust of other valuers at that company years later.

I shouldn't have done it. I should have just let it go. I should have let them think they had won. I should have given him a way of hiding his embarrassment from me. In the years to come, I'd have been able to drop in comments, like, 'do you remember that time when you valued this prop for £120k and within a week I got it valued by another company for £160k? That would have done a much better job without causing me so much grief, and he would have been more realistic going forward.

I was in the right and he was an idiot, but just being in the right is not always enough. Sometimes you have to roll with the punches in this game. If I'd had more sense, I would have had a weapon to continually beat him with, but I simply threw it away! You have to look for the good in every single bad situation.

Opportunity favours those who are prepared. On another matter two weeks ago, I had an e-mail from Greg commenting on a message forwarded from Julian, saying, 'I have no issue with this, but it is your decision.' The message that Julian had sent him said, in effect, that the owner of a prop next to one of ours wanted to take away our right of access to our rear garden.

We had never used this right and in fact I had not even known we had it. They had offered to cover our legal cost. Julian had said, if you have no objections I am going to say yes.

I got on the phone to Julian and had a go at him for approaching Greg, as I make all property direction decisions. He apologised and then we discussed it. I said, we may not use that right of way now, but should we ever sell the house in the future, that right of way may be very important to a potential purchaser. The right of way has a value to me and if I am to give it up I want to be compensated by at least £5k.

Also, I said, put yourself in the purchaser's position. He must have a good reason for wanting this right of way and at the very least it will be increasing the value of their home. We agreed to start negotiations at £10k and eventually, in a full 60 seconds of negotiations. We settled on £9k.

I saw an opportunity neither Greg nor Julian had seen and I took it. I was able to do that because I sit around and wait for opportunities to present themselves to me. I am not preoccupied by unnecessary grief so my mind is open to opportunities when they come along. I find by doing this, somehow I get a lot more of them.

Getting back to my poor valuation, if I had taken that valuers' poor valuation and waited for the correct opportunity to re-package it, roll it up into a tube and insert it in a certain part of his anatomy, I would have created the desired effect and made myself some more money to boot. I would have had to wait, but I would have out-flanked him.   In my youthful exuberance I waged a full frontal assault, which I lost!   The moral is to pick your battles in this game, and be sure of the outcome before going to war.

So, the valuer goes out there and you've given him the information.   You are now presenting the property to him in the best light.   Isn't this a wonderful flat?   Yes.   We have done all this refurb to it.   Yeah.   Blah-de-blah. This is your sales pitch.   This is your time to sell him on how nice the flat is, in what an upcoming area it is, how the first tenant who saw it rented it. How you were easily able to rent it for a high rent. How the estate agents have said if you wanted to sell it, they would put it on the market for £X and expect you to get at least £X for it. Get your pitch right, not too over the top, just great salesmanship. This bit adds a fortune to your wealth.

For all of you people out there who are saying, 'I could not do that; I am not a salesman.' Yes you are. Everybody on earth is a salesman; you have to be one to survive.

Those instincts are in you and if you cannot find them, then do everything else I have said to do to get your property ready to be valued.   After that, go to my forum on the website and see what advice you will get by saying, 'I have a valuation next week and I am worried about presenting myself to the valuer.'   When you get the response, you should not be worried any more.

If you still have doubts, just as you are about to meet the guy, think about this: Ok, in the next 15 minutes I have the opportunity to convince this complete stranger of the value I believe my property is worth.   When I get it right I will have done very nicely and that money will allow me to go and buy another property. If I get it wrong I am going to have to wait another two years to get hold of £8-£13k. Do I want to wait another two years for that money?

Hello Mr Valuer, what a wonderful day it is today, I cannot believe how nice the weather is for this time of year. I am sorry I am in such a good mood, but my cousin had her baby this morning. You get the point? Be positive!

You have done everything to guarantee that you are going to get your £100k val. You are pretty sure you are going to get £105k and you might touch £110k.

In the summer, 85% of our values hit target, the target being £105 - £115k for this sort of deal. 10% percent get £100k, and 5% fail and get £95k and we cannot use the valuation. From the 85%, 70% of those hit the lower target and 30% hit the top. In other words, the percentages are there if you prepare properly. If you do not prepare, it's a completely different thing.

There is no point trying to get your property to value up if the flat next door is up for sale for £75k. The valuer cannot conceive that this other flat is being sold below market value because the vendor needs to sell. For some reason, 90%-95% of valuers simply do not understand what a motivated seller is.

On occasion, I have been a victim of my own success. Valuers have cited other properties I was purchasing (unbeknown to them) as reasons why my property was not worth what I wanted it to value for. Getting round those sorts of problems is definitely for an advanced version of the book, as too much knowledge of a subject can hold you back at the beginning. I am showing you what you need to know to win, and get your first few successes. After that, your own skill will carry you on to more.

I have cost myself a lot of time waiting for a property to value because I was buying more property on the same road. Now I buy a property, go away, buy somewhere else and then go back and buy more property when I have completed and refinanced my first property.

One particular road we did in Littlehampton crucified us for about 12 months for that particular reason. They said, well, property does not sell on this road for more than £75k. And I said, no, it is because I am buying every one of them that they are so cheap!

They saw the light late last year and the property market in that road jumped up from £75k to £115k in about five weeks, thanks to a little trick I used to try to sell some of my properties in the road for what they were really worth.

Back to our story. You have presented your property in its best light. Now you are at the mercy of the gods-that-are-valuers. You wait. The valuation comes back and he says, yes, it valued at £110k, which is your best case scenario. He is going to give you 85% of that, so that means you have a £93.5k loan.

You take off the existing mortgage of £50k, you take back the £10k you put in to refurbish and close the deal, you take back the revaluation £350 (reval), you pay the solicitors costs of £600 and what are you left with? You have £32.05k as opposed to the £18.729k you would have had from selling it. If it had valued for £105k you would have got £4.25k less, and if it had valued for £100k you would have got £8.5k less.

Let us take £8.5k from £32.05k. That leaves £23.55k. Still more than we would have got if we had sold and we still have equity in the property and we have not chopped our asset up for firewood. We can go back in 2-5 years time and have some more.

But let us go further. Let us say it would only value for what we sold it for, which was £94k. We would need to subtract £13.579k from the £32.05k figure, giving us a total of £18.471.

Even if we just refinanced it for what we could have sold it for, we would have got nearly as much money as we did by selling it and we would still have the property! I do not know about you, but I think that a loss of £258 would be money well spent. And that loss would only happen if we got our valuation wrong.

I put this down to show traditional property investors that by not understanding the business they are really in and getting carried away without properly understanding the math, they are costing themselves a great deal of money.

Sorry guys. Hopefully, you will understand it now that I have broken it down, but even if it is still too warped a concept for you to handle right now, perhaps you should just try it on your next prop. Just do me a favour and before you do your maths on it, look at it realistically and write down every expense, all the expected tax and project forward to the end. Believe me, you will end up a lot richer if you do, as selling property is really for amateurs and the only reason to really sell a property is cashflow. If you are still eager to sell, are you trying to tell me that you haven't cash flowed the property correctly from the start?

When you next think about selling a property you already own, then if it's for any other reason than cashflow you are probably wrong to be selling it. The best way of really getting this into you that I have found is this, **'When You sell Your property, You are transferring Your wealth to someone else!'**

Do you like giving **Your** wealth away, because that is exactly what **You** are doing?

Don't worry 999 times out of 1,000 they will then go on to transfer the wealth you've given them to someone else too. So it's not as if they've won and you've lost, no you've both lost! The only way to break this cycle of 99% of people giving their wealth away is to do the simplest thing. And that is **not to sell.**

It takes effort to sell, but it only requires mental effort **to not sell**. So 999 people out of 1,000 have to go out of their way to get rid of their wealth. Now this is the madness of accepting something as the truth just because the herd does. Why do you think only 1% of people retire rich? Well they are the ones who do it differently from the rest of the herd. Ask yourself a question, how's your current plan in life working out for you? If you want a different result then you need to do it a different way!

Another point to remember is that the experts will tell you that the market has peaked and there is a crash coming. Well there is no top of the market. Other than for a short period of time, and short term investing is not what true property investing is all about. If you want to make money then that is a reasonably good way of doing it, but it takes too much effort for me. If you want to create wealth and have more money for free every so often for the rest of your life then you must dismiss the thought of selling as it's just too expensive!

I really do laugh when I hear property investors tell me that they sold at the peak and made a fortune in the 90's. I say to them, 'That's excellent, you were fortunate to make so much money when everyone else was doing so badly!' They agree with me and then I say, 'But what are those properties worth today?' To which they reply, 'Oh they're worth three or four times what I sold them for now!'

Do you see just how little this person who would be perceived as an expert really knows about what they are doing? This idiot started the conversation by telling me they sold at the peak and finished it by saying they were worth three or four times as much. Conclusion, there are more delusional people in property investing than you would ever believe, which is why I say that 99% of Property Investors don't know how they made their money and probably never will.

The main conclusion though is that there is no peak, and there never will be!

Here is another little concept for you to try to get your heads around: **Property is free even if you have no tenant in it!**

How does that work then, eh??? It's quite simple really but sooo powerful when you know how to use it.

So what is the average interest rate for the last 30 years? Let's say it's 8.5%.

What is the average house price inflation for the last 30 years? It's actually 11.74% but let us say it is 11%.

Take one from the other and property inflation has outstripped your mortgage expense by 2.5%/year, even with the property sitting empty!

So property is therefore FREE!

All property is about is the single most important thing in any business: cashflow. But unlike businesses where, 'cashflow is king,' in property **'cashflow is the <u>only</u> thing!'** As history clearly proves to us if we are clever enough to use it as a guide.

Now let's say you have a £100k property and it goes up at 11% per annum. So you make £11k. Your mortgage rate is 8.5%. So it costs you £8.5k. Your tenant pays £500/month or £6k a year. So you are losing £2.5k a year or £208/mth. Well traditional property investing would say this is appalling and you must sell the property as it is eating you alive.

However, if you can plan your cashflow correctly then this loss is only a cashflow loss as you are generating £17k/year with expenses of £8k/year, so your net gain is £9k/year. So I would say you are investing into this long term asset £2k/year.

Now where is it written down that you must by law make a rental profit on a property? Obviously it isn't. The problem is it is accepted as the norm and if you don't get a profit then you are doing it wrong.

Now when you invest in a pension or some planned stock market investments you don't expect your investment to cover its monthly expenses do you? You are happy to pay in one, two, three hundred or more each and every month and this is into something that you don't really understand. In fact most people are abdicating control of their money to someone else and paying a fee to do so. And are being left with a buy hold and pray strategy.

Why is it that it is acceptable by the money people in this country for you to fund that investment, when in all honesty the risk is far greater and yet if you have to put £1/mth into your property investment then you are doing it wrong? Have they an ulterior motive perhaps, but I'm not here to discuss that. So why not choose to invest that money into your own asset creation instead. Who says you have to do it their way?

This point is the main reason why the buy to let market will become the chosen path for so many more people over the next 10 to 15 years. And why it will remain so strong- even though people don't really understand it and the media is so good at telling them that they can't make money in long term property investing. Their brains are seeing through this propaganda to the truth and they are doing this without knowing they even are.

So what is the catch then? The catch is, 'Our limited understanding of what is really going on!'

From a refinance, you just got as much as you would have done from selling the property and you have kept the property. You have still got the equity in it. Its main two purposes now are: 1) It is your lender's comfort factor 2) because you are in a long-term business it goes on your balance sheet. It still counts. It is irrelevant whether you can actually realise it or not.

So what do you get to do with all that money that comes in? Do you write a cheque to the taxman for his share? Oh, no, you do not because you have not sold the property. So, where is the tax then? Where is the tax you have got to pay? You have not made a gain so there is no tax. You can now take that money and put it on a horse if you want. And you can claim tax relief on the interest up to the purchase price of the property when it entered the rental market. For clarity, it can enter in a few ways. The most common is that you bought it as a buy to let in which case the price you paid for it is the maximum you can refinance it to and claim tax relief on the interest payments. The other common way is when you keep your residential property and then let it out. For those properties you can refinance it and claim tax relief on it to 100% of the value when it entered the rental market.

But that doesn't mean when that is all used up you can't continue to release further equity. It just means you can't claim the tax relief on the interest.

So let's say you released £10k and that took your equity to 110% of the time it first went into the rental market. And let's say you were paying 6% interest on the money, so £600/year. Assuming you are a 40% tax rate payer then you will not be able to claim tax relief on that interest payment, so £240/year. Which is hardly a reason to not withdraw the £10k. This is yet another reason why this is just a cashflow business.

So is this a fantastic loophole or what? We think it is brilliant. Basically, I live from equity withdrawal. Last year I refinanced, I do not know approx, £1.4 million. I took about £400k out for myself to live on and the remainder of the money went back into developing and buying more properties. My tax bill for that £400k that I lived on, bought fast cars with, went on holiday with, bought clothes with was £0.

If you plan correctly, tax is a flexible expense and you would be amazed how fast your wealth can be created if you do not have to give 40% of your surplus to the chancellor. Tax is a flexible expense and you can choose what you have to pay in this country, so why would anyone ever want to evade tax? The only reason must be because they do not understand the system!

So, would having the equity tax free make a difference to you? Has this one point alone made at least the value of this book 1,000 times over, every year for the rest of your life? Only if you apply the knowledge right! So why has no-one told you this stuff before? Obviously you property investors already know this loophole, but are you using it to the max? Are you paying £0 tax? I always like to under promise and over deliver.

So let's say you want to have £20k/year after tax income from property with the greatest degree of certainty you can get in this world. Then it is all down to maths. I bank on being able to release 2% of my equity each year. So we know the growth each year will average 11.74% and we know even the low predictions are for over 5% growth over the next 20 years.

I'm not going to go into depth as to why the property market has extreme upward price pressure and why if anything this is going to bend the 11.74% upwards rather than downwards. I'm just going to say that a shift in the demographics in this country and mainly too few houses being built and worse than that, too few being built in the wrong area are in my opinion going to at least continue the trend or enlarge it over the next 20 years. There are of course dozens of other factors but these are the two that affect the market the most. I could write a book on my conclusions over market predictions and I have a record of pointing out accurately where the market was going on a large scale as a whole, and on individual small pockets. I've said on my blog in the past about areas in a towns and I predicted areas of extraordinary growth like Northern Ireland or Scotland.

If I happen to be buying in an area that is going to experience sudden growth then that is a bonus to me, but it is not essential or even necessary. But if I wanted to use this speculation strategy then I could do.

To be quite honest I find it easy to predict what is going to happen and I struggle to understand why the economists are so good at getting it wrong. I can only put it down to a lack of understanding of what they are predicting and so in effect they are basing their assumptions and maths from the wrong starting point. That of course means their conclusions end up in the wrong place.

So back to the point. It is reasonable to assume that releasing 2% of your portfolio value annually is about as certain as you can get in this world, and probably more certain than you having the same job next year.

So therefore it's now quite simple, you want £20k/anum after tax (which of course means that if this was earned income then you would need a lot more), so you need a £1,000k portfolio. That's five properties worth £200k or ten properties worth £100k. Pretty simple really! If you want more then just do the maths and ask yourself the question, can I find the time to do this once to create the income for the rest of my life?

So this little loophole that they can't stop, despite wanting to, means tax free money for you and me as long as we never sell. This and other tax strategies, as well as market predictions I will be discussing and revealing on my website.

Yes, that was a shameless promotion but it will make you money. Just one tip a year from me will save you more money each year than the cost of the site, let alone the years of future profit.

But if you don't have the time to actually read what I write then it will be a waste of your money. As far as I'm concerned I want to help site members make at least £10k/year or a 15% growth in their net worth annually or it is not worth them being a member.

I know it seems like a hyped up brag against the low cost of the site but it's not hard really. It's just getting you to stop taking steps in the wrong direction and getting you to head the right way. Like all the business mentors I've had in my life, they dispensed knowledge and it was down to me to pick it up and use it. As far as I'm concerned, my site tools will make you wealthier and are worth more than the cost of the site alone, and then my insight into the market is the best predictor I've found. The community

427

side of it is a bonus; it's the tools, that when used and applied will increase your wealth.

How do I know? Well they worked for me and have worked for everyone who has used them properly. So yes this is a shameless promotion, but it is difficult for me to not say it as it is, like everything else I've said in this book - it makes you money!

Now don't get me wrong, it makes me money too but I believe in the Universal laws. I read a few years ago that I could never out give the Universe and that the law of reciprocation would mean that I could have everything I wanted if I helped enough other people get what they wanted. So by me creating wealth for someone else, this means that automatically a debt that the Universe would owe me is created.

So I decided to write a book and build a site that would make everyone a lot more money than the expense it cost them. I.e. For every £1k I make the end user would make £100k or much more, thereby creating a debt that supposedly the Universe owes me. Now I'm not ever expecting that debt to be recovered as frankly I don't need to worry about that, all I need to focus on are ways to create other people money and I am then automatically rewarded.

As a believer in those laws, I know that they also work in reverse, so if I cost people money without them creating wealth, then this will take wealth from me. This is obviously to be avoided at all costs! So I must always trade something that costs X but is worth X++++++.

But before you start thinking I am this great philanthropist who goes out helping others to create wealth,

I want you to understand that I did this for selfish reasons, and I am a strong believer in the virtue of selfishness. They may be noble and create wealth in a lot of people but I did it to feed me first. The fact that I get to help you on the way is a wonderful bonus to me but it was not my primary goal. My primary goal is for you to pay me money for my knowledge and as such you can be assured that my intention is to always provide you with knowledge that makes you money, as I want you to keep paying me.

I don't know why other people in the knowledge industry find this so difficult to say because if I didn't say it to you, then I feel I would be pulling the wool over your eyes. As far as I'm concerned, money is the way I keep score. The more I am paid then the better I have been at creating wealth for others. There will always be the British herd hatred/dislike for anyone who makes money as this seems to be the accepted norm. I think this will be certainly some of the reason why 99% of people in this country retire poor!

This brings into play the law of attraction which has been an underlying theme throughout this book. If currently you are highly likely to be one of those 99% that will retire poor and you do not like the thought of other people getting wealthy, then in effect you may dislike wealthy people. Ask yourself a question, 'if I don't like wealthy people and I am trying to become one, then am I actually fighting my own beliefs? And therefore am I actually holding myself back?'

The law of attraction basically means that you get what you think about most. If you think 'I hate being poor' then guess what, you'll be poor. If you think 'I hate being fat', then guess what, you stay fat. However, if you see yourself as a thin person or a rich person and are willing to put the effort in to create that image for yourself then you will create it. So if you want to be poor, then surround yourself with poor people and you will have what you desire. If you want to be rich then you have to surround yourself with rich people. To me this is so obvious, but for some reason it eludes 99% of people.

I remember when Mike first told us how much money he wanted us to pay him in return for his time. I thought it was outrageous - we had never paid that much for advice. I thought especially as he was already rich why did he need to charge us so much for what he could give away for free.

Well the fact that it was costing me so much money made me be ready and waiting for him to arrive and made me pay attention 100% of the time he was there. It also made me put in place things he taught us sometimes within minutes of him leaving. Basically I am tight and I therefore wanted value for my money!

Do you think I would have gotten so much, been so attentive and taken so much action if Mike had given us his time for free? Would you?

I now call this money 'hurt money' as it has to hurt for me to pay proper attention to it and I think that is true of the vast majority of people. If something is free to you, then subconsciously you hold it in low value and pay little attention to it. If something has cost you so much that it hurts, then you consider it has high value and you pay lots of attention to it. Therefore by default it helps you the most.

I am still cheap and I like getting things for free as I am still trying to apply this same lesson I have learnt here to other areas of my life. But I recognize that it can take time to change my culture. I try and apply the same rule to my investment in myself as I do when buying some building material; will the money I am spending here add at least the same value to me that it is costing me and will it give me at least a 300% return on my investment. After that, it is just down to the time I have available as to whether I invest the money.

So if you are one of those people then you are going to have trouble creating wealth for yourself if you don't like wealthy people. I strongly suggest you look at your beliefs and see where they have come from because, as I often say to people, it is no trouble getting a new concept into someone's mind; the trouble is in   getting the old rubbish out!

Okay, now how much work you put into mitigating your tax liability pays you dividends year after year. It is a clear and present wealth creation strategy that very few of us are doing enough with. You never ever have to evade a tax. You avoid tax, but you always do it playing by the rules. The government wants you to avoid the tax. That is why they give tax breaks in the first place. Believe me, in all the time I have been doing this, I have never found the Inland Revenue anything other than helpful.

And if you are unsure about my advice on this point, simply pick up the phone to the Inland Revenue and ask them about it. When they say, yes, you can do that, ask them to put it in writing so that, if you ever have a tax investigation, you can go, well, we asked you if what we were doing was the right thing to do and here is your reply.

These people are not to be feared, they will help you. These are nice people. I love the taxman. I think he is great. He is my best friend because he has the rule book and he has shown us all the rules of the game. All we have to do is play within them.

So, unless you sell, you never have to pay tax on that asset, because you never 'crystallise' your gain. You can claim tax relief on some of the interest, but you will never pay tax on the vast majority you have released unless you sell. If you sell, tax will be due on it, on the lot, on every penny you have had. So to avoid that, you need another strategy!

They make the rules and we play by them. But that is my favourite loophole of all time. It does not get any better than that, does it? Because for every £1 I receive, somebody who is on 40% tax has had to earn £1.60. So, my life moves further forward faster because the tax I do not pay compounds the gain I make.

My mentor, Mike, said, 'In this world you can make much more money if you are an honest man than if you are a dishonest man'. And we live by that. It's integrity, integrity, integrity. As far as we are concerned, it is simply the way it is. You do not have to be sly. You do not have to be underhanded. You just have to be honest. You have to know the rules and if you play by the rules, you can make a lot more money being honest than you ever can being dishonest. Trust me; I am in this for the money.

I want to buy and keep buying forever because I am getting a little wiser and being even more tax efficient, every year. But, the main thing is, I just keep buying. All of the time. I do not sell, I try to never sell. Never sell unless you blooming well have to for cashflow reasons. If you blooming have to, you then have to mitigate your tax.

To all you people out there who are still paying your 40% tax, your accountant is not doing his job! You do not need to pay all that tax, people! There are ways around mitigating at the very least some of it.

So, which would you rather do?

OPTION A - would you rather sell the property, pay the tax and have your £18.73k, or OPTION B - keep the property, do not pay any tax and have £32.05k instead? Oh, and have the equity as well, which is 15%, so another £16.5k. Which would you rather do?

So what is wrong with you property experts out there? Don't you get this? Is it too simple to be believed, is that it? Why do you sell, when it ends up costing you money? Stop thinking you know everything about what you are doing and start learning; you have got some of the basics wrong!

Because, if you still believe you are further ahead by selling property to create wealth, you need to go back to the start of this book and start reading again, because you haven't got it. If you still do not understand the point of all this, then you people really do not get it.

I was at an Open Day recently and this lady came up to me and said, 'In the promotional e-mail you sent me, you said you were going to teach even Property Investors something they did not know.'

I said, 'Yes, I did.'

And she said, 'Well I came along because I wondered, what I don't know, as I am a successful property investor and I own several properties.'

I said, 'Well the main thing I am trying to teach property investors is to never sell.'

She said, 'Oh, yes I know that. Actually what I am doing at the moment is I am trying to sell this property so that I can buy more and hang on to them as I think that's a good idea.'

Well, what could I say to her? She had totally missed the point I was making; she had listened but had not heard. In her reply to me, in the first sentence, she said she not only knew how beneficial it was to hold onto property, she was going to sell one in order to buy and keep others. What could I say to this amateur?

I keep saying this but traditional Property Investors do not seem to be able to grasp it, as they think they understand it already, but they do not.

Since first writing this book I have received emails weekly, if not daily, from people who have owned property for years, sometimes even more property than I own who have said 'Up until I read your book I didn't understand what I was doing.' I consider these real compliments, but more importantly they back up what I am saying, and that is that over 99% of Property Investors do not understand the business they are in.

That is why the real wealth in property is yet to be created, probably by one of you. Because if you can accept this fact, accept it deep in your bones and then apply these skills, you will have more wealth each and every year for the rest of your life.

If you have still got a bit in you that says, 'Yes, but I really want to sell that property', then you still have not got it. I have still not managed to make the message clear to you. Do not look to sell it, look to fund it and re-value it properly.

Now, hopefully, this book will get it through to you. If it does not, come to one of the Open Days because you can hear people speaking it and telling you about it and living it. And you can say, hang on a minute, this is real. This actually does happen and it can happen for me too. This can happen despite you, all you have to do is not get sucked into the jet engine of popular opinion that you need to sell something to make money.

The facts prove my case. In property, you do not need to sell something to make more money now and unbelievable money later.

And to repeat this essential point again, **You actually can make more money by not selling property than you can by selling it**.

All you have to do to have it happen for you is believe it. You do not need to understand it, just believe it. You sow the seed once and you reap the harvest every 18 months or so for the rest of your life.

Money For Nothing And Your Property For Free!

I say to people never sell, but that is on the assumption that you bought the property in the first place with the intention of never selling as part of your portfolio, as there can be instances (not many) when there is a justifiable reason to sell. They are ONLY to do with Cash flow.

So if you think you need to sell, then you should probably meet all of these conditions for doing so: -

1. You have a property which is producing a miniscule yield and would eat into too much of your cash flow
2. You are in a position where you can sell it and pay no tax
3. You are intending to use the surplus cash to buy property to a higher value than you already own
4. The property you buy will be producing a yield that protects a weak cash flow
5. Keeping your existing property would slow down your portfolio growth

There may be some other reasons but if they do not involve cash flow in some way, then never sell.

My Favourite Part

When I get paid is my favourite part. And it should be yours too, because if you are going into property for any other reason than getting paid, then frankly you have emotions involved and there is no room for them in Property Investing. So, to you and me, our favourite bit is when we get paid.

That is why I am so good at it; it is the bit I like most! I have been fortunate enough to be able to help a lot of people with this strategy. One of my proudest moments was when I was able to help my parents.

My parents were very good with money. They had always been traditional investors (not property investors). They had ISAs, PEPs, stocks, shares, that sort of thing. They did not need my help with that as they were quite comfortable with their non-encumbered property and significant portfolio income.

How I was able to help them was by taking the management of their money away from them and manage their money properly, turning their one property worth £160k into nine properties now worth around £2 million, with about £650k equity in them. At the same time, I was able to move them to a new home; the house they have now is twice the size of the one they had.

At the moment, we are planning a big extension on that house to turn it from a three-bed detached on a large plot into a five-bed detached on a large plot to make it the perfect place my mum has always wanted to have. I was able to do all of that, all of it in under one year. At the same time, I have mitigated all their inheritance tax liability and there is no inheritance tax to pay on their estate at all. I'm not going to cover Inheritance Tax in this book, but needless to say I have found a pretty good way to never pay it myself, but to defer it forever. This info is available on the site in My Inheritance Tax Plan, or it will be available in more depth in 2008 in a free e-book.

Another short story is when my father-in-law was made redundant. He struggled for 12 to 18 months to try and find work in his old industry, all the time eating into his savings to survive. Basically, the experience he had meant nothing in the industry he was in. Because of his age, plenty of younger people were being offered jobs he was not.

I knew I could help him, but my wife did not think they would want my help. I had to offer as I could not sit by and watch them struggle, so I offered and to our surprise they said yes. I am a big believer in 'A prophet not being recognised in his own home', it being far easier to accept the help of a complete stranger than a family member, but to their credit they saw past knowing me as their son-in-law and recognised me for the successful Property Investor I had become.

So I released the equity from their house and I have done a similar thing for them as I did with my parents. I made it so that my father-in-law never has to go back to work again. He lives a life of ease now, which is as it should be. He does voluntary work and things he is interested in. And property, the real power of property, has enabled me to do that through refinancing.

You can do this, too. I do this sort of thing and I help people with it and it changes their lives. And if you can change people's lives for the better, I think it makes you a better person. That is in my opinion.

I try to do as much good as I can. And I see it as my responsibility to make as much money as possible so I can therefore give and help more.

I am also a believer in the Universal laws and in this instance the law of Reciprocity, which is 'You get what you give'. With this book I am combining it with the understanding that I can't out give the Universe. Therefore by writing this book, I have created so much wealth in so many people that effectively I have created a debt that the Universe owes me and can't ever repay me in full. Don't get me wrong. I'm never intending to collect, I will receive what I should receive based on the value of my contribution. Got a bit deep there, and that's not really for this book, just thought you'd want to know one of the reasons I'm giving you all the knowledge you need to become wealthy.

My skill in property has enabled me to do this for both sets of parents and now hopefully you too. Thanks to this skill, constantly refined and applied, in my parents' lifetime, I have become the man my Uncle Dave said I would be.

My parents have always stood by me, when they saw me fail, and when they saw me go through horrible personal tragedies. Now, their faith has borne fruit. They have seen me succeed beyond belief and have told me how proud they are of me. And I consider that to be one of my greatest possessions.

It is my hope that these skills will allow you too to achieve the sort of inner pleasure I have managed to get for myself through their application and continued use. Just knowing about this revaluation thing can project you through life like a turbo charger, and I encourage you to have fun with it.

If you cut down that tree, that seed you planted, then you make your money once. You are taking the profits and you are paying your tax. Why do that when you can have your cake and eat it too? Why not, instead of chopping that wonderful fruit-bearing tree up for firewood and burning it once to keep you warm, why don't you just let it bear fruit every few years and wait for time to pay you all that money? Look at property as if it is a fruit tree, if you look after it, then it will always bear you fruit.

Occasionally it will provide you with seeds that you plant to produce another tree, which will bear you fruit. You can use just one fruit tree to build an ever expanding orchard, for you, for your family and for whoever you choose to help. So why would you ever want to cut your fruit tree down and sell it for firewood?

Try to always remember: -

Fruit For Nothing And Your Fruit Tree's Free.

It is up to you though! As far as I am concerned, my favourite bit is the bit when I get paid. And the fact that I don't have to sell anything, I do not have to deal with sales to be able to get paid. Why, that is just fantastic. When a thing like that is not only possible, but legal into the bargain, what the hell does anybody want to sell for?

The skill I am showing you here is the bit that eludes most so-called professional property investors. This is the bit that makes all the difference, turning the so-called professional into the super rich investor. When I saw the truth, I knew in an instant which one I wanted to be.

Most so-called professionals would like to keep their property, but as their money is tied up in it they think they need to turn it to make a profit. This is because they do not really understand the benefits of revaluation or the loopholes available in the tax.

I would rather be in a position where I do not make a profit now, have the money instead and keep the property. It seems a lot more logical to me. It might be a little bit more difficult to understand, but remember, understanding something is often overrated. You do not need to understand every aspect of it to make money; all you need is belief and a willingness not to do anything that will stop it happening automatically. In property, you and your emotions are your wealth creating strategy's worst enemy!

31

But, but, but…

But, but, but. Stop it. Get over it and create wealth.

Oh, my God, I am losing money each month. I bought this property. I have rented it out. Basically, I had a big void on it. The money in this budget has gone through the roof. I am now losing money each month. I am losing £50 a month; £600 a year I am losing. I must sell!

Where do we start? Well first off, you should try not to do this. Self-made billionaire, Martin Davis, said in an interview with Forbes Magazine when he was asked about making money, that he only has one simple rule, and that is do not lose money.

This is the only thing that is easy to do with money. Anybody can manage to lose it. I fully agree, losing money, now that is easy! Do not need any skills for that, right? That Brewster's Millions thing? Walk in the park. Thirty million, no worries, no sweat. Do that with ease. I could probably do that without getting off my sofa. Easy-peasy. Losing money, is really, really simple.

Right?

You do not want to lose it. You try not to do it in the first place. So, you always make sure you do your due diligence from the start. But, if you have ended up losing money, I think it deserves a little further exploration. Let us look at it from another point of view. Let us look at what is really going on.

Let us say you are going backwards, £50 a month, £600 pounds a year on a property. I am not going to assume you have got any other properties at the moment. I am just going to assume you have got just this one.

First off, let us look at it from a tax point of view. From that perspective, you can carry this loss forward until the day you die. So let us say next year the maintenance budget comes down and you go back into profit. Or the year after that you increase the rent and the mortgage payment stays the same. Or the interest rates come down and you gain a profit where you can cover your loss then. So, yes it is a loss, but it is not a major one and as long as you can cashflow it, is it so bad?

Let us say that none of that happens and you stay losing £600 a year for the rest of your life on £100k property. It is not the ideal situation. You know, some would say you should sell that property.

I would say, fair enough. But I would also suggest that before you sell, you should look to refinance that property through a cheaper lender. You should look to increase the rent. You should look to speak to the managing agent and find out the reason for the high maintenance costs to see if that will add value to your home, so you can look at it from a positive point of view. You can look at trying to acquire the freehold if the managing agent is spending money they do not need to spend. There are loads of different ways to look at it.

How I would look at it, though, is this way. This is how I <u>choose</u> to look it. This is that choice thing again, a very powerful word.

£600 paid in a year to make me a £10k a year on average for the rest of my life. Hmmm? Is that a good savings plan or what? Let's see now. I get tax relief on that £600 after all. So, what's that worth? That is probably worth a fair bit more. So, that £600 is probably not really costing me £600. It is probably only actually costing me about £350 - £400. So £350 - £400 lost to make £10k a year tax free for the rest of my life. I do not know about you, but I think that is still not a bad investment. And when you consider this against a 'conventional' pension plan, how on earth could you ever, in a million years hope to achieve a 2500% profit on your money? Property is not just 'the real alternative to Pensions', it goes much deeper than that.

What everyone should be saying is this, ***'Can we really consider pensions as an alternative to property?'***

In this world the skill is in asking the right question!

Quick side track on pensions!

I did some research when I was preparing for this book. I asked a pension expert for a quote on a pension.

I asked what premium I would have to pay if I was 30 years old in order to receive a pension of £20,000 per annum in today's terms if I was retiring at both 55 or 60 years of age.

- This would be of course a pre-tax income.
- This is a level premium contract with the end pension increasing by 5% per annum.
- I was quoted for a pension that would not pay if I was off sick.
- I was quoted for a mid-band statutory growth rate.

The answer came back: -
Retiring at age 55 the cost would be £516 per month
So if I want to retire at 55, with a £20k per annum income I will have to pay £6,192 per year or £154,800 in total.

Or

Retiring at age 60 the cost would be £325 per month
So if I want to retire at 60, with a £20k per annum income I will have to pay £3,900 per year or £117,000 in total.

Now let's compare what property can do, in comparison.

- To receive £20k / year from property at 11.74% annual growth I would need to own £171,000 of property. (That's not even one average property!)
- To receive £20k / year from property at 10% annual growth I would need to own £200k of property.
- To receive £20k / year from property at 5% annual growth I would need to own £400k of property. (This is about 3 one bedroom flats)
- To receive £20k / year from property at 2.5% annual growth I would need to own £800k of property. (This is 5 – 6 one bedroom flats)

Now I don't know about you, but I have far more confidence in my £800k property portfolio going up in value by a mere 2.5% each year, than I ever would have in me actually receiving £20,000 per year return on a pension!

And remember my portfolio rising is tax free!

Just because we have always been doing something one way does not have any bearing on whether it is the right way or not. As Stephen Hawking said, 'It is not clear that intelligence has any long term survival value.'

I personally know that property will increase at its true rate of 11.74%/year, but I only look to withdraw 2%/year from my own portfolio. Somewhat conservative I know! But if you'd like to use my strategy then here it is: -

1. Decide what you want in the way of annual after tax money
2. Be realistic and work out what you really want, remember you can always have more once you've achieved your first goal (I believe in audacious goal setting, but there really is no need in Property Investing as it's so simple ☺)
3. Divide the figure you've come up with in half and times it by one hundred, and that is the size of portfolio you need to build

Let's say it is £20k

£20k divided by 2 = £10k, times 100 = £1,000k. So if you want to receive £20k/anum on my really conservative growth strategy you need to build a £1,000,000 property portfolio.

Back to the point…

You didn't intend to lose money and believe me; you didn't want it to happen. But, it happened. So, what is your tax liability going to be on that property at the end of the year? Nothing, right?

Let us say you do it for 10 years and you have made a total of £6k of losses. And then you end up buying some property and you make loads and loads of rental gains on those properties. Well, you can claim all that £6k as a loss against any rental gain any time in the future. Not bad, eh? You can carry forward tax loses until you die!

So you are saving, as if you were putting it into a building society. Yes, I know it's a generalisation, but it is the intention and sentiment that matters here when we are discussing these sorts of small sums. Remember, if you did not have the tenant in the property, it would still be free, but you would have to cash flow more into it. And you only get that cash flow back every so often. You know, every year or 18 months or so, forever.

Do you see what I am saying? Because property is free, the fact that you've got to fund it £600 a year does not really matter. Because the property funds it from planned equity withdrawal. If the property is going up in value at 10% percent a year on average over seven years, you would have made a lot, lot more than you lost. In those seven years, you will lose £7.2k. If you have only got a property worth £100k, it's going to be worth £200k in seven years' time. That is it. It is that simple. So, is it such a bad thing, to lose a little money occasionally? Especially when you have tax relief and other ways to try and mitigate the loss?

I look at this sort of thing as if I am just paying it into my pension. Because those properties are a pension to me, a better one than anyone else could ever provide me with. Another of Mike's sayings was nobody looks after your money as well as you do.

32

Can't Someone Else Do It?

Well, one of the ideas of this book was to give you all the info you need to go and buy property the easy way that I do. I also gave you the really easy way where you do not have to do anything other than buy property, with just 2 – 3 hours work.

I haven't filled in all the blanks, but you should not fear them (even though I know some of you will!). You need to know I believe in the law of reciprocity and if I was to lead you down the wrong way then I would be paid back for that at my level.

So I am telling you that you can do it. There are hundreds of members on my site and thousands of previous book buyers who have and are doing it right now. Just go to the site and read the countless posts that say what members are doing! So, so can you! You do not need to be a special person, you just need to believe you can.

I know those blanks are not reasons to fear the unknown. And I know that they are not big enough to stop you moving forward. If they were, I would have included them in this book!!!

Coming from the position of someone who has filled in the blanks, they are nothing to be scared of. If you just step forward with the knowledge I have shared with you here, then you will fill those blanks in yourself. Yes you may make mistakes, but don't worry, every one of us does – mistakes are good. It is how we learn. And guess what? We survived, and so will you.

The blanks would fill up this book with a lot of stuff that would take the inspiration element off of it. And the point of this book is not to fill in every blank, but to get you to just buy one! That's it. If you already own plenty, then just buy more because I've freed you from the bull**it that surrounds property investment.

But I know that just buying one property will change the mindset of people that don't own it. It will make **you** see that **you** the average person can control **your** future. That **you** don't need the government, or the lottery, or anyone else to protect **you** or **your** family in **your** old age. That **you** can control it **yourself**. That **you** can be wealthy, if **you** choose to be!

It's up to **you** whether **you** believe in **you** or not!

Now I am going to give you a third, bonus way you can do it. This is the way I now do it and as a Property Investor I wouldn't have it any other way. And I'm going to be pushing you further here, to recognise the truth about your situation as I would rather have a few more of you upset with me, but more of you Property Investors. I didn't write this book to win a popularity contest, I wrote it to make you start buying property.

For myself I decided that there had to be an even better way to invest in property, as I found it too much like hard work after about six months. Unfortunately, this way looked like it was going to cost me more, and it did at the start, as it will do you. But after the initial cost the returns have been far greater than I ever could have done myself.

33

The Property Buying Machine?

This is the short story of how Passive Investments came to be. I used to read books while sitting in my swimming pool first thing in the morning. I have always been an early riser and I find the morning my most creative time of day. We had bought about 50 properties by then and we were very busy. So first thing in the morning became my "me" time and I learned things.

So I am in there one autumn morning reading Michael Gerber's <u>The E-Myth.</u> For those of you who don't know, this book is simply a must read. Not just for people in business, but for those contemplating it, for those who would like to one day go into it and for everybody else who would like opportunity to come their way one day.

The book is about dispelling the idea that everyone who sets up a business is an entrepreneur. I used to hate that word. When people called me that it made me crazy. I saw so many entrepreneurs fail in the 80's that I did not even want to hear the word. I have got over it now, as people refer to me as an entrepreneur all the time and I have had to learn to accept it, and I do now take it in the way it is meant.

Anyway Gerber's book showed me how to systemise my business and turn it from what mine was – 'just a job' into a business. It is just logical and my frustration when reading it was based on the fact that I should have known all that. But then isn't that always the case with profound knowledge?

At the time, we still had our manufacturing businesses and I was looking at ways of E-Mything those businesses. I hit a large number of stone walls when I tried because that much change is painful for an existing business, especially when you have failed to get everyone facing the same direction to start with.

However, I started thinking about what I was doing in property. At the time, I no longer really worked at the manufacturing business. I had decided I wanted to focus my efforts on being a property investor. Greg and I chatted and decided that he would downsize and remove our old business and I would focus on building our portfolios.

That morning as I was reading, I was quite stressed. I thought about all the people and all the things I was dealing with as I looked for new properties. I was dealing with negotiating the properties. I was dealing with the conveyancing. I was dealing with the solicitors. I was dealing with the exchange, the completion. I was dealing with the refurbishment. I was dealing with the tenants. I was dealing with the tenant issues. I was dealing with the voids. I was dealing with the revaluations. I was dealing with the refinancing. I was dealing with the valuers. I was dealing with time, rounding the money up so that we could afford to buy the new property coming in from the refinance of the old one and of course I was dealing with several refurbishments. I was busy!

And it was like, whoa. I had it going off all over the place, all the time. It is amazing but when you decide to buy 50+ properties in a year, you create a lot of work for yourself and everyone around you! And in a very short space of time, I had created myself a full-time job just handling what was going on there. I had already decided that a full time job was not what I wanted ever again. I had tried working for an income and earning money, and quite frankly, I was not very good at it. I much prefer not being restricted and find creating money much easier.

So I broke it down into seven stages. They are finding the property, which I quite liked doing. There is handling the conveyancing, I do not really like that. There is dealing with the solicitors and exchange, I do not really like that. Dealing with the solicitors and the completions, I do not really like that. There is handling the refurbishments, I do not really like that. There is handling the tenants and getting the rentals done, I really dislike that area. There is refinancing the property, I do not really like that either.

And finally, there is the getting paid bit. Well, I just love that bit.

I thought this business would be fantastic if I could just do the getting paid bit and do the buying the property bit when I wanted to. Because I still really enjoyed the buying the property bit. Everything else I did not really want to do, but it came with the Property Investment business and I had just accepted the idea that I had to do all of it if it was going to work.

So I started to think about it. And I thought, well, wouldn't it be good if I had a business that did all of that for me and I just got paid? If you think about it, it is the goal of every business to just get paid. I had previously sworn I would never go into business again as it was too much like hard work.

But this time I was going to be the only customer. And then if I built this business, this 'Property Buying Machine' as I described it to myself, then I could just do the bit that I like, which is the getting paid bit.

So I sat/wallowed there and I thought, yeah, if I set this up and I systemised it so that everybody had a system and everybody knew what they had to do, I reckon I could get to the stage within a few years of not needing to be there and have all of the benefits but none of the work. Then I could go and spend all my time doing the bit I wanted, which was finding more deals and making more money, all the time acquiring more and more property. And obviously using other people's efforts I would obtain a much better return on my primary investment, my time! Cool!

So, I told Greg about the idea and he said, 'Well, what do you want?' I said, 'Well, more or less, I want what we have got going on at the moment,' because I was not doing all this myself at the time. I had Lindsay and Pete helping me, as well as another lady who worked for us at the time called Kelly. And there was David, a chartered accountant we had brought in, who was running the accounts.

Basically, as I thought about it, I realised that we had already built a business without consciously putting a plan of action in place. As we had nothing in place, we were able to redesign it from scratch and start again. We had no real business at this stage, we built it from the ground up. Our advantage was we had a company with 106 employees at the time so we were able to pull the skill sets required straight out of our other companies. Well at least to start with!

I went out and employed Julian to come in and run the acquisitions for me, and the rental management side of it. So, we now had a properties manager and an acquisitions manager in one person. The intention was that, in time, he would just be doing acquisitions and we would employ a property manager.

We had several building teams handling their own projects and then one of the guys, Max, stuck his head up above the rest and the job fitted him quite well. He went on to make the small works job his own before moving on to his own business in Property Investing last year. Being a Property Investor himself, he looked at things from a certain point of view – the point with profit in mind. This is essential to the refurb element.

Pete was handling the valuations and talking to some of the estate agents before Julian came along. He was also looking for ways for us to bring in clients to our other businesses through networking.

The other key member of the team was Steve, who had run another company for me. When I sold the manufacturing element out from under him it killed his business off, but he was too good to let go so we brought him in to run the research and development side of 'Our Property Buying Machine'. He is still with us today and is now running Client services and it is his job to police the rest of the company to make sure we deliver on our promises.

I broke the system down and redesigned the whole system from the ground up so that all I had to do was okay the purchases. First, I had to teach Julian what we wanted in a property. I had to make sure that he bought the right thing. After that, it was a case of the rest of it was going to be handled in stages.

We developed the system over a period of time, as we were purchasing a lot more property. All I wanted was a property buying machine where I got paid. That was it. Brilliant.

Along the way Pete had said, you know, clients will want to come in and have us do this for them. I must admit, I thought what the hell do I want clients for, I am too busy making money to bother with the hassle associated with helping clients.

Anyway, when we more or less finished the initial concept, it was functioning. Don't get me wrong, there were still loads and loads of systems to be created and de-bugged, and we are still creating them now and changing/adapting and improving them.

But, when we had the basic format done and in place, we worked it out that we had about £250k a year overhead to run all of this. I said, 'Well that does not really matter as we're making huge sums of money each year.' As I said, it cost us at the start, but now we were beginning to see the benefits of other people's efforts. I have found this leverage to be one of the greatest, if not the greatest' leverage of all.

Then we thought, well, hang on a minute. If we took on clients and they paid us enough, then they could pay for our property-buying machine. We would make them plenty of money by having them utilising our system, and we would get our system for our use for free. I thought, brilliant, a win – win deal. That is a great idea. But would anybody actually be that interested in having us do it for them? Pete and our new friend Nicola both thought they would. Greg and I were far less certain.

So Pete and Nicola did a test and very successfully demonstrated that we had a potential market. We went to the drawing board and started to design our service. This took over a year and cost quite a lot of money to define as there was no one for us to copy. We wanted to define our market some more so we then held a few Open Days in the conservatory at our offices in Ashington (there's a picture of it on the front of the book). The food was great but we had limited success. We did not really think too much about it, we just figured it would take a while to get our message across.

So in 2005 we were ready and were attending a Property Investment show the following month. We decided to organise a few Open Days after the show. Greg had come back from holiday at Christmas and said, 'We are doing this all wrong. People are not seeing the value in our product. We need to get a lot more professional and show people the true value of what we do.' He said, 'I think this is happening because I do not believe that we actually know the true value of what we do ourselves.' He was right and it was the turning point.

Then a friend, Gill Fielding, came to an Open Day in January and said, 'I love your product, I'll buy one now. But you don't know how to sell it and I'd like to help you to get it off the ground as what you are doing will really help people.'

Gill taught us how to come across far more professionally and advanced our business a few years in just a couple of months.

So we re-designed what we were offering people. Our core principle was that it had to be something we would buy ourselves. We thought, we will sell a portfolio building service for £30k and cover our overheads, which would have obviously increased by then. We knew we would probably be able to sell 10 to 12 of those a year. That would then cover all of our costs and give us our very own property buying machine where we could develop the system further. Then whatever I am doing in my life, wherever I am doing it, my property buying machine would be working for me, primarily, and secondly working for a limited number of clients to create wealth for them. Then in the future, we would get back-end fees on the property as well. In other words our share of the property we bought for them would be in the growth. The idea was that, after the up front fee our clients would never part with the money themselves as we would get their properties to pay it. We thought it was a winner and we thought we filled a gap in the market but it was still to be tested.

Because we are in a long-term business, we did not like the idea of selling somebody something and then when you have sold it, that is the end of it. To us this is like the buy and sell strategy of some Property Investors. The way we looked at it was, that if we did a good job, then at the end of the contract we would have made our clients a large amount of money. They would want to stay on as clients and pay us more fees to keep on doing it for them. This is the main reason we decided to limit this service to just 500 clients over 5 years.

We thought this really is a win – win deal. They make £150 - £300k, we get our overheads covered. Several years later we get paid a very nice share of the profit and do you think they will want to give some of the profit we have made them back so that we can do it again for them? Well, of course they will. It was one of the best win – win deals we had ever seen, even if I do say so myself. So we had designed a service that we ourselves would buy.

We thought our clients, as long as we continue to under promise and over deliver, are always going to want to stay as clients because when you make that sort of money for people, why would they not want to continue being clients? As Gill Fielding says, 'I have never seen an investment that performs as well as this one!'

So, we looked at it and thought, fair enough. We think we know what we have got here. Our unique selling point was the fact that we buy under market value. It was only four months later that we figured out that was not our unique selling point at all, that was merely a benefit of our service. It was our clients that actually told us what our Unique Selling Point was, but they had to keep telling us because we did not get it.

Our unique selling point was the fact that we did everything for them. The lot, they only got involved if they wanted to. The service that I had designed for myself, because I wanted all the best bits of property investing with none of the bad bits, was our USP, and that is why people buy it – we never sell it! We do not need to and we don't want to. All we need to do is tell people how it works and how it can benefit them.

So, if you really want to know, 'can someone else do it?' the answer is yes, we can. So if you do not want to open Pandora's Box and unleash the grief of learning it and getting it right, then you can simply pay us to do it. Well, we thought, there would be just a few people a year who would want us to do it for them.

In that first year we decided to offer our service to 100 people and believed that in the first year we would hopefully bring in a massive total of just 12 clients. We envisaged it taking three years to find 100 clients, as we had realised that we only wanted people who really wanted us to do this for them, and we imagined they would be few and far between. The 500 was really just an idea that we didn't think would actually happen.

At our first presentation at the end of March 2005, a total of nine people went ahead with our product. We thought there had to be a mistake and that people had been carried away with the emotion of the day. Two weeks later at the second open day, 14 people went ahead, with one person buying two places. We thought that had to be wrong as well. Two weeks after that, 13 people went ahead taking 17 places and we finally understood that people wanted our service.

They were inspired by what we had to offer. We didn't realise this at the time but we had created a whole new sub-industry. We only found that out later when I tried to market the business.

Anyway, after our three successful open days we had a wonderful meeting where we decided, okay, we had not really ever intended to go back into business as we were all Property Investors at our core. But our clients were giving us a clear sign that they thought our business was sound. So we agreed to set up a company just to do this for people.

Passive Investments Limited was born in May 2005. We moved all of the clients straight into that and decided that we needed to plan a proper strategy to develop our company system and to make our company 'Bullet Proof'. It was decided that transparency would be at our core and that we would develop our systems around that principle. We decided to keep taking on clients until we reached our target for that year and think again, nearer Christmas.

As the developer of the system, I thought this was fantastic as it gave me funding that I could spend on infrastructure and systems development. I had long believed that if you wanted to be the best, you shouldn't try and compete with anyone other than yourself and just keep getting better and better. Then whatever competition was left would always struggle to compete with you. Ray Croc, the founder of McDonalds, was asked when he was interviewed, 'Are you not concerned about all of the people copying your system?' To which he replied, 'No, I can invent faster than they can copy!' I know exactly what he means.

2006 got off to a good start and in this year we had the advantage of some clients who had gone through the first cycle. You have to understand, in the first year people bought our service with very little proof that we could deliver on our promises other than the historical information of our ever growing portfolio. As each week went by, however, more and more proof was delivered and our newsletter continued to demonstrate the returns we were making for people.

I spent most of the year working on marketing and bringing new clients in. I had been convinced that writing a book, which is primarily trying to help people, would then automatically produce the spin off benefit of helping me to find Passive clients. I knew by sharing with everyone so freely how we do it and how they could too that a small percentage would want us to do it for them.

I knew that when we fully explained the process, people would see the power of it, and some would decide as I did that they would want the getting paid bit and would be quite happy to have the property pay for our service for them. Because that's all I wanted to start with when I came up with the idea. I knew that people wouldn't or might not want to do it for themselves and so they would pay my Property Buying Machine to do it for them. I knew they would rather have experts working on their behalf using a system they understood, rather than go through the pain of building their own system. It seemed logical to me.

So 2006 was spent testing out different marketing approaches whilst I was waiting for the book to be finished. I was having to put up with the ridicule of everyone saying, 'No one will buy the book! It won't change everyone's opinion that much!' And other somewhat more derogatory remarks ☺

But I knew the content and the power of the book. They hadn't read it after all, so how could they? So I just kept smiling and saying, 'Just you wait and see!'

Well, the proper release happened on Dec 13th 2006. About two months later we had a waiting list and have had one ever since. We have also never done any other promoting since then other than this book, so we were able to disband the marketing department. This gave us more time to focus on improving the business instead. I have not been big headed at all by rubbing everyone's nose in it, well not as much as they deserve anyway!

So 2007 got off to a great start, our systems became tighter and Greg is currently going through the whole company bringing all departments to an even greater level of service. We have also just gone live with our bespoke client management software, which will provide an unrivalled level of transparency for our clients in the near future.

One of the advantages of our company is that we are in a business that gives us the time and money required to continually improve the systems. We are preparing the company currently to bring in a CEO and then hand this area over to him. This is so that we can both just do the directing. We are also increasing the staff levels so that we have more people than is required to carry out the work.

We have found that trying to bring two separate offices of the company up to a new speed together at the same time is very hard and so are moving shortly into a new single office close to Worthing town centre. This is a beautiful Grade II listed house, big enough to handle our growth to 500 clients or more.

Anyway, now I'm going to cover exactly how what we do for ourselves, is exactly what we do for our clients, and how this isn't going to actually cost them any money for us to do it for them. They will have to cashflow it, and they will have to cashflow some of our fees, but the property portfolio we buy for them will pay this money back over time.

We've become very good at spotting our ideal clients. They are the ones who are realists, who frankly see the benefit in what we offer, they also want us to do this for them and they trust us to just get on with it. They are not in a rush and they know it is just a certain way to solve a problem for them.

We were never doing this to create an income originally or create a company that would have a value of any sort. We were just doing this so that we had our own property buying machine with the overheads covered. It's funny how things work out though. Passive Investments was set up for me and Greg and our wives and our children, because we did not want to do it. We wanted to buy more property and we wanted to leverage our time to buy more property. The only reason this was set up was to protect us and our families and secure our futures, and for our future generations.

It has turned out to be something everybody seems to want or need. We have clients now from all walks of life; doctors, surgeons, fraud investigation officers, policemen, nurses, teachers, independent financial advisors, accountants, dentists, business owners, company directors, estate agents and software designers to name but a few - and loads, and loads of a group of people who I never thought would be interested in what we do... Property Investors.

When we designed our service we assumed that Property Investors would not be interested. Why pay us to do it when they can do it for themselves. What we have found is that over 50% of our clients are already property investors. And it took them explaining it to us for us to understand why they wanted to pay us to do it for them. To use an amalgam of their own words, 'What, all I have to pay you is an upfront fee and you'll do everything? Well after the first property this is virtually paid for and everything else you do for me afterwards is free! This is a no-brainer! You do all the work, the properties you buy me pay for it, they end up paying you the fee as well, so all I'm doing is cash flowing the fee and the purchasing fund. You don't want to take over the management of my existing portfolio as well, do you?' We hadn't expected that!

Our clients come to us and we ask them why they want us to do this? A heart surgeon said to us, 'Well, I have got to face facts, haven't I?' He said, 'I want to get into property. I am dying to get into property. But I have not had the time. I cannot and will not get around to it. So I thought, if I do not do this with you, I am never going to get into property. I have evaluated every other offering out there that people do and, basically, yours is the only one whose people are actually doing it for themselves and not just doing it to make money, and I like that.' He had spoken to plenty of clients who are doing it with us and then said, 'So I figure that if you are doing it yourself and if these people I have spoken to are finding it so good, you cannot all be wrong!'

So, that was it and he became a client. And the other clients we have all more or less say the same thing. They all are either just wanting more property with no grief or they are dying to get into property, but just literally will not do it or do not want to do it themselves.

And if they will not do it themselves, they are happy to pay my company to do it for them for a fee and a part of the growth. And because of the way property works, the fees that they pay us are basically paid for over time by the property anyway, so it is just cashflow. So their returns are enormous. That is it. That is what this whole book is about, that property makes money over time. There are only two ways in property you can really ever lose:

1. Not enough cashflow
2. You sold the property

So we know that you are not going to sell, because that would be just silly – so all you have to do with the cashflow is borrow more than you need to invest - 50% more!

34

Is It Worth It?

All any of us actually need, to be secure in the future and have a real 'pension', is five small properties. Just imagine for a second that you were 40 years old and it was 1980 and I said this to you. Just imagine you had taken my advice. Over the following five years you did a very aggressive strategy of buying one small property a year and re-financing them as necessary. By 1985 you would have finished your aggressive, no sorry, you're really easy relaxed strategy.

By 1990, even with the crash, you would still have had all your money out. You would have paid, in my area, approximately £100k for the props. Now let us say you did not touch them, until now. They would still have £80k of mortgages on them, because we have already agreed a mortgage is a good thing to have. So you look at them today and they are worth £600k. You speak to a mortgage advisor and he says he can get you an 85% mortgage. You can have £500k less your outstanding mortgage, a total of £420k.

You think to yourself, I want to have £1k a week after tax forever. So you draw that money from your mortgage drawdown monthly or quarterly or whenever you want it, it is entirely up to you. You can have the £420k tomorrow if you want it, tax-free of course.

But let us just say you stick to £1k a week and no more. So in eight years, after taking £1k a week, you are now 73 years old, the money would be gone right? I mean, I am not taking any rent whatsoever into any of these calculations. So you are 73 (don't worry about mortgages, because there are plenty of ways to refinance), your properties have gone up, let us say 8.5% / year. So now they are worth £1,152k. You see another mortgage advisor and he re-finances them to £979k. Your outstanding mortgage is £500k, so you have now got another £479k. The cost of living's gone up a bit, so you take £1.25k a week tax-free as your pension. This time you have enough to last only 7.3 years. You are now 80 years old. So you repeat the process. Properties have grown by 10% per year this time.

Your portfolio is now worth £2,245k. Again you re-finance to £1,908k and you owe £979k. This leaves you another £929k. The cost of living has gone up again, so you now want £1.5k a week tax-free. This money would then last nearly 12 years.

So in 12 years you return to your portfolio, you're 92 years old, property has only grown at 6% over those 12 years. You see a new mortgage advisor, because your old one has retired.

Your portfolio at that growth is £4,158k and 85% of it is £3,534k. You owe £1,908k and when it is paid off you've got £1,626k. Cost of living has gone up and that means that in your 92nd year, if you decide you want to go out and party, you will need more money. You decide to take £2k a week. That lasts you for another 15.5 years. You're now 107 years old.

That got a little boring did it not? After all, we all knew where I was going with it. Surely we all realised what was going to be the end result. Then why doesn't anybody talk about it? Why did it take until 2006 for someone to tell everyone that property was free?

Well what we do is charge you a fee upfront of £37,500 to build you a portfolio of five previously owned properties over a six year period.

We buy all of them significantly below market value, and we return all the deposit funds that you also have to provide, back to you after each property is bought, refurbished and refinanced.

When you become a client, you go on our purchasing list which is run on a first come first served basis. When your name reaches the top you are offered a property and you provide the deposit funds, refurbishment cost etc so that we may acquire the property for you in your name. The maximum you will ever need to provide is £30,000 (current average is £22,000) and this will be returned to you after each refinance.

Then your name once again goes on the purchasing list to buy the second of your five properties and this continues until your portfolio is complete. At this point all you will have parted with is our original £37,500 fee.

Quite often, people are put off by this fee so one of our clients said we really should explain what value the fee is providing people, as we weren't doing that.

Well, first off our fee doesn't really make us our profits, because if you were to break this out over the six years we are building your portfolio then it would work out to £120.19/week.   Split over the five properties this is

£7,500/property or £24.03/week for us to find, arrange the mortgage, progress chase it to completion, refurbish the property, make the refinance happen very quickly, arrange your first remortgage, find a tenant for it, manage the managing agent, handle the problem phone calls, handle any legal issues, identify when the property can release more equity, refinance it again, arrange the remortgage and last, but by no means least, manage your expectations.

So would you do that for £24.03/week?

No, and neither do we. That is the front end fee and that contributes towards our costs of building your portfolio. Where we make our profit is by doing our job well and sharing in the growth on your property - only after you have had all of your money back first, and only when your property can comfortably afford to give it to us. So this is a big time commitment from us.

And don't think we will be wanting to take our profits too early. Our service is about making you happy, because if we make you enough money then you will ask us to carry on and make you some more. Over the first six years we are really learning to work with each other and this will prove in the same way as living with someone before you get married whether you want to become life long partners or not. Please remember we are property investors first, so we look at lifetime returns on our investments and we look at our Passive clients in exactly the same way.

At the Open Day, Greg delivers the details of our service in a light-hearted way and then after that, we go to extraordinary lengths to make sure that you are happy with everything before becoming a client. We don't want people lying awake at night wondering if they have done the right thing, two years into the contract waking up in a cold sweat going, 'Right just three more properties to go and I'll be through this!' We are not in the business of just taking on people who can afford our service/ We are looking for partners rather than clients, and as anyone who has ever tried finding a business partner will know, not everyone has partner qualities ☺

We called our company Passive Investments for a reason, and the reason is that it is Passive. You get on with your life whilst we build you a portfolio. It really is that simple.

Becoming a client gives you certainty and takes away the worry about whether you will actually do it. The safety comes with our 100% track record and the security is that we have our own portfolios on the line here as well. We are in this together, because we set Passive up to protect us and our families and we would never do anything to put them at risk. Your other security is that it is in our interest to make this happen for you. If we don't, then we really don't get to make our full money, as the fees your properties will pay us is a lot more than the original £37,500 that you have parted with at the start.

Let's take it apart a little further and explain where we really add value.

So it is £7,500/property

Assuming you can actually find a source of properties 25%+ below market value (actually, in real life) the absolute minimum anyone would charge you would be

2.5% + VAT. Our average purchase price at the moment is £90,000: -

£2,643

We will save you at least 20% on your refurbishment budget (in most beginners' cases we'd probably do it for half the cost). Currently our average refurb is running at £4,500:-

£900

Our emotional detachment will save another sum of money that you would have otherwise spent on the refurb, probably a lot more than this, but we'll say:-

£500

We think that not having to deal with the builder at all is worth at least: -

£750

We will certainly save you on the revaluations at least one val fee on each refinance: -

£700

We think that all the preparation and the attending of the valuations is easily worth: –

£750

We will achieve a far lower void rate each year than you would, probably two weeks a year:-

£1,000

Our ongoing management will save you money on extra property expenses throughout the six years: -

£500

Our six years financial management of your portfolio is easily worth: -

£300

So in total, £8,043 is the minimum we think we are saving you before we even start to look at the time saving which obviously has a considerable value.

But really, we will probably buy the property for £10,000 less than you would, and we will probably get it to value for £10,000 more than you would. So even with our back end fees included, our service adds more than it will cost you.

But what's the most valuable bit of all???

No Pain, because we do it all! For those of you who I haven't inspired enough, or you realise that you just want the money and nothing else, then you want what I did. A machine I could just take home, plug into the wall and have it throw money at me when it was warmed up!

Ninety nine per cent of the people rushing around from meeting to meeting, having business phone calls, getting stressed or just working in normal job, will fail to ever reach the goal they are trying to achieve.

This is a disgraceful state of affairs, that the system we are taught to follow **fails 99% of the time**. All you need to do to escape joining them as failures is to do it the really easy way for yourself. Or the easy way. Or pay us £37,500 to do it for you. Then even if you take the crazy minimum growth at just 2% a year property market growth you will make a minimum of £20k/year tax free after just 10 years!

A sea of change is sweeping across the way people prepare for their pensions and you can either be part of it, or you can sit on the sidelines forever, with you and your family being left further behind because you did not take the opportunity up when it was so clearly presented to you.

You've probably stepped up to the brink before, and then turned away. I know I did! Several times in fact! Don't you owe it to yourself and your family to grasp the knowledge that I'm sharing with you here and use it to change your life and their lives/ You don't need me, and you don't need Passive, but you must do something, otherwise your chances of having a life of choice grow less with each passing day.

I ask people which was the hardest property to buy, and they all reply the first one. And I say no, it isn't. Your first one was easy compared with the hardest one. It was easy because you needed it. However, you don't need an investment property in the same way. So your first investment property is the hardest property you will ever buy - because you have to step way outside your comfort zone, when you don't need to.

I have to admit my strategy is boring and you don't have to be very clever, but I think you will agree it is easy for all of us to achieve this. When you do it right however, I've come to understand that getting wealthy should be boring, because you have become good at it. Well, this does it for you and it pays you while it's doing it. Does it get any better?

35

So What's The Alternative?

So all you need is to find a way to buy and hang on to five small properties and then you are done – stop worrying about a pension, there is no investment around that's this easy <u>and</u> this good! So why is it, when the maths are so simple and the result so obvious that most so called experts say, they don't think you can consider property as a real alternative to pensions? Surely they have all got it backwards. Surely it's **'how can we really consider the stock market as a real alternative to property?**

I find that a very powerful statement.

Let's think about it another way. If for example, let's say, Norwich Union said to you, we need you to stick £37,500 into a pension and provide £30,000 cashflow from time to time. Then, after six years you will have created a pension plan worth over a quarter of a million that pays you out a minimum of £20,000 tax free a year for the rest of your life. How many do you think they would sell?

They would **own** the pension market in this country, and that could easily cause all of the others to go out of business, which of course we know couldn't happen.

So let's get this straight. You don't have to put money in for 40 years to have the pension., You get to just put a lump sum in once and six to ten years later, you are able to withdraw annually in cash more than the average wage in this country!

Just think about how powerful that could be for people? Just think about what a culture change would happen in this country if this became a commonly accepted way to do it. The average person being able to retire with just ten years of work. Well the bad news would be that only a small percentage of the population could do it. And the good news for you is that the media and all conventional financial institutions are continually doing their best to convince the population that this is not possible. So the fact that you have found this industry means you have more of a chance of retiring financially free than virtually the rest of the population.

Why not phone up a large and respected insurance company like Norwich Union and say you want a pension that in ten years will give you after tax earnings of £20,000 a year for the rest of your life (even if you are 18 years old at the start ☺). Property investment is not governed by the same rules as a pension. You don't have to wait till you're 50, 60 or 70 to start taking your money and you don't need to buy an annuity which in my opinion is - well I want to say robbery, but that'll probably offend- so I'll say somewhat unfair. You can take this when you want!

Anyway, when they've stopped laughing at you, then you can ask them how much? When you ask this, what you are doing is saying to a builder, yes I want you to build me Wembley Stadium in between football seasons!

Can you imagine how much money you would need to put in to get £20k/year from them after only six to 10 years? I'd imagine you would need to have contributions and growth of hundreds of thousands of pounds over a 10 year period, tying your money up in what is essentially the stock market. That's if you can get an answer! And then what's the guarantee of it actually working? Following the Northern Rock crisis and now the hedge funds in my opinion being dangerously over geared, and one or some of them failing doesn't really bear thinking about. Makes what we are doing for normal people at Passive look too good to be true, doesn't it?

Well it isn't. It's profoundly simple and sometimes the simplest systems can easily beat the most complex hedge fund management and pension companies. And I know where I'd rather have my future investment. Ask yourself, would you rather have your money invested in a hedge fund that gears its investment of your money to something like 99.99% at times in order to possibly return you after charges, a pathetic 10% a year. Having the money that you continue to put in regularly, diversified into countless different stocks and shares that you don't know or possibly even understand. Or would you rather have zero of your own money tied up in a property that you can see and touch in a market that you at least understand, which is protected by people whose interest is in your investment succeeding as they don't get at their real profit unless they get it right? And bear in mind, that you don't pay this profit. The properties they've bought for you do it instead!

It's not too hard to see why we have a waiting list for our service, as the demand for what we do is obvious. We can only and are only willing to take on a limited number of new clients a month, otherwise the quality of our service may suffer. If you think I've been selling this too hard then don't buy from us, buy from someone else or do it yourself, just do it though. Our service is simply a choice for some of you.

Following the stats we have been able to pull together since first releasing this book there seems to be four groups of people. Those who do it themselves. This covers 8% for certain and probably a further 12%, so our stats are pointing to 20% of people who read this book take action and go into property. This obviously out performs every other self help book I've ever heard of, and I think that is probably down to the way it has been written to inspire instead of motivate, the profound information in the book's content and the way the book was sold in the first place. This stat is something that I am very proud of.

Next you have the people who decide to have us do it all for them. Currently 1 in 88 book buyers become a Passive client. Some of these also do it for themselves at the same time because they are looking for the certainty of us doing it, but they are so fired up that they also want to do it themselves. Another achievement I am very proud of.

Then you have the remaining 80-ish percent of people who make up the other two groups. Those who have and have not read the book, and then have not taken any action. **And will not take any action**. The question you need to be asking yourself right now is, are you doomed to be one of those?

And I can tell you what you are ALL thinking, 'No it won't be me, I'm doing this!' This always reminds me of a line in the movie Pulp Fiction about boxing being a sport full of so many unrealistic people, who all want to be the world champion.

Now the odds of success are obviously greater here than in the world of boxing. After all you have a 20% chance of success. But 80%, the vast majority, will (after being fed up with your current life plan not being worthy of what you want for yourself and your family) have struggled to find another way. You eventually stumbled across property investing, then further dug and found this book, and have been shown profound knowledge that will change your life, and shows how easily it is to obtain the money.

And STILL, four out of five of you will go back to your lives and even though you were at the brink of taking the right path, you will turn back and return to your comfort zone. And you will have passed up certainly the best opportunity you will ever have to break out of the mould that the system has created for you.

This is what I am not proud of, and this is why I have spent such a long time doing a re-work of this book and been somewhat more forceful in my efforts to get you to take action because I want more of you to have a life of choice. Doing this has shown me that the market shifts so much that I need to do a re-work annually to make sure this book remains up to date with what works now.

Do you really think that there will be a better opportunity for you to create great wealth?

Do you really think your financial plans should be based on the six lottery numbers?

Do you really want to leave your future to blind chance?

Do you really care so little about your future that you will not invest the time you need to invest right now to secure it?

Or even if you don't have the time or the inclination then those people with a little equity have been shown another way. My job is to increase the figures from 20% of my readers changing their lives to a lot more than that.

I don't care whether we do it for you, or you do it for yourself. As you can see, all I need to do is sell another 88 books at £20 to find another Passive client. My future and Passive's future are certain. Yours is not. Do it yourself, do it with us, or do both, but don't do nothing. What were the odds of you finding material like this that makes so clear what you need to do?

You don't want to be one of the 99% of people who retire poor in this country, and you don't want to be in the 80% of readers who don't take action. If you do nothing else, then **just buy one!**   That is all it will take for you to see how easy this really is!

By buying one, it will give you confidence to buy another, and then another and pretty soon you'll find that to secure yourself all you need is five small properties. Given enough time, they will produce enough money for you to retire for the rest of your life. Why do you think we designed our service to give people five properties? We know it is all that is needed to secure your life.

You know that the £20,000 a year represents just 2% per year annual growth, so ask yourself : is this a really conservative growth expectation?

Traditional pensions simply cannot compete, so why are they being pushed so hard? They are pensions for the masses, not everyone can buy property, but everyone who has been clever enough, fortunate enough, or by mistake picked up and read this book, can and should.

The decision on choosing our service is not about the decision to buy. That is obvious. It is something that I would choose myself, therefore I know it is a good deal. The decision is really whether you are going to do it yourself or have us do it for you. Doing it yourself is what this book is about. In this book I've shown you that you can do it yourself. It is not hard. And I have tried to break it down as simply as possible, so that people are not scared of it and people actually go out there and actually do it. I have also provided the membership site to help you through the hardest bit which is 'Starting' and then to provide continued guidance for you as long as you want it. I really have made this easy for you!

But to those of you who don't want to do it yourself, but are quite convinced after reading this book, that I know what I am talking about. I suggest you try and come along to one of our Open Days at Gatwick.

We hold one of these every three weeks for around 25 people and we only release the days one at a time by email. We do this because of the demand to attend the days and the fact that we can only take on a limited number of new clients per month. So I say, try because these usually fill up within a few hours of emailing.

If you would like a few more details of what Passive does, then all the details of our service can be found on the website: www.PassiveInvestments.co.uk

I suggest you sign up for the Passive client newsletter. By reading what comes out, you can study us from a distance and see if you like what we do and how we treat our clients. When you sign up for the newsletter there's a link to a page with all the previous newsletters, so you'll be able to get a real feel for what we do.

When you register you should also instantly get last quarter's newsletter and the next quarters will be sent to you. Then sit back and watch us for six or seven months. Just watch what is happening, don't rush in, check our service and see if it fits you before trying to come to an Open Day.

If you don't want to do this yourself, I suggest you come to us. Because by paying my company to do it for you, you will have got into property and that is the purpose of this book, to get and keep you in property. This is not rocket science. It is just don't wait to buy property. Buy property and wait.

What's more, when I first wrote this book I knew that it would inspire some competitors to set up in business. Being responsible for marketing, it was very hard to be the first company in the market. Just imagine you were the first company selling bottled water. It's hard to build a market place because you have to first educate people into the advantages of paying for water, over getting it free from the tap. But if you are the fourth or fifth company, then all you have to do is sell the differences between you and your competitors. So having no competitors had its own very unique set of problems ☺

Well, since releasing the book there are now three new companies saying they do what we do and I expect a handful more over the next few years. Frankly, there is room for us all. So if our waiting list is too long, then another company in this industry we inadvertently created, are offering a similar service. I cannot speak for their systems or ability, only your due diligence will do that. But my reason for telling you of their existence is that you must get into property investing - so any choice is probably better than no choice.

Now, you have got to this point in the book. Well done. Most people will never get this far with self help books. You know that property is the right thing to get into and you know and understand why that is, so choose one of the three roads to go down and just do it. Please don't be one of the 80% who will choose the fourth and do nothing.

If you can't or won't do that, then write it on a calendar for one year from today and make sure you put the date you first set the goal on. This is so that you can track back the date and this will hopefully inspire you in the future, should you fail to get started on this easy goal now.

Just do it, write it in the calendar, write it in your diary, put it in your Outlook right now. Go to your Outlook and go, okay, I am going to sign up for his newsletter. If I have not at least started on property investing in one year's time, then I am going to go and see them and I am going to buy their service, if that's what it takes to secure my future.

Don't get me wrong. It will be more money next year, because we put the price up each year. But if you doubt it at the moment, then give yourself a year to see if the messages and the hooks I have put into the book get you to start buying. If you doubt what I say about the property market, then sit back and watch it rise again over the next year. Once again, following the Northern Rock troubles, the talk has turned to a property market slowdown. The trouble is these so-called experts don't understand what they are talking about, so how can they ever make an accurate prediction? So don't listen to them. It is always a good time to buy as long as you buy at the right price. That's easy for me to say but, because of all the information that bombards you, it might be very difficult for you to understand. The funny thing is, it really is that simple. The property market doesn't matter, but a single property does. I wrote an article on the site about how property investors don't buy in the property market, if you want that point further explained. Anyway…

You can do this yourself!
You do not need Passive!
You do not need other companies!
You do not need me!
This is simple!
You KNOW that!

You Just Need To Believe You Can!

But if you are not going to do anything THEN it is better to come to us than to live with the regret !

You know I'm right. I know I'm right because I've been there too. You have to make the decision and choose what is important to you. I mean, most of our clients chose to use our service because their time is more important to them, just as mine was to me. And they do not want to go through the pain of the apprenticeship.

I'm not sorry to labour this point because it is as important as oxygen is to us:

The point is: you actually have to do something

Now that you are aware that this is easy and you can do it, you simply must take action, please! You owe it to yourself to be financially free, you owe it to everyone around you as well. Just imagine the life you could lead and the good you could do, if you removed the problem of needing to work for money in your life. It really does make you think doesn't it? If it hasn't, then I suggest you read it again and just imagine what your life would be like if you took action.

Our clients took action. They secured it. Having done it, they were able to say, that's it. It is done. I now have some certainty in my financial future, thanks to property. I am speaking as a man who owns a lot of properties. I know what just five properties can do for people.

Five was not enough for me. I wanted a lot more than that. You don't need to do it the way I have done it. The way I have done it is just **nuts**. It is not necessary.

The way I am showing people to do it, the way I have told you to do it in this book, will work fine. You will make more money than you ever need to make, from property - if you just start taking action. The sooner you do it, the sooner you will have the results. It is that simple.

Do not listen to the rubbish fed to you by people in the pub. They know nothing about the property market. I have shown you the property market. The ups and downs of the market are pretty much irrelevant over a long enough period of time. My advice is to forget the property market. It's not important!

Now, when people say to me, I can't afford to do that, I know it is because they have not figured out how to fund it yet. It is not because they can't afford to do it. They just haven't figured out how to do it. Well, if you haven't got the money or if you just want to have more of it, then you can use the systems, tools, and knowledge on my site to acquire all the funds you need. But if you don't use them as instructed and you are not methodical, then they will not work. I can only show you the door here; it is down to you to walk through.

If you want to get passionate about this, if you want to change your life, change your family's lives, make your life easy in the near future, and I mean easy, if you are 35 years old now, a five-portfolio bought today in 20 years' time could be worth £5 million at the real rate of growth 11.74% / year. You will still have all the mortgages on it. You will still have them, and probably have £400k of mortgages. But it will be done.

So for £37.5k, or whatever the fee is that year, in the end, you will have a £5 million portfolio. And if you are using equity to fund it, then it is only money that you are taking from one property and placing in several others somewhere else so it's not as if you are really parting with money either, is it? How can anyone possibly say no to that?

Of course you have got the fourth choice:

Don't do it and live with the regret!

I meet readers regularly and I can say that they tell me, without fail, that the most powerful line in the book, was where I wrote: - **Within 12 weeks of reading this book, if you have not bought a property, you are not going to - unless you re-read the book..** This line has inspired so many people to do it, and I hope it inspires you.

So there it is. You know how to do it the easy way and the really easy way. If you can't be bothered or you haven't got the time, you can pay Passive or one of our new competitors to do it for you. And if you want an excellent reason why you should trust me to build your business for you, I will let you into a little secret: The real reason I am doing this for people and why they can rely on me to get the job done, is the reason I have been in it from the beginning. Here it is: the unvarnished truth:

I am in it for the money!

We will take on 144 clients a year at Passive. In a little over two years we will have 500 clients and be buying 500 properties/year. In each of these properties we will own a share of the growth representing at least £15k. We make a small amount of money on the refurbishment costs and of course, we are paid our upfront fees.

At the end of the six year term, our clients will have the opportunity to have us continue to build their portfolios or go it alone. Those who leave us will be replaced by those eagerly waiting in the wings. By mistake we have created a phenomenal business, which produces us far more than we ever thought it would do financially. It also feeds a desire we have to help other people break out of the mould and it helps us to make people wealthy. It really does tick all of the boxes for Greg and me, but at the end of the day we wouldn't do this if we weren't paid really well to do so.

Trust me: I am in this for the money!

None of what I have said includes the possibility of franchising our service, taking it abroad, rolling it out in many other ways. We may consider doing this, but to be quite honest we haven't decided yet as we never intended to go into business in the first place, and currently all we are focusing on is delivering an amazing service to our clients.

This is a system. It is still semi-reliant on me and Greg at the moment to do the bits we both do. But within the next two-three years, our system will be complete to 99%. It will be a bullet-proof transparent company that will continue to improve and adapt to the changing market and make itself as indestructible as is ever possible.

The back-end fees on property mean that we protect it that way as well. That means that this is a long-term protected company. I was in business for years before discovering a better way, and I can think of no better way of guaranteeing success than if both the companies and the clients' interests are served in the same way.

All of us are in this for the money. The strength that the company has and that our clients have, is in knowing that we are all in this for the money. It is our purpose for Passive to provide a service to our clients which gives them more options in their lives. By us making each and every client a significant amount of money each and every time we purchase them a property, we secure our long term goals and of course, we help to secure theirs.

Personally I find it very rewarding when the system I conceived for myself gives one of my clients yet another infinite return on their investment. It is something that both Greg and I are very proud of.

So, it is your choice. Stop reading and start bl***y buying yourself, or get someone else to do it. Whichever you choose to do, make sure you choose to start buying property and planning to set yourself free.

As Warren Buffet says, *'Someone's sitting in the shade today because someone planted a tree a long time ago.'* Go and start your own orchard by planting your first tree.

If you either start - or do not start for whatever reason - then I suggest you become a member of my website and let me and all the other members help you to achieve what you want financially, and share many more techniques in Property Investing and much more that there just wasn't time to cover in this book.

And finally <u>always remember what property really is...</u>

**Money for Nothing
and Your Property for Free!**

I hope you enjoyed the book and have fun with the knowledge.

Sincerely,

Andy Shaw

P.S. My burning hope is that the end of this book is really the beginning of an exciting new opportunity for you to change your financial life forever. My burning hope is this book inspires you to take positive action.

Don't let it become yet another collection of unfinished hopes on a dusty bookshelf. Don't let that happen!

Take one small action step now:

Make sure you visit my website at <u>www.AndyShaw.com</u> - and leave me a comment about what you intend to do now.

Put it in writing and make a small commitment, even if it's anonymous, to take positive action.

Then subscribe to my free blog and online newsletter. That way we can stay in contact, and I can continue to help you move towards your financial goals.

You'll receive important property investment advice and financial intelligence that has already helped a lot of people to take financial control of their lives.

Do it now, don't procrastinate. Procrastination is the biggest killer of dreams, don't let it kill yours. Head over to www.AndyShaw.com right away... I'll see you there!

Bonus

Frequently Asked Question Section: -

I was asked by book readers to put the answers to some of the most frequently asked questions in this edition, so I hope you find these useful. Each question has been answered on the site in far more depth and also, at times, in different ways. So for greater explanations, I suggest going there.

Q: I can't find below market value property!
A: Then you are not following the technique I showed in the book because they are there. I got everyone to focus on the newspapers as that is the way to learn the area very quickly but once you know the area, the internet is a fast way to sort properties. I use the site www.Rightmove.co.uk then I structure my search to cover within three miles, flats and apartments and lowest price.

First find a property that is at the bottom end of the price range. Say a one- bed flat for £85,000. Then use the Can You Buy It tool on the site to see what value you will need for the flat so that you recover all your outlay. Roughly, this is going to be a value of £110k to £115k.

So all you need to look for is comparable property to the value of £115k and you have probably identified a below market value property. Now you've got to go and see if it really is or not.

The Can You Should You Buy It tool will evaluate the deals for you and make sure you unemotionally decide whether or not to buy a property. I designed it myself to make sure I never tied up money in a property.

With the web search above and the deal evaluation tool, you'll be able to locate deals very quickly. But you will not know the market and the area anywhere near as well if you do not use the paper technique I explained. It appears (guess only) that about 45% of people use the paper technique and find deals easily. Then, another 55% say they can't find Below Market Value deals (BMVs).

Q: What do I do about this bit…?
A: You'll get the answer you are looking for if you just re-read that section of the book.

I strongly recommend at least one re-read of the book. When I read books that have so much profound knowledge in them, I always find that re-reading allows me a much greater level of understanding.

Plenty of the people who have taken my strategy and really worked it have told me that they have read the book several times and constantly keep it on hand for referral. Repetition is a master skill and for some reason we need to hear things three to seven times before we change our patterns.

Q: What mortgages should I go for first?
A: Never tie yourself into a Mortgage with redemption penalties to start with. Take a discounted mortgage that you can refinance straight away after completion.

Then on re-finance, go for a very cheap mortgage that ties you in for two or three years.

Every month I update my choice of purchase lender and re-finance lender. Mortgages change all the time so this makes sure that you at least know what deals I'm using.

Be very careful choosing your broker. Don't choose one just because you know them. You want one who specialises in the area you are going into. And I cannot recommend highly enough that you go to a Mortgage Packager instead of an IFA, or make sure your IFA will go through a Mortgage Packager. Why? Because a Mortgage Packager arranges the whole deal before it gets submitted to a lender and this detached situation adds huge value.

On the website there is also a vast amount of information on mortgages and mortgage packagers.

Q: Can you recommend me a broker/packager?
A: I recommend one on the site and it is in the mortgages section. I'm not putting it here, otherwise they will be bombarded with calls that lead nowhere. So I haven't made it too easy to find in the mortgages section.

Q: Should I do this in a limited company?
A: No.

Q: Why not?
A: You are doing this for the money that you can get at for free. If you do it in a limited company then the money is not yours, it is your limited company's' and you cannot get at your money without selling. Therefore what would be the point? I listened to experts at one point and put quite a

few properties into a limited company. I now call that portfolio 'My Useless Portfolio!'

Q: When will I know if a property crash is about to happen?
A: Just keep an eye on my site blog where I regularly give my opinion on what's currently really going on. The idea is that you use my insight to keep up with what is going on. Then over time when you see my predictions work out, hopefully this will give you greater confidence in the future.

Q: Should I open a separate bank account for my portfolio?
A: Yes, run everything separately from your domestic bank account.

Q: I'm releasing plenty of extra cash from my first re-mortgage but I'll have a rental shortfall of £1,000 per year. Should I increase my cashflow reserve?

A: Yes, in this instance put 3 to 5 years of shortfall into a separate high interest reserve account. Do what you want with the rest. Annually review your rental shortfall reserve and make sure you have a minimum of three years reserve in it.

Q: What is the most important area to focus on first?
A: Cashflow is the most important. It is the Only thing that matters.

Q: I've got a poor credit file, how can I do this?
A: The easiest way is to do it in someone else's name and draw up a Declaration of Trust document so that you can cover your legal interest in the property. If that is not possible, or not palatable, then you can use the Cross firing

section on the website to rebuild your credit history in the shortest time possible. This should take 6 to 12 months depending on the level of poor credit.

Q: I have no money and a lot of debt; can I still get into property?

A: The easiest way out of this is to use the Cross firing system which really works like a magnet, attracting credit facilities to you. But it is no get rich quick scheme and neither is the whole property buying system, just a certain way of achieving your goals. You can still use the systems in here but you would just need to do it in someone else's name and draw up a declaration of trust to protect your legal interest in the property.

If you don't have anyone who wants to do this with you right now, learn to use the techniques to locate deals. Then you will be able to sell these deals at a profit and/or joint venture partners will find someone with those skills, just as they do me.

If you still want to do it in your name then the site also includes sections on Credit Cards and Personal Loans. Using the cross firing techniques will give you the best chance of obtaining credit by only going to the lenders that really want to lend. This is the biggest thing about applying for credit and you don't want to apply when a lender doesn't have any money to lend.

You want to approach them when they are in what I call a Lending Frenzy. This means they've borrowed a lot of money and need to get it on the street fast. Therefore, their lending criteria is at its most relaxed. This is the time to attempt to raise finance from them. So what I do on the site is identify which lenders are at that point so that your success rate increases somewhat ☺

Q: What are you doing regarding Inheritance tax?

A: I suggest you read My Inheritance Tax Plan, which is on the site because I have found the best way to have your cake and eat it, and then pass it on to your children in a way that means that they have the smallest bill possible - but they actually never pay the bill themselves. In essence you can defer your inheritance tax bill forever (this is pure gold!).

Q: Can you give me a bullet point of list of what to do in what order?
A:
- Raise funds
  o Use the crossfiring to build your profile
  o Release equity
  o Raise from credit cards
  o Raise overdraft limits
  o Look into other fund raising opportunities like friends and family
- Make sure you can get the mortgage you want
- Find a solicitor who understands what you are trying to do
- Find some BMVs
- Go and start viewing
- Negotiate a deal
- Hold it together throughout exchange
- Go and find a builder before exchange
- Go and find several managing agents to handle your property

- Exchange and complete
- Carry out the refurb
- Get the revaluation done
- Get the property let out
- Find some more BMVs….

Q: Have you got a glossary of terms?

A: Yes there is one on the site, but if you go to Google and search 'Property Glossary' then you can find plenty of them.

Q: I am getting on in years now. Have I left it too late to get involved in property?

A: No, you have not left it too late.
There are two distinct routes you can take..

1)
You can buy in your own name. If you have 8 - 10 years+ before your 75th Birthday this will work very well as long as you buy the properties below market value.

Property doubles every 7 years, so if you released £100,000 from your own home now and left £34,000 in the bank as a spare contingency cashflow, you could use the £66,000 to invest in two properties each year for five years.

At the end of five years, you would have no money tied up (because you release it at one property per year via equity release) and a portfolio of 10 properties.

Let's say you were forced to sell five of them at the age of 75 to release equity because you had to repay all of the mortgages (which is criminal by the way). That would clear the other mortgages and pay your tax bill. Then you would be left with five properties with no mortgages on them producing an income of £3,000/month.

So clearly this strategy would mean that you were living out your days with a reasonable income and occasionally, if you wanted to, you could sell a property.

However, there are a growing number of lenders who lend on buy-to-let now irrespective of age and recently, a 102-year-old man was given a 25 year interest only mortgage. If he held that loan to term, he would be the oldest person who supposedly ever lived. The full article is on the site and it shows that there are several mainstream lenders who will lend this way. And as the lenders start to understand what they are doing a little more, then more will emerge.

2)
If however, you were really clever, you could purchase in someone else's name so that you had the use of the equity released until you passed away. Then, thanks to the benefit of using their name, they would be rewarded with the remaining equity in the property (i.e. no inheritance tax.) This essentially means you can have your cake and eat it, regardless of your age.
Obviously you would need to seek legal advice as this is outside the normal way of doing things and your accountant/solicitor would have to be happy with the person who remained the owner upon your death. You would also need the revenue's okay that they were happy with this so that you avoid inheritance tax.

Likewise, you would need a legal contract with the person whose name was on the property so that they couldn't go and sell it before you've finished with it. But all of that can be sorted by your solicitor, and if your solicitor says that it can't be done, then I suggest you get a second opinion because what they could be really saying is, 'I don't know how to do that and I'm afraid to tell you I don't, in case you go somewhere else.'

Hopefully that should inspire you to go now and seek out the advice needed to make property ownership a must in your life. After all it is always a good time to buy property. So you have not left it too late!

Q: I do not live in the UK; will your approach work overseas?

A: My system focuses on the specifics of the UK as this is where I built the bulk of my portfolio.

That said however, the majority of what I discuss in this book covers Property Investment and a profound understanding of it. So there are no reasons I know of why the vast majority of the system would not be applicable in other countries.

Q: I need one-on-one help. Do you do personal coaching?
A: It was giving one-on-one coaching that helped lead me to write the book, and create the membership site.

I was so depressed with the amount of time I invested in someone and their lack of progress in the direction that I was sending them that I came to the conclusion that one – on-one would not work for me. I wanted to touch a lot more people with the time I had available for this project. I knew I could not dent the figures of 99% of people retiring poor, if I did it one person at a time.

I also find a real advantage in the written word because people can't answer back before they have fully read my answer. Then, if they do answer back, they have usually had a chance to digest what I have said rather than just firing back a question without understanding the answer I have given.

I have found it is human nature to love the sound of your own voice and as such, people are often just waiting for the noise to finish so that they can ask another question, without listening to the previous answer.

I also found that by sharing my thinking on my site, people actually take the info and really make use of it. This serves as guidance but does not lead them to rely totally on me as I am only there if they run into trouble and that is only where the mastermind group are unable to help. The rest they do themselves.

Lastly for me to give one-on-one time is not leveraging my time efficiently and I doubt anyone would want to pay the sort of money that I would have to charge to make one-on-one coaching viable to me.

Q: Do you hold seminars?

A: We don't hold seminars as I do not find them very viable for the time they take up. However, after I released the book, I was deluged by emails asking for a seminar. These came from people who said they loved the info but they felt that they would learn more from visual/audio or one-on-one than they would from the written word.

We felt that by doing one seminar we could solve a number of issues for people, 1) we could get on film people finding below market value deals in their own home towns, which would further enhance our message that this is achievable. 2) I know that some people learn more from a visual or audio medium. 3) By creating the DVD we could do the work once and get paid forever, making one seminar very viable.

This should be released towards the end of 2007.

Q: Okay Andy I get it. But how on earth do I convince my partner that this isn't just another get rich quick scheme?

A: This one is tricky, because each person seems to react differently so if I give a few different approaches then you can pick one that is applicable.

When people read my book they find that finally they have found something that is so profound that they know it will work. They know it is not a get rich quick scheme and they know it will certainly work for them. The problem is that their parents, or their partner, or friends, or their children say something like, 'Yeah righto Son! Well I don't want you risking your future on another get rich quick scheme!'

You, however, know it is not. So how do you go about convincing them. Well firstly, try not to get too excited. I know that's hard, but play the information down. Be more subtle and let them come to their own conclusions and realise for themselves that the info is gold dust.

First, try and get them to read the book, because due to the info contained within it and because of the way it is written, people accept it very easily. I have received dozens of emails from professional property people saying they were certain that they would find the info boring or worse, rubbish and they now understand what they are doing to a far greater level.

However, if they WILL NOT read the book, then when you get to one of the most profound parts that you know they will automatically accept, get them to read just that page. Try and get them to read it out loud as well because as they do so, you can discuss it with them. They will believe the sound of their own voice more than any other. And when they read the profound bits they will really sink in. Then, when you find another bit in the book do the same again.

Also talk calmly while you are reading it, pointing out how you have turned left on occasions when the book now shows you that you should have turned right. In other words get them to see how a previous decision may have been a mistake.

Let them reach that conclusion for themselves. Don't force your opinions onto them. Your goal is for them to be dragging you into doing this, your goal is for this to be their idea - then you really have a partner.

If they won't even entertain it, then go straight to the core and ask for their support as you are quite willing to discuss things with them that you do not like or disagree with. In other words make them feel unreasonable, then it is human nature for decent people to want to be reasonable. So just say something like, 'I would like to do this and would appreciate your support.'

Once you've done all of that and they still don't believe it, or they won't listen, then say, 'Well I want to do this but I want to protect us if I'm wrong. So how about we ring fence our money and I do this with just this much of our equity? You can use the line, 'Well it is half mine.' But this is not a winning line unless followed up with 'And I don't ask for your support often!'

If your partner is certain that this is another get rich quick scheme and they won't read the book then use that against them. In the art of war you take someone else's weapons and make them yours, therefore creating an advantage. Actually if you need to overcome an objectionable partner then I suggest you read the revised edition of Sun Tzu's 'The Art of War', as this will show you many ways to out flank problem opponents. It will also help with your strategy in negotiating with estate agents.

For example if they won't read the book, you can say, 'Well you won't even read the book, so how can you even comment on whether it is a get rich quick scheme or not! Why not just read the book and then we will both have all of the knowledge and then we can discuss it sensibly?' This approach may just work.

Frankly there are hundreds of different ways to win the argument, especially when it comes down to the knowledge in the book as that beats all arguments, so the only ones you have to work on are whether or not they believe that you are capable of applying it.

Then if you come back with something profound like, 'Well if we carry on doing the same thing then we will not ever be able to retire financially free and have the life we deserve! We need to do something a little differently if we want a different result. I suggest you come and look at some of the comments that the membership site members have said about what they are doing. So it is not just him who says it's possible. There are hundreds of normal people making this happen too.'

If all that fails then say, 'Well, shall we try and go along to an Open Day and see if we want his company to do it for us?' The way Greg explains things in an entertaining way in just a few hours could be enough to convince your partner that they should read the book.

There really are angles on angles here and it is down to you to think outside the box. Another way is to say, 'I've found this system that could change our lives but it seems like a lot of work to make it happen. However, if you were able to help with a couple of the easier bits then I think I may be able to attempt it!'

Alternatively you could just go and find some BMV deals and then say, 'I didn't believe what this book said but I tried it and it worked Look at this…'

I could go on and on, but I think you've had enough! Every time you come up against one of these annoying types of problems there will be a solution and the answer is probably hidden in the question.

All you have to do is put yourself in their shoes and you should find the button you need to press to get your partner's support. After all you are doing this for their benefit too. So just believe they will support you and then start to ask for their support and if you really believe they will support you, then you may find this a lot easier than you think.

I found the people I least thought would be interested in doing this wanted to do it, and the people I thought would jump in with both feet, ran a mile. So just relax and believe you can and you can.

NOTES

NOTES

<u>NOTES</u>

DREAMS THAT VEIL

December, 1911: Twelve-year-old Eliza Brannan eagerly awaits the return of her brother Roderick from university, a welcome but brief diversion from her otherwise cosy existence in the heart of Northamptonshire with her widowed mother and cousin Dorothea. Roderick and Dorothea are growing up fast, forging lives and loves of their own, and Eliza feels left behind. When an unexpected proposal of marriage leads Dorothea to a search for her long-lost father in the slums of London, Eliza begins to realize that the world is a bigger and more frightening place than she could ever have imagined.

SPECIAL MESSAGE TO READERS

THE ULVERSCROFT FOUNDATION
(registered UK charity number 264873)
was established in 1972 to provide funds for
research, diagnosis and treatment of eye diseases.
Examples of major projects funded by
the Ulverscroft Foundation are:-

- The Children's Eye Unit at Moorfields Eye Hospital, London
- The Ulverscroft Children's Eye Unit at Great Ormond Street Hospital for Sick Children
- Funding research into eye diseases and treatment at the Department of Ophthalmology, University of Leicester
- The Ulverscroft Vision Research Group, Institute of Child Health
- Twin operating theatres at the Western Ophthalmic Hospital, London
- The Chair of Ophthalmology at the Royal Australian College of Ophthalmologists

You can help further the work of the Foundation
by making a donation or leaving a legacy.
Every contribution is gratefully received. If you
would like to help support the Foundation or
require further information, please contact:

THE ULVERSCROFT FOUNDATION
The Green, Bradgate Road, Anstey
Leicester LE7 7FU, England
Tel: (0116) 236 4325

website: www.foundation.ulverscroft.com